Once a Day
EVERY DAY...

FOR A
WOMAN
of
GRACE

The quoted ideas expressed in this book (but not Scripture verses) are not, in all cases, exact quotations, as some have been edited for clarity and brevity. In all cases, the author has attempted to maintain the speaker's original intent. In some cases, quoted material for this book was obtained from secondary sources, primarily print media. While every effort was made to ensure the accuracy of these sources, the accuracy cannot be guaranteed. For additions, deletions, corrections, or clarifications in future editions of this text, please write Freeman-Smith.

The Holy Bible, King James Version

The Holy Bible, New King James Version (NKJV) Copyright © 1982 by Thomas Nelson, Inc. Used by permission.

New century Version®. (NCV) Copyright © 1987, 1988, 1991 by Word Publishing, a division of Thomas Nelson, Inc. All rights reserved. Used by permission.

The Holman Christian Standard Bible™ (HCSB) Copyright © 1999, 2000, 2001 by Holman Bible Publishers. Used by permission.

The Holy Bible, New International Version®. (NIV) Copyright © 1973, 1978, 1984 International Bible Society. Used by permission of Zondervan. All rights reserved.

The Holy Bible. New Living Translation (NLT) copyright © 1996 Tyndale Charitable Trust. Used by permission of Tyndale House Publishers.

The New American Standard Bible®, (NASB) Copyright © 1960, 1962, 1963, 1968, 1971, 1972, 1973, 1975, 1977, 1995 by The Lockman Foundation. Used by permission.

Scripture taken from The Message. (MSG) Copyright © 1993, 1994, 1995, 1996, 2000, 2001, 2002. Used by permission of NavPress Publishing Group.

Cover Design by Kim Russell / Wahoo Designs
Page Layout by Bart Dawson

ISBN 978-1-60587-441-8

Printed in the United States of America

1 2 3 4 5—CHG—16 15 14 13 12

Trust in the Lord with all your heart,
and do not rely on your own understanding;
think about Him in all your ways,
and He will guide you on the right paths.

—

Proverbs 3:5-6 HCSB

Once a Day
EVERY DAY...

FOR A
WOMAN
of
GRACE

INTRODUCTION

Your life here on earth is an all-too-brief journey from the cradle to the grave. When you make that journey with God—and when you encourage your family members to do the same—you will avail yourself of the peace and abundance that God offers to those who invite Him into their hearts.

In your hands, you hold a book that contains 365 devotional readings for women of grace. During the next year, please try this experiment: read a page from this book each day. If you're already committed to a daily time of worship, this book will enrich that experience. If you are not, the simple act of giving God a few minutes each morning will change the direction and the quality of your life.

Each day provides opportunities to put the Creator where He belongs: at the center of your life. When you do, you will worship Him, not just with words, but with deeds. And you will be richly rewarded.

This book is intended to remind you of the eternal promises that are found in God's Holy Word and of God's never-ending love for you. May these pages be a blessing to you, and may you, in turn, be a blessing to those whom God has seen fit to place along your path.

READ THE BIBLE IN A YEAR

Reading the Bible from cover to cover in 365 days is a worthy goal for every Christian, including you. If you complete the suggested Bible readings found on each page of this book, you will, in 365 days, finish both the Old and New Testaments.

Each day provides yet another opportunity to study God's Word, to follow His path, and to reacquaint yourself with His promises. When you do these things, you will be richly blessed. So take the time to read His Word once a day, every day. No exceptions.

SPENDING TIME WITH GOD EVERY DAY

He said to him, "You shall love the Lord your God with all your heart, with all your soul, and with all your mind. This is the greatest and most important commandment."

Matthew 22:37-38 HCSB

When it comes to spending time with God, are you a "squeezer" or a "pleaser"? Do you squeeze God into your schedule with a prayer before meals (and maybe, if you've got the time, with a quick visit to church on Sunday)? Or do you please God by talking to Him far more often than that? If you're wise, you'll form the habit of spending time with God every day. When you do, it will change your life.

When you begin each day with your head bowed and your heart lifted, you remind yourself of God's love, His protection, and His commandments. And if you are wise, you will use your morning prayer time to align your priorities for the coming day with the teachings and commandments of God's Holy Word.

This book asks that you give your undivided attention to God at least once a day every day. And make no mistake about it: the emphasis in the previous sentence should be placed on the words "at least." Even if you're the busiest woman on Planet Earth, you can still carve out time for God. And when you think about it, isn't that the very least you should do?

Spiritual worship is focusing all we are on all He is.

Beth Moore

A TIMELY TIP

Finding time for God takes time . . . and it's up to you to find it. The world is constantly vying for your attention, and sometimes the noise can be deafening. Remember the words of Elisabeth Elliot; she said, "The world is full of noise. Let us learn the art of silence, stillness, and solitude."

YOUR JOURNEY WITH GOD

For it is God who is working among you both the willing and the working for His good purpose.

Philippians 2:13 HCSB

Your life is a journey, and every step of the way, God is with you. If you seek to live in accordance with God's will for your life—and you should—then you will live in accordance with His commandments. You will study God's Word, and you will be watchful for His signs. You will associate with fellow Christians who will encourage your spiritual growth, and you will listen to that inner voice that speaks to you in the quiet moments of your daily devotionals.

Sometimes, God's plans seem unmistakably clear to you. But other times, He may lead you through the wilderness before He directs you to the Promised Land. So be patient and keep seeking His will for your life. When you do, you'll be amazed at the marvelous things that an all-powerful, all-knowing God can do.

God intends to use you in wonderful, unexpected ways if you let Him. The decision to seek God's plan and to follow it is yours and yours alone. The consequences of that decision have implications that are both profound and eternal, so choose carefully.

With God, it's never "Plan B" or "second best." It's always "Plan A." And, if we let Him, He'll make something beautiful of our lives.

Gloria Gaither

A TIMELY TIP

God has a plan for the world and for you. When you discover His plan for your life—and when you follow in the footsteps of His Son—you will be rewarded. The place where God is leading you is the place where you must go.

A LOVE THAT CHANGES EVERYTHING

Your old life is dead. Your new life, which is your real life—even though invisible to spectators—is with Christ in God. He is your life.

Colossians 3:3 MSG

What does the love of Christ mean to His believers? It changes everything. His love is perfect and steadfast. Even though we are fallible, and wayward, the Good Shepherd cares for us still. Even though we have fallen far short of the Father's commandments, Christ loves us with a power and depth that is beyond our understanding. And, as we accept Christ's love and walk in Christ's footsteps, our lives bear testimony to His power and to His grace. Yes, Christ's love changes everything; may we invite Him into our hearts so it can then change everything in us.

This hard place in which you perhaps find yourself is the very place in which God is giving you opportunity to look only to Him, to spend time in prayer, and to learn long-suffering, gentleness, meekness—in short, to learn the depths of the love that Christ Himself has poured out on all of us.

Elisabeth Elliot

Jesus is all compassion. He never betrays us.

Catherine Marshall

A TIMELY TIP

Jesus loves you. Period. His love is amazing, it's wonderful, and it's meant for you.

Day 4

THE IMPORTANCE OF PRAYER

Be anxious for nothing, but in everything by prayer and supplication, with thanksgiving, let your requests be made known to God.

Philippians 4:6 NKJV

Prayer is a powerful tool for communicating with our Creator; it is an opportunity to commune with the Giver of all things good. Prayer is not a thing to be taken lightly or to be used infrequently. Prayer should never be reserved for mealtimes or for bedtimes; it should be an ever-present focus in our daily lives.

Daily prayer and meditation is a matter of will and habit. You must willingly organize your time by carving out quiet moments with God, and you must form the habit of daily worship. When you do, you'll discover that no time is more precious than the silent moments you spend with your Heavenly Father.

A prayerful heart and an obedient heart will learn, very slowly and not without sorrow, to stake everything on God Himself.

Elisabeth Elliot

Prayer is our pathway not only to divine protection, but also to a personal, intimate relationship with God.

Shirley Dobson

A TIMELY TIP

When you are praying, the position of your eyelids makes little or no difference. Of course it's good to close your eyes and bow your head whenever you can, but it's also good to offer quick prayers to God with your eyes—and your heart—wide open.

A FRESH OPPORTUNITY

Therefore we were buried with Him by baptism into death, in order that, just as Christ was raised from the dead by the glory of the Father, so we too may walk in a new way of life.

Romans 6:4 HCSB

God's Word is clear: When we genuinely invite Him to reign over our hearts, and when we accept His transforming love, we are forever changed. When we welcome Christ into our hearts, an old life ends and a new way of living—along with a completely new way of viewing the world—begins.

Each morning offers a fresh opportunity to invite Christ, yet once again, to rule over our hearts and our days. Each morning presents yet another opportunity to take up His cross and follow in His footsteps. Today, let us rejoice in the new life that is ours through Christ, and let us follow Him, step by step, on the path that He first walked.

If you are God's child, you are no longer bound to your past or to what you were. You are a brand new creature in Christ Jesus.

Kay Arthur

Today is the day of salvation. Some people miss heaven by only eighteen inches—the distance between their heads and their hearts.

Corrie ten Boom

A TIMELY TIP

If you're a thoughtful believer, you'll make it a habit to praise God many times each day, beginning with your morning devotional.

BEYOND THE DAILY GRIND

*Come to Me, all you who are weary and burdened, and I will give you rest.
Take My yoke upon you and learn from Me, because I am gentle and humble
in heart, and you will find rest for your souls. For My yoke is easy and My
burden is light.*

Matthew 11:28-30 HCSB

Even the most inspired women can, from time to time, find themselves running on empty. Why? Because the inevitable demands of daily life can drain us of our strength and rob us of the joy that is rightfully ours in Christ. Thankfully, God stands ready to renew our spirits, even on the darkest of days. God's Word is clear: When we genuinely lift our hearts and prayers to Him, He renews our strength.

Are you seeking a renewed sense purpose? Turn your heart toward God in prayer. Are you weak or worried? Take the time to delve deeply into God's Holy Word. Are you spiritually depleted? Call upon fellow believers to support you, and call upon Christ to renew your spirit and your life. When you do, you'll discover that the Creator of the universe stands always ready and always able to create a new sense of wonderment and joy in you.

The moment you wake up each morning, all your wishes and hopes for the day rush at you like wild animals. And the first job each morning consists in shoving it all back; in listening to that other voice, taking that other point of view, letting that other, larger, stronger, quieter life coming flowing in.

C. S. Lewis

A TIMELY TIP

You need a regular appointment with your Creator. God is ready to talk to you, and you should prepare yourself each morning to talk to Him.

ENTHUSIASTIC SERVICE

Do your work with enthusiasm. Work as if you were serving the Lord, not as if you were serving only men and women.

Ephesians 6:7 NCV

D
o you see each day as a glorious opportunity to serve God and to do His will? Are you enthused about life, or do you struggle through each day giving scarcely a thought to God's blessings? Are you constantly praising God for His gifts, and are you sharing His Good News with the world? And are you excited about the possibilities for service that God has placed before you, whether at home, at work, at church, or at school? You should be.

You are the recipient of Christ's sacrificial love. Accept it enthusiastically and share it fervently. Jesus deserves your enthusiasm; the world deserves it; and you deserve the experience of sharing it.

The proper perspective creates within us a spirit of reaching outside of ourselves with joy and enthusiasm.

Luci Swindoll

There seems to be a chilling fear of holy enthusiasm among the people of God. We try to tell how happy we are—but we remain so well-controlled that there are very few waves of glory experienced in our midst.

A. W. Tozer

A TIMELY TIP

Be enthusiastic about your faith. John Wesley wrote, "You don't have to advertise a fire. Get on fire for God and the world will come to watch you burn." When you allow yourself to become extremely enthusiastic about your faith, other people will notice—and so will God.

Day 8

IN THE FOOTSTEPS OF THE SAVIOR

The one who loves his life will lose it, and the one who hates his life in this world will keep it for eternal life. If anyone serves Me, he must follow Me. Where I am, there My servant also will be. If anyone serves Me, the Father will honor him.

John 12:25-26 HCSB

Whom will you walk with today? Will you walk with people who worship the ways of the world? Or will you walk with the Son of God? Jesus walks with you. Are you walking with Him? Hopefully, you will choose to walk with Him today and every day of your life. God's Word promises that when you follow in Christ's footsteps, you will learn how to live freely and lightly (Matthew 11:28-30).

Are you worried about the day ahead? Be confident in God's power. He will never desert you. Are you concerned about the future? Be courageous and call upon God. He will protect you. Are you confused? Listen to the quiet voice of your Heavenly Father. He is not a God of confusion. So talk with God; listen to Him; and walk with His Son—starting now.

Will you, with a glad and eager surrender, hand yourself and all that concerns you over into his hands? If you will do this, your soul will begin to know something of the joy of union with Christ.

Hannah Whitall Smith

A TIMELY TIP

If you want to follow in Christ's footsteps . . . welcome Him into your heart, obey His commandments, and share His never-ending love.

PERFECT WISDOM

Therefore, everyone who hears these words of Mine and acts on them will be like a sensible man who built his house on the rock. The rain fell, the rivers rose, and the winds blew and pounded that house. Yet it didn't collapse, because its foundation was on the rock.

Matthew 7:24-25 HCSB

Where will you place your trust today? Will you trust in the wisdom of fallible men and women, or will you place your faith in God's perfect wisdom? Where you choose to place your trust will determine the direction and quality of your life.

Are you tired? Discouraged? Fearful? Be comforted and trust God. Are you worried or anxious? Be confident in God's power and trust His Holy Word. Are you confused? Listen to the quiet voice of your Heavenly Father. He is not a God of confusion. Talk with Him; listen to Him; trust Him. He is steadfast, and He is your protector . . . forever.

Decisions which are made in the light of God's Word are stable and show wisdom.

Vonette Bright

I need the spiritual revival that comes from spending quiet time alone with Jesus in prayer and in thoughtful meditation on His Word.

Anne Graham Lotz

A TIMELY TIP

God's wisdom is perfect, and it's available to you. So if you want to become wise, become a student of God's Word and a follower of His Son.

 *Day 10*

USING YOUR GIFTS

I remind you to keep ablaze the gift of God that is in you.

2 Timothy 1:6 HCSB

All women possess special gifts and talents; you are no exception. But, your gift is no guarantee of success; it must be cultivated and nurtured; otherwise, it will go unused . . . and God's gift to you will be squandered.

Today, accept this challenge: value the talent that God has given you, nourish it, make it grow, and share it with the world. After all, the best way to say "Thank You" for God's gift is to use it.

What we are is God's gift to us. What we become is our gift to God.

Anonymous

You are the only person on earth who can use your ability.

Zig Ziglar

A TIMELY TIP

You are the sole owner of your own set of talents and opportunities. God has given you your own particular gifts—the rest is up to you.

WHY HE SENT HIS SON

For all have sinned, and fall short of the glory of God, being justified freely by His grace through the redemption that is in Christ Jesus . . . .

Romans 3:23-24 NKJV

Despite our shortcomings, God sent His Son so that we might be redeemed from our sins. In doing so, our Heavenly Father demonstrated His infinite mercy and His infinite love. We have received countless gifts from God, but none can compare with the gift of salvation. God's grace is the ultimate gift, and we owe Him the ultimate in thanksgiving.

Christ sacrificed His life on the cross so that we might have eternal life. This gift, freely given from God's only begotten Son, is the priceless possession of everyone who accepts Him as Lord and Savior. We return our Savior's love by welcoming Him into our hearts and sharing His message and His love. When we do so, we are blessed here on earth and throughout all eternity.

Number one, God brought me here. It is by His will that I am in this place. In that fact I will rest. Number two, He will keep me here in His love and give me grace to behave as His child. Number three, He will make the trial a blessing, teaching me the lessons He intends for me to learn and working in me the grace He means to bestow. Number four, in His good time He can bring me out again. How and when, He knows. So, let me say I am here.

Andrew Murray

A TIMELY TIP

God's grace is always available. Jim Cymbala writes, "No one is beyond his grace. No situation, anywhere on earth, it too hard for God." If you sincerely seek God's grace, He will give it freely. So ask, and you will receive.

CELEBRATING OTHERS

Therefore encourage one another and build each other up as you are already doing.

1 Thessalonians 5:11 HCSB

D o you delight in the victories of others? You should. Each day provides countless opportunities to encourage others and to praise their good works. When you do so, you not only spread seeds of joy and happiness, you also obey the commandments of God's Holy Word.

As Christians, we are called upon to spread the Good News of Christ, and we are also called to spread a message of encouragement and hope to the world. So, let us be cheerful Christians with smiles on our faces and encouraging words on our lips. By blessing others, we also bless ourselves, and, at the same time, we do honor to the One who gave His life for us.

A single word, if spoken in a friendly spirit, may be sufficient to turn one from dangerous error.

Fanny Crosby

One of the best ways to encourage someone who's hurting is with your ears—by listening.

Barbara Johnson

A TIMELY TIP

Do you want to be successful and go far in life? Encourage others to do the same. You can't lift other people up without lifting yourself up, too. And remember the words of Oswald Chambers: "God grant that we may not hinder those who are battling their way slowly into the light."

WHAT DOESN'T CHANGE

Jesus Christ is the same yesterday, today, and forever.

Hebrews 13:8 HCSB

Our world is in a state of constant change. God is not. At times, the world seems to be trembling beneath our feet. But we can be comforted in the knowledge that our Heavenly Father is the rock that cannot be shaken. His Word promises, "I am the Lord, I do not change" (Malachi 3:6 NKJV).

Every day that we live, we mortals encounter a multitude of changes—some good, some not so good, some downright disheartening. On those occasions when us must endure life-changing personal losses that leave us breathless, there is a place we can turn for comfort and assurance—we can turn to God. When we do, our loving Heavenly Father stands ready to protect us, to comfort us, to guide us, and, in time, to heal us.

Conditions are always changing; therefore, I must not be dependent upon conditions. What matters supremely is my soul and my relationship to God.

Corrie ten Boom

When you're through changing, you're through!

John Maxwell

A TIMELY TIP

Change is inevitable . . . you can either roll with it or be rolled over by it. Choose the former.

TODAY'S BIBLE READING
Old Testament: Genesis 34-35
New Testament: Matthew 10:1-24

CLAIMING THE JOY

A cheerful heart has a continual feast.

Proverbs 15:15 HCSB

On some days, as every woman knows, it's hard to be cheerful. Sometimes, as the demands of the world increase and our energy sags, we feel less like "cheering up" and more like "tearing up." But even in our darkest hours, we can turn to God, and He will give us comfort.

Few things in life are more sad, or, for that matter, more absurd, than a grumpy Christian. Christ promises us lives of abundance and joy, but He does not force His joy upon us. We must claim His joy for ourselves, and when we do, Jesus, in turn, fills our spirits with His power and His love.

When we place Jesus at the center of our lives and trust Him as our personal Savior, He will transform us, not just for today, but for all eternity. Then we, as God's children, can share Christ's joy and His message with a world that needs both.

God is good, and heaven is forever. And if those two facts don't cheer you up, nothing will.

Marie T. Freeman

If we find ourselves imprisoned, then, we may be sure of this: that it is not our earthly environment that constitutes our prison-house, for the soul's wings scorn all paltry bars and walls of earth's making. The only thing that can really imprison the soul is something that hinders its upward flight.

Hannah Whitall Smith

A TIMELY TIP

Cheerfulness is its own reward—but not its only reward.

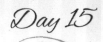

THE MASTER'S TOUCH

Everything is possible to the one who believes.

Mark 9:23 HCSB

When a suffering woman sought healing by simply touching the hem of His garment, Jesus turned and said, "Daughter, be of good comfort; thy faith hath made thee whole" (Matthew 9:22 KJV). We, too, can be made whole when we place our faith completely and unwaveringly in the person of Jesus Christ.

Concentration camp survivor Corrie ten Boom relied on faith during her ten months of imprisonment and torture. Later, despite the fact that four of her family members had died in Nazi death camps, Corrie's faith was unshaken. She wrote, "There is no pit so deep that God's love is not deeper still." Christians take note: Genuine faith in God means faith in all circumstances, happy or sad, joyful or tragic.

If your faith is being tested to the point of breaking, know that your Savior is near. If you reach out to Him in faith, He will give you peace and heal your broken spirit. Be content to touch even the smallest fragment of the Master's garment, and He will make you whole.

He wants us to have a faith that does not complain while waiting, but rejoices because we know our times are in His hands—nail-scarred hands that labor for our highest good.

Kay Arthur

A TIMELY TIP

Don't be embarrassed to discuss your faith: You need not have attended seminary to have worthwhile opinions about your faith.

WHEN THE JOURNEY IS DIFFICULT

For whatever is born of God overcomes the world. And this is the victory that has overcome the world—our faith.

1 John 5:4 NKJV

All of us face times of adversity. On occasion, we all must endure the disappointments and tragedies that befall believers and nonbelievers alike. The reassuring words of 1 John 5:4 remind us that when we accept God's grace, we overcome the passing hardships of this world by relying upon His strength, His love, and His promise of eternal life.

When we face the inevitable difficulties of life-here-on-earth, God stands ready to protect us. Our responsibility, of course, is to ask Him for protection. When we call upon Him in heartfelt prayer, He will answer—in His own time and according to His own plan—and He will heal us. And while we are waiting for God's plans to unfold and for His healing touch to restore us, we can be comforted in the knowledge that our Creator can overcome any obstacle, even if we cannot. Let us take God at His word, and let us trust Him.

Crisis brings us face to face with our inadequacy and our inadequacy in turn leads us to the inexhaustible sufficiency of God.

Catherine Marshall

A TIMELY TIP

Remember that ultimately you and you alone are responsible for controlling your appetites. Others may warn you, help you, or encourage you, but in the end, the habits that rule your life are the very same habits that you yourself have formed. Thankfully, since you formed these habits, you can also break them—if you decide to do so.

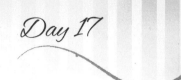
DISCIPLINE YOURSELF

Discipline yourself for the purpose of godliness.

1 Timothy 4:7 NASB

Are you a self-disciplined woman? If so, congratulations . . . your disciplined approach to life can help you build a more meaningful relationship with God. Why? Because God expects all His believers (including you) to lead lives of disciplined obedience to Him . . . and He rewards those believers who do.

Sometimes, it's hard to be dignified and disciplined. Why? Because you live in a world where many prominent people want you to believe that dignified, self-disciplined behavior is going out of style. But don't deceive yourself: self-discipline never goes out of style.

Your greatest accomplishments will probably require heaping helpings of self-discipline—which, by the way, is perfectly fine with God. After all, He knows that you're up to the task, and He has big plans for you. God will do His part to fulfill those plans, and the rest, of course, depends upon you.

Work is doing it. Discipline is doing it every day. Diligence is doing it well every day.

Dave Ramsey

In the very place where God has put us, whatever its limitations, whatever kind of work it may be, we may indeed serve the Lord Christ.

Elisabeth Elliot

A TIMELY TIP

A disciplined lifestyle gives you more control: The more disciplined you become, the more you can take control over your life (which, by the way, is far better than letting your life take control over you).

Day 18

PATS ON THE BACK

So then, we must pursue what promotes peace and what builds up one another.

Romans 14:19 HCSB

L ife is a team sport, and all of us need occasional pats on the back from our teammates. In the book of Ephesians, Paul writes, "Do not let any unwholesome talk come out of your mouths, but only what is helpful for building others up according to their needs, that it may benefit those who listen" (4:29 NIV). Paul reminds us that when we choose our words carefully, we can have a powerful impact on those around us.

Since we don't always know who needs our help, the best strategy is to encourage all the people who cross our paths. So today, be a world-class source of encouragement to everyone you meet. Never has the need been greater.

Don't forget that a single sentence, spoken at the right moment, can change somebody's whole perspective on life. A little encouragement can go a long, long way.

Marie T. Freeman

Always stay connected to people and seek out things that bring you joy. Dream with abandon. Pray confidently.

Barbara Johnson

A TIMELY TIP

Think carefully about the things you say so that your words can be a "gift of encouragement" to others. Your friends and family members need encouraging words . . . from you.

Day 19

YOUR SHINING LIGHT

While ye have light, believe in the light, that ye may be the children of light.

John 12:36 KJV

The Bible says that you are "the light that gives light to the world." What kind of light have you been giving off? Hopefully, you've been a good example for everybody to see. Why? Because the world needs all the light it can get, and that includes your light, too!

Christ showed enduring love for you by willingly sacrificing His own life so that you might have eternal life. As a response to His sacrifice, you should love Him, praise Him, and share His message of salvation with your neighbors and with the world. So let your light shine today and every day. When you do, God will bless you now and forever.

Light is stronger than darkness—darkness cannot "comprehend" or "overcome" it.

Anne Graham Lotz

When we are in a situation where Jesus is all we have, we soon discover he is all we really need.

Gigi Graham Tchividjian

A TIMELY TIP

Leadership is a responsibility that must not be taken lightly. If you choose to lead others, you should first choose to follow Jesus.

IN HIS HANDS

For whatever is born of God overcomes the world. And this is the victory that has overcome the world—our faith.

1 John 5:4 NKJV

The first element of a successful life is faith: faith in God, faith in His Son, and faith in His promises. If we place our lives in God's hands, our faith is rewarded in ways that we—as human beings with clouded vision and limited understanding—can scarcely comprehend. But, if we seek to rely solely upon our own resources, or if we seek earthly success outside the boundaries of God's commandments, we reap a bitter harvest for ourselves and for our loved ones.

Do you desire the abundance and success that God has promised? Then trust Him today and every day that you live. Then, when you have entrusted your future to the Giver of all things good, rest assured that your future is secure, not only for today, but also for all eternity.

Faith is seeing light with the eyes of your heart, when the eyes of your body see only darkness.

Barbara Johnson

God uses our most stumbling, faltering faith-steps as the open door to His doing for us "more than we ask or think."

Catherine Marshall

A TIMELY TIP

Feelings come and feelings go, but God never changes. So when you have a choice between trusting your feelings or trusting God, trust God.

Day 21

THE LORD IS NEAR

Draw near to God, and He will draw near to you.

James 4:8 HCSB

Since God is everywhere, we are free to sense His presence whenever we take the time to quiet our souls and turn our prayers to Him. But sometimes, amid the incessant demands of everyday life, we turn our thoughts far from God; when we do, we suffer.

Do you set aside quiet moments each day to offer praise to your Creator? As a woman who has received the gift of God's grace, you most certainly should. Silence is a gift that you give to yourself and to God. During these moments of stillness, you will often sense the infinite love and power of your Creator—and He, in turn, will speak directly to your heart.

The familiar words of Psalm 46:10 remind us to "Be still, and know that I am God." When we do so, we encounter the awesome presence of our loving Heavenly Father, and we are comforted in the knowledge that God is not just near. He is here.

God walks with us. He scoops us up in His arms or simply sits with us in silent strength until we cannot avoid the awesome recognition that yes, even now, He is here.

Gloria Gaither

God wants to be in our leisure time as much as He is in our churches and in our work.

Beth Moore

A TIMELY TIP

Perhaps you have become wrapped up in the world's problems or your own problems. If so, it's time to open yourself up to God. When you do, God will bless you and comfort you.

Day 22

SEEKING HIS WILL

Teach me to do Your will, for You are my God; Your Spirit is good. Lead me in the land of uprightness.

Psalm 143:10 NKJV

God has a plan for our world and our lives. God does not do things by accident; He is willful and intentional. Unfortunately for us, we cannot always understand the will of God. Why? Because we are mortal beings with limited understanding. Although we cannot fully comprehend the will of God, we should always trust the will of God.

As this day unfolds, seek God's will and obey His Word. When you entrust your life to Him without reservation, He will give you the courage to meet any challenge, the strength to endure any trial, and the wisdom to live in His righteousness and in His peace.

The only safe place is in the center of God's will. It is not only the safest place. It is also the most rewarding and the most satisfying place to be.

Gigi Graham Tchividjian

Jesus told us that only in God's will would we have real freedom.

Catherine Marshall

A TIMELY TIP

When you place yourself in the center of God's will . . . He will provide for your needs and direct your path.

GOOD HABITS, BAD HABITS

Do not be deceived: "Evil company corrupts good habits."

1 Corinthians 15:33 NKJV

It's an old saying and a true one: First, you make your habits, and then your habits make you. Some habits will inevitably bring you closer to God; other habits will lead you away from the path He has chosen for you. If you sincerely desire to improve your spiritual health, you must honestly examine the habits that make up the fabric of your day. And you must abandon those habits that are displeasing to God.

If you trust God, and if you keep asking for His help, He can transform your life. If you sincerely ask Him to help you, the same God who created the universe will help you defeat the harmful habits that have heretofore defeated you. So, if at first you don't succeed, keep praying. God is listening, and He's ready to help you become a better person if you ask Him . . . so ask today.

If you want to form a new habit, get to work. If you want to break a bad habit, get on your knees.

Marie T. Freeman

Since behaviors become habits, make them work with you and not against you.

E. Stanley Jones

A TIMELY TIP

Choose your habits carefully. Habits are easier to make than they are to break, so be careful!

CHOOSING THE GOOD LIFE

And in that day you will ask Me nothing. Most assuredly, I say to you, whatever you ask the Father in My name He will give you. Until now you have asked nothing in My name. Ask, and you will receive, that your joy may be full.

John 16:23-24 NKJV

God offers us abundance through His Son, Jesus. Whether or not we accept God's abundance is, of course, up to each of us. When we entrust our hearts and our days to the One who created us, we experience abundance through the grace and sacrifice of His Son, Jesus. But, when we turn our thoughts and our energies away from God's commandments, we inevitably forfeit the spiritual abundance that might otherwise be ours.

What is your focus today? Are you focused on God's Word and His will for your life? Or are you focused on the distractions and temptations of a difficult world. The answer to this question will, to a surprising extent, determine the quality and the direction of your day.

If you sincerely seek the spiritual abundance that your Savior offers, then follow Him completely and without reservation. When you do, you will receive the love, the life, and the abundance that He has promised.

It would be wrong to have a "poverty complex," for to think ourselves paupers is to deny either the King's riches or to deny our being His children.

Catherine Marshall

A TIMELY TIP

Don't miss out on God's abundance. Every day is a beautifully wrapped gift from God. Unwrap it; use it; and give thanks to the Giver.

TO JUDGE OR NOT TO JUDGE

When they persisted in questioning Him, He stood up and said to them, "The one without sin among you should be the first to throw a stone at her."

John 8:7 HCSB

The warning of Matthew 7:1 is clear: "Judge not, that ye be not judged" (KJV). Yet even the most devoted Christians may fall prey to a powerful yet subtle temptation: the temptation to judge others. But as obedient followers of Christ, we are commanded to refrain from such behavior.

As Jesus came upon a young woman who had been condemned by the Pharisees, He spoke not only to the crowd that was gathered there, but also to all generations when He warned, "He that is without sin among you, let him first cast a stone at her" (John 8:7 KJV). Christ's message is clear, and it applies not only to the Pharisees of ancient times, but also to us.

Judging draws the judgment of others.

Catherine Marshall

Christians think they are prosecuting attorneys or judges, when, in reality, God has called all of us to be witnesses.

Warren Wiersbe

A TIMELY TIP

To the extent you judge others, so, too, will you be judged. So you must, to the best of your ability, refrain from judgmental thoughts and words.

Day 26

NEVER-ENDING LOVE

And we have this command from Him: the one who loves God must also love his brother.

1 John 4:21 HCSB

C. S. Lewis observed, "A man's spiritual health is exactly proportional to his love for God." If we are to enjoy the spiritual health that God intends for us, we must praise Him, we must love Him, and we must obey Him.

When we worship God faithfully and obediently, we invite His love into our hearts. When we truly worship God, we allow Him to rule over our days and our lives. In turn, we grow to love God even more deeply as we sense His love for us.

Today, open your heart to the Father. And let your obedience be a fitting response to His never-ending love.

When we develop an authentic love relationship with God, we will not be able to keep Him compartmentalized in "churchy," religious categories.

Beth Moore

To love God is to love His will.

Elisabeth Elliot

A TIMELY TIP

Because God first loved you, you should love Him. And one way that you demonstrate your love is by obeying Him.

OUR ACTIONS AND OUR BELIEFS

As you have therefore received Christ Jesus the Lord, so walk in Him, rooted and built up in Him and established in the faith, as you have been taught, abounding in it with thanksgiving.

Colossians 2:6-7 NKJV

As Christians, we must do our best to make sure that our actions are accurate reflections of our beliefs. Our theology must be demonstrated, not only by our words but, more importantly, by our actions. In short, we should be practical believers, quick to act whenever we see an opportunity to serve God.

We may proclaim our beliefs to our hearts' content, but our proclamations will mean nothing—to others or to ourselves—unless we accompany our words with deeds that match. The sermons that we live are far more compelling than the ones we preach. So remember this: whether you like it or not, your life is an accurate reflection of your creed. If this fact gives you cause for concern, don't bother talking about the changes that you intend to make—make them. And then, when your good deeds speak for themselves—as they most certainly will—don't interrupt.

Although God causes all things to work together for good for His children, He still holds us accountable for our behavior.

Kay Arthur

Either God's Word keeps you from sin, or sin keeps you from God's Word.

Corrie ten Boom

A TIMELY TIP

How can you guard your steps? By walking with Jesus every day of your life.

Day 28

LIFE'S ROADMAP

All Scripture is inspired by God and is profitable for teaching, for rebuking, for correcting, for training in righteousness, so that the man of God may be complete, equipped for every good work.

2 Timothy 3:16-17 HCSB

God's Word is unlike any other book. The Bible is a roadmap for life here on earth and for life eternal. As Christians, we are called upon to study God's Holy Word, to trust its promises, to follow its commandments, and to share its Good News with the world.

As women who seek to follow in the footsteps of the One from Galilee, we must study the Bible and meditate upon its meaning for our lives. Otherwise, we deprive ourselves of a priceless gift from our Creator. God's Holy Word is, indeed, a life-changing, one-of-a-kind treasure. And, a passing acquaintance with the Good Book is insufficient for Christians who seek to obey God's Word and to understand His will.

The Reference Point for the Christian is the Bible. All values, judgments, and attitudes must be gauged in relationship to this Reference Point.

Ruth Bell Graham

BIBLE: Basic Instructions Before Leaving Earth.

Anonymous

A TIMELY TIP

God intends for you to use His Word as your guidebook for life . . . your intentions should be the same.

THIS IS HIS DAY

This is the day the Lord has made; let us rejoice and be glad in it.

Psalm 118:24 HCSB

The 118th Psalm reminds us that today, like every other day, is a cause for celebration. God gives us this day; He fills it to the brim with possibilities, and He challenges us to use it for His purposes. The day is presented to us fresh and clean at midnight, free of charge, but we must beware: Today is a non-renewable resource—once it's gone, it's gone forever. Our responsibility, of course, is to use this day in the service of God's will and according to His commandments.

Today, treasure the time that God has given you. Give Him the glory and the praise and the thanksgiving that He deserves. And search for the hidden possibilities that God has placed along your path. This day is a priceless gift from God, so use it joyfully and encourage others to do likewise. After all, this is the day the Lord has made . . . .

If you can forgive the person you were, accept the person you are, and believe in the person you will become, you are headed for joy. So celebrate your life.

Barbara Johnson

The highest and most desirable state of the soul is to praise God in celebration for being alive.

Luci Swindol

A TIMELY TIP

If you don't feel like celebrating, start counting your blessings. Before long, you'll realize that you have plenty of reasons to celebrate.

CHARACTER-BUILDING TAKES TIME

For this very reason, make every effort to supplement your faith with goodness, goodness with knowledge, knowledge with self-control, self-control with endurance, endurance with godliness.

2 Peter 1:5-6 HCSB

Character is built slowly over a lifetime. It is the sum of every right decision, every honest word, every noble thought, and every heartfelt prayer. It is forged on the anvil of honorable work and polished by the twin virtues of generosity and humility. Character is a precious thing—difficult to build but easy to tear down.

As believers in Christ, we must seek to live each day with discipline, honesty, and faith. When we do, integrity becomes a habit. And God smiles.

There is something about having endured great loss that brings purity of purpose and strength of character.

Barbara Johnson

Each one of us is God's special work of art. Through us, He teaches and inspires, delights and encourages, informs and uplifts all those who view our lives. God, the master artist, is most concerned about expressing Himself—His thoughts and His intentions—through what He paints in our characters.

Joni Eareckson Tada

A TIMELY TIP

When your words are honest and your intentions are pure, you have nothing to fear.

CHOICES THAT PLEASE GOD

I have set before you life and death, blessing and curse. Choose life so that you and your descendants may live, love the Lord your God, obey Him, and remain faithful to Him. For He is your life, and He will prolong your life in the land the Lord swore to give to your fathers Abraham, Isaac, and Jacob.

Deuteronomy 30:19-20 HCSB

Sometimes, because you're an imperfect human being, you may become so wrapped up in meeting society's expectations that you fail to focus on God's expectations. To do so is a mistake of major proportions—don't make it. Instead, seek God's guidance as you focus your energies on becoming the best "you" that you can possibly be. And, when it comes to matters of conscience, seek approval not from your peers, but from your Creator.

Whom will you try to please today: God or man? Your primary obligation is not to please imperfect men and women. Your obligation is to strive diligently to meet the expectations of an all-knowing and perfect God. Trust Him always. Love Him always. Praise Him always. And make choices that please Him. Always.

Commitment to His lordship on Easter, at revivals, or even every Sunday is not enough. We must choose this day—and every day—whom we will serve. This deliberate act of the will is the inevitable choice between habitual fellowship and habitual failure.

Beth Moore

A TIMELY TIP

First you make choices . . . and pretty soon those choices begin to shape your life. That's why you must make smart choices . . . or face the consequences of making dumb ones.

Day 32

BUILDING FELLOWSHIP

It is good and pleasant when God's people live together in peace!

Psalm 133:1 NCV

Fellowship with other believers should be an integral part of your everyday life. Your association with fellow Christians should be uplifting, enlightening, encouraging, and consistent.

Are you an active member of your own fellowship? Are you a builder of bridges inside the four walls of your church and outside it? Do you contribute to God's glory by contributing your time and your talents to a close-knit band of believers? Hopefully so. The fellowship of believers is intended to be a powerful tool for spreading God's Good News and uplifting His children. And God intends for you to be a fully contributing member of that fellowship. Your intentions should be the same.

Be united with other Christians. A wall with loose bricks is not good. The bricks must be cemented together.

Corrie ten Boom

In God's economy you will be hard-pressed to find many examples of successful "Lone Rangers."

Luci Swindoll

A TIMELY TIP

God intends for you to be an active member of your fellowship. Your intentions should be the same.

EXTREME CHANGES

Then He said to them all, "If anyone wants to come with Me, he must deny himself, take up his cross daily, and follow Me."

Luke 9:23 HCSB

Jesus made an extreme sacrifice for you. Are you willing to make extreme changes in your life for Him? Can you honestly say that you're passionate about your faith and that you're really following Jesus? Hopefully so. But if you're preoccupied with other things—or if you're strictly a one-day-a-week Christian—then you're in need of an extreme spiritual makeover!

Nothing is more important than your wholehearted commitment to your Creator and to His only begotten Son. Your faith must never be an afterthought; it must be your ultimate priority, your ultimate possession, and your ultimate passion. You are the recipient of Christ's love. Accept it enthusiastically and share it passionately. Jesus deserves your extreme enthusiasm; the world deserves it; and you deserve the experience of sharing it.

The Christian faith is meant to be lived moment by moment. It isn't some broad, general outline—it's a long walk with a real Person. Details count: passing thoughts, small sacrifices, a few encouraging words, little acts of kindness, brief victories over nagging sins.

Joni Eareckson Tada

A TIMELY TIP

Think about your relationship with Jesus: what it is, and what it can be. Then, as you embark upon the next phase of your life's journey, be sure to walk with your Savior every step of the way.

Day 34

TODAY'S BIBLE READING
Old Testament: Exodus 31-33
New Testament: Matthew 22:23-46

FRIENDSHIPS THAT HONOR GOD

If your life honors the name of Jesus, he will honor you.

2 Thessalonians 1:12 MSG

Some friendships help us honor God; these friendships should be nurtured. Other friendships place us in situations where we are tempted to dishonor God by disobeying His commandments; friendships such as these have the potential to do us great harm.

Because we tend to become like our friends, we must choose our friends carefully. Because our friends influence us in ways that are both subtle and powerful, we must ensure that our friendships are pleasing to God. When we spend our days in the presence of godly believers, we are blessed, not only by those friends, but also by our Creator.

The best times in life are made a thousand times better when shared with a dear friend.

Luci Swindoll

Inasmuch as anyone pushes you nearer to God, he or she is your friend.

Barbara Johnson

A TIMELY TIP

Take the time to reconnect with old friends. They'll be glad you did, and so, too, will you.

THE MIRACLE WORKER

Jesus said to them, "I have shown you many great miracles from the Father."
John 10:32 NIV

God is a miracle worker. Throughout history He has intervened in the course of human events in ways that cannot be explained by science or human rationale. And He's still doing so today.

God's miracles are not limited to special occasions, nor are they witnessed by a select few. God is crafting His wonders all around us: the miracle of the birth of a new baby; the miracle of a world renewing itself with every sunrise; the miracle of lives transformed by God's love and grace. Each day, God's handiwork is evident for all to see and experience.

Today, seize the opportunity to inspect God's hand at work. His miracles come in a variety of shapes and sizes, so keep your eyes and your heart open. Be watchful, and you'll soon be amazed.

There is Someone who makes possible what seems completely impossible.
Catherine Marshall

Faith means believing in realities that go beyond sense and sight. It is the awareness of unseen divine realities all around you.
Joni Eareckson Tada

A TIMELY TIP

God is in the business of doing miraculous things. You should never be afraid to ask Him for a miracle.

THE ULTIMATE INSTRUCTION MANUAL

The one who has contempt for instruction will pay the penalty, but the one who respects a command will be rewarded.

Proverbs 13:13 HCSB

The Holy Bible contains thorough instructions which, if followed, lead to fulfillment, righteousness, and salvation. But, if we choose to ignore God's commandments, the results are as predictable as they are tragic.

A righteous life has many components: faith, honesty, generosity, love, kindness, humility, gratitude, and worship, to name but a few. If we seek to follow the steps of our Savior, Jesus Christ, we must seek to live according to His commandments. Let us follow God's commandments, and let us conduct our lives in such a way that we might be shining examples for those who have not yet found Christ.

Let us remember therefore this lesson: That to worship our God sincerely we must evermore begin by hearkening to His voice, and by giving ear to what He commands us. For if every man goes after his own way, we shall wander. We may well run, but we shall never be a whit nearer to the right way, but rather farther away from it.

John Calvin

A TIMELY TIP

Remember this: God has given us His commandments for a reason: to obey them. These commandments are not suggestions, helpful hints, or friendly reminders—they are rules we must live by . . . or else!

Day 37

THE LAST WORD

For God has not given us a spirit of fearfulness, but one of power, love, and sound judgment. So don't be ashamed of the testimony about our Lord, or of me His prisoner. Instead, share in suffering for the gospel, relying on the power of God.

2 Timothy 1:7-8 HCSB

All of us may find our courage tested by the inevitable disappointments and tragedies of life. After all, ours is a world filled with uncertainty, hardship, sickness, and danger. Old Man Trouble, it seems, is never too far from the front door.

When we focus upon our fears and our doubts, we may find many reasons to lie awake at night and fret about the uncertainties of the coming day. A better strategy, of course, is to focus not upon our fears, but instead upon our God.

God is your shield and your strength; you are His forever. So don't focus your thoughts upon the fears of the day. Instead, trust God's plan and His eternal love for you. And remember: God is good, and He has the last word.

God shields us from most of the things we fear, but when He chooses not to shield us, He unfailingly allots grace in the measure needed.

Elisabeth Elliot

Fear lurks in the shadows of every area of life. The future may look very threatening. Jesus says, "Stop being afraid. Trust me!"

Charles Swindoll

A TIMELY TIP

Are you feeling anxious or fearful? If so, trust God more. Entrust the future—your future—to God.

YOU ARE BLESSED

I will make them and the area around My hill a blessing: I will send down showers in their season—showers of blessing.

Ezekiel 34:26 HCSB

If you sat down and began counting your blessings, how long would it take? A very, very long time! Your blessings include life, freedom, family, friends, talents, and possessions, for starters. But, your greatest blessing—a gift that is yours for the asking—is God's gift of salvation through Christ Jesus.

Today, begin making a list of your blessings. You most certainly will not be able to make a complete list, but take a few moments and jot down as many blessings as you can. Then give thanks to the giver of all good things: God. His love for you is eternal, as are His gifts. And it's never too soon—or too late—to offer Him thanks.

Oh! what a Savior, gracious to all, / Oh! how His blessings round us fall, / Gently to comfort, kindly to cheer, / Sleeping or waking, God is near.

Fanny Crosby

Count your blessings! Recounts are OK . . .

Anonymous

A TIMELY TIP

If you need a little cheering up, start counting your blessings. In truth, you really have too many blessings to count, but it never hurts to try.

THE POWER OF FAITH

Believe in the Lord your God, and you will be established; believe in His prophets, and you will succeed.

2 Chronicles 20:20 HCSB

Every life—including yours—is a series of successes and failures, celebrations and disappointments, joys and sorrows. Every step of the way, through every triumph and tragedy, God will stand by your side and strengthen you . . . if you have faith in Him. Jesus taught His disciples that if they had faith, they could move mountains. You can too.

When you place your faith, your trust, indeed your life in the hands of Christ Jesus, you'll be amazed at the marvelous things He can do with you and through you. So strengthen your faith through praise, through worship, through Bible study, and through prayer. And trust God's plans. With Him, all things are possible, and He stands ready to open a world of possibilities to you . . . if you have faith.

Faith is an act of the will, a choice, based on the unbreakable Word of a God who cannot lie, and who showed what love and obedience and sacrifice mean, in the person of Jesus Christ.

Elisabeth Elliot

Faith is strengthened only when we ourselves exercise it.

Catherine Marshall

A TIMELY TIP

If you don't have faith, you'll never move mountains. But if you do have faith, there's no limit to the things that you and God, working together, can accomplish.

NEW BEGINNINGS

Do not remember the former things, nor consider the things of old. Behold, I will do a new thing.

Isaiah 43:18-19 NKJV

Each new day offers countless opportunities to serve God, to seek His will, and to obey His teachings. But each day also offers countless opportunities to stray from God's commandments and to wander far from His path.

Sometimes, we wander aimlessly in a wilderness of our own making, but God has better plans of us. And, whenever we ask Him to renew our strength and guide our steps, He does so.

Consider this day a new beginning. Consider it a fresh start, a renewed opportunity to serve your Creator with willing hands and a loving heart. Ask God to renew your sense of purpose as He guides your steps. Today is a glorious opportunity to serve your Father in heaven. Seize that opportunity while you can; tomorrow may indeed be too late.

If the leaves had not been let go to fall and wither, if the tree had not consented to be a skeleton for many months, there would be no new life rising, no bud, no flower, no fruit, no seed, no new generation.

Elisabeth Elliot

No matter how badly we have failed, we can always get up and begin again. Our God is the God of new beginnings.

Warren Wiersbe

A TIMELY TIP

If you're going into a new phase of life, be sure to make God your partner. If you do, He'll guide your steps, He'll help carry your burdens, and He'll help you focus on the things that really matter.

OPTIMISM NOW!

And now, dear brothers and sisters, let me say one more thing as I close this letter. Fix your thoughts on what is true and honorable and right. Think about things that are pure and lovely and admirable. Think about things that are excellent and worthy of praise.

Philippians 4:8 NLT

As Christian women, we have every reason to rejoice. God is in His heaven; Christ has risen, and we are the sheep of His flock. But, when the demands of life seem great and our resources seem small by comparison, we may find ourselves exhausted, discouraged, or both.

What's your attitude today? Are you fearful, angry, or worried. Are you confused, bitter, or pessimistic? If so, God wants to have a little chat with you.

God wants you to experience His joy and abundance. But, God will not force His joy upon you; you must claim it for yourself. So today, and every day thereafter, celebrate this life that God has given you. Think optimistically about yourself and your future. Give thanks to the One who has given you everything, and trust in your heart that He wants to give you so much more.

Developing a positive attitude means working continually to find what is uplifting and encouraging.

Barbara Johnson

Every major spiritual battle is in the mind.

Charles Stanley

A TIMELY TIP

If you want to improve the quality of your thoughts, ask God to help you.

COURTESY MATTERS

Out of respect for Christ, be courteously reverent to one another.

Ephesians 5:21 MSG

Did Christ instruct us in matters of etiquette and courtesy? Of course He did. Christ's instructions are clear: "In everything, therefore, treat people the same way you want them to treat you, for this is the Law and the Prophets" (Matthew 7:12 NASB). Jesus did not say, "In some things, treat people as you wish to be treated." And, He did not say, "From time to time, treat others with kindness." Christ said that we should treat others as we wish to be treated in every aspect of our daily lives. This, of course, is a tall order indeed, but as Christians, we are commanded to do our best.

Today, be a little kinder than necessary to family members, friends, and total strangers. And, as you consider all the things that Christ has done in your life, honor Him with your words and with your deeds. He expects no less, and He deserves no less.

Courtesy is contagious.

Marie T. Freeman

Only the courteous can love, but it is love that makes them courteous.

C. S. Lewis

A TIMELY TIP

Remember: courtesy isn't optional. If you disagree, do so without being disagreeable; if you're angry, hold your tongue; if you're frustrated or tired, don't argue . . . take a nap.

BEYOND THE DIFFICULTIES

When you are in distress and all these things have happened to you, you will return to the Lord your God in later days and obey Him. He will not leave you, destroy you, or forget the covenant with your fathers that He swore to them by oath, because the Lord your God is a compassionate God.

Deuteronomy 4:30-31 HCSB

Sometimes the traffic jams, and sometimes the dog gobbles the homework. But, when we find ourselves overtaken by the minor frustrations of life, we must catch ourselves, take a deep breath, and lift our thoughts upward. Although we are here on earth struggling to rise above the distractions of the day, we need never struggle alone. God is here—eternally and faithfully, with infinite patience and love—and, if we reach out to Him, He will restore perspective and peace to our souls.

If you find yourself enduring difficult circumstances, remember that God remains in His heaven. If you become discouraged with the direction of your day or your life, lift your thoughts and prayers to Him. He will guide you through your difficulties and beyond them.

Do the unpleasant work first and enjoy the rest of the day.

Marie T. Freeman

Recently I've been learning that life comes down to this: God is in everything. Regardless of what difficulties I am experiencing at the moment, or what things aren't as I would like them to be, I look at the circumstances and say, "Lord, what are you trying to teach me?"

Catherine Marshall

A TIMELY TIP

Difficult days come and go. Stay the course. The sun is shining somewhere, and will soon shine on you.

SHOUT FOR JOY

Shout triumphantly to the Lord, all the earth. Serve the Lord with gladness; come before Him with joyful songs.

Psalm 100:1-2 HCSB

The 100th Psalm reminds us that the entire earth should "Shout for joy to the Lord." As God's children, we are blessed beyond measure, but sometimes, as busy women living in a demanding world, we are slow to count our gifts and even slower to give thanks to the Giver.

Our blessings include life and health, family and friends, freedom and possessions—for starters. And, the gifts we receive from God are multiplied when we share them. May we always give thanks to God for His blessings, and may we always demonstrate our gratitude by sharing our gifts with others. The 118th Psalm reminds us that, "This is the day which the LORD has made; let us rejoice and be glad in it" (v. 24, NASB). May we celebrate this day and the One who created it.

If you can forgive the person you were, accept the person you are, and believe in the person you will become, you are headed for joy. So celebrate your life.

Barbara Johnson

God knows everything. He can manage everything, and He loves us. Surely this is enough for a fullness of joy that is beyond words.

Hannah Whitall Smith

A TIMELY TIP

Every day should be a cause for celebration. By celebrating the gift of life, you protect your heart from the dangers of pessimism, regret, hopelessness, and bitterness.

TURNING AWAY FROM ANGER

My dear brothers and sisters, always be willing to listen and slow to speak. Do not become angry easily, because anger will not help you live the right kind of life God wants.

James 1:19-20 NCV

Perhaps God gave each of us one mouth and two ears in order that we might listen twice as much as we speak. Unfortunately, many of us do otherwise, especially when we become angry.

Anger is a natural human emotion that is sometimes necessary and appropriate. Even Jesus Himself became angered when He confronted the moneychangers in the temple. But, more often than not, our frustrations are of the more mundane variety. When you are tempted to lose your temper over the minor inconveniences of life, don't. Turn away from anger, and turn instead to God.

When the winds are cold, and the days are long, / And thy soul from care would hide, / Fly back, fly back, to thy Father then, / And beneath His wings abide.

Fanny Crosby

Anger is the fluid that love bleeds when you cut it.

C. S. Lewis

A TIMELY TIP

When you lose your temper . . . you lose.

Day 46

FEARING GOD

The fear of the Lord is the beginning of knowledge.

Proverbs 1:7 HCSB

Are you a woman who possesses a healthy, fearful respect for God's power? Hopefully so. After all, God's Word teaches that the fear of the Lord is the beginning of knowledge (Proverbs 1:7).

When we fear the Creator—and when we honor Him by obeying His commandments—we receive God's approval and His blessings. But, when we ignore Him or disobey His commandments, we invite disastrous consequences. God's hand shapes the universe, and it shapes our lives. As believers, we must cultivate a sincere respect for God's awesome power. The fear of the Lord is, indeed, the beginning of knowledge. So today, as you face the realities of everyday life, remember this: until you acquire a healthy, respectful fear of God's power, your education is incomplete, and so is your faith.

Spiritual worship comes from our very core and is fueled by an awesome reverence and desire for God.

Beth Moore

A healthy fear of God will do much to deter us from sin.

Charles Swindoll

A TIMELY TIP

When you possess a healthy fear of God, He will guide your steps and guard your heart.

NOURISHED BY THE WORD

You will be a good servant of Christ Jesus, nourished by the words of the faith and of the good teaching that you have followed.

1 Timothy 4:6 HCSB

Do you read your Bible a lot . . . or not? The answer to this simple question will determine, to a surprising extent, the quality of your life and the direction of your faith.

As you establish priorities for life, you must decide whether God's Word will be a bright spotlight that guides your path every day or a tiny nightlight that occasionally flickers in the dark. The decision to study the Bible—or not—is yours and yours alone. But make no mistake: how you choose to use your Bible will have a profound impact on you and your loved ones.

The Bible is the ultimate guide for life; make it your guidebook as well. When you do; you can be comforted in the knowledge that your steps are guided by a Source of wisdom and truth that never fails.

Knowing God involves an intimate, personal relationship that is developed over time through prayer and getting answers to prayer, through Bible study and applying its teaching to our lives, through obedience and experiencing the power of God, through moment-by-moment submission to Him that results in a moment-by-moment filling of the Holy Spirit.

Anne Graham Lotz

A TIMELY TIP

The Bible is God's roadmap for life here on earth and for life eternal. How you choose to use your Bible is, of course, up to you . . . and so are the consequences. So today, challenge your faith by making sure that you're spending quality time each day studying God's Word.

TOO BUSY

Careful planning puts you ahead in the long run; hurry and scurry puts you further behind.

Proverbs 21:5 MSG

Are you one of those women who is simply too busy for your own good? Has the hectic pace of life robbed you of the peace that might otherwise be yours through Jesus Christ? If so, you're doing a disservice to yourself and your family.

Through His Son Jesus, God offers you a peace that passes human understanding, but He won't force His peace upon you; in order to experience it, you must slow down long enough to sense His presence and His love.

Today, as a gift to yourself, to your family, and to the world, be still and claim the inner peace that is your spiritual birthright—the peace of Jesus Christ. It is offered freely; it has been paid for in full; it is yours for the asking. So ask. And then share.

How much of our lives are, well, so daily. How often our hours are filled with the mundane, seemingly unimportant things that have to be done, whether at home or work. These very "daily" tasks could become a celebration of praise. "It is through consecration," someone has said, "that drudgery is made divine."

Gigi Graham Tchividjian

A TIMELY TIP

Do first things first, and keep your focus on high-priority tasks. And remember this: your highest priority should be your relationship with God and His Son.

THE GIFT OF CHEERFULNESS

Worry is a heavy load, but a kind word cheers you up.

Proverbs 12:25 NCV

Cheerfulness is a gift that we give to others and to ourselves. And, as believers who have been saved by a risen Christ, why shouldn't we be cheerful? The answer, of course, is that we have every reason to honor our Savior with joy in our hearts, smiles on our faces, and words of celebration on our lips.

Christ promises us lives of abundance and joy if we accept His love and His grace. Yet sometimes, even the most righteous among us are beset by fits of ill temper and frustration. During these moments, we may not feel like turning our thoughts and prayers to Christ, but that's precisely what we should do. When we do so, we simply can't stay grumpy for long.

We may run, walk, stumble, drive, or fly, but let us never lose sight of the reason for the journey, or miss a chance to see a rainbow on the way.

Gloria Gaither

Be assured, my dear friend, that it is no joy to God in seeing you with a dreary countenance.

C. H. Spurgeon

A TIMELY TIP

Do you need a little cheering up? If so, find somebody else who needs cheering up, too. Then, do your best to brighten that person's day. When you do, you'll discover that cheering up other people is a wonderful way to cheer yourself up, too.

A GROWING RELATIONSHIP WITH GOD

But grow in the grace and knowledge of our Lord and Savior Jesus Christ. To Him be the glory both now and to the day of eternity.

2 Peter 3:18 HCSB

Your relationship with God is ongoing; it unfolds day by day, and it offers countless opportunities to grow closer to Him . . . or not. As each new day unfolds, you are confronted with a wide range of decisions: how you will behave, where you will direct your thoughts, with whom you will associate, and what you will choose to worship. These choices, along with many others like them, are yours and yours alone. How you choose determines how your relationship with God will unfold.

Are you continuing to grow in your love and knowledge of the Lord, or are you "satisfied" with the current state of your spiritual health? Hopefully, you're determined to make yourself a growing Christian. Your Savior deserves no less, and neither, by the way, do you.

We set our eyes on the finish line, forgetting the past, and straining toward the mark of spiritual maturity and fruitfulness.

Vonette Bright

The Holy Spirit testifies of Jesus. So when you are filled with the Holy Spirit, you speak about our Lord and really live to His honor.

Corrie ten Boom

A TIMELY TIP

The difference between theological dogma and faith with works is the difference between stagnant religion and joyful Christianity.

HIS COMFORTING HAND

But God, who comforts the humble, comforted us . . . .

2 Corinthians 7:6 HCSB

If you have been touched by the transforming hand of Jesus, then you have every reason to live courageously. Still, even if you are a dedicated Christian, you may find yourself discouraged by the inevitable disappointments and tragedies that occur in the lives of believers and non-believers alike.

The next time you find your courage tested to the limit, lean upon God's promises. Trust His Son. Remember that God is always near and that He is your protector and your deliverer. When you are worried, anxious, or afraid, call upon Him and accept the touch of His comforting hand. Remember that God rules both mountaintops and valleys—with limitless wisdom and love—now and forever.

Put your hand into the hand of God. He gives the calmness and serenity of heart and soul.

Mrs. Charles E. Cowman

When God allows extraordinary trials for His people, He prepares extraordinary comforts for them.

Corrie ten Boom

A TIMELY TIP

Perhaps you have become wrapped up in the world's problems or your own problems. If so, it's time to focus more on your spiritual blessings as you open yourself up to God. When you do, God will bless you and comfort you.

THE NEED TO BE DISCIPLINED

Do you not know that the runners in a stadium all race, but only one receives the prize? Run in such a way that you may win. Now everyone who competes exercises self-control in everything. However, they do it to receive a perishable crown, but we an imperishable one.

1 Corinthians 9:24-25 HCSB

God is clear: we must exercise self-discipline in all matters. Self-discipline is not simply a proven way to get ahead, it's also an integral part of God's plan for our lives. If we genuinely seek to be faithful stewards of our time, our talents, and our resources, we must adopt a disciplined approach to life. Otherwise, our talents are wasted and our resources are squandered.

Our greatest rewards result from hard work and perseverance. May we, as disciplined believers, be willing to work for the rewards we so earnestly desire.

Personal humility is a spiritual discipline and the hallmark of the service of Jesus.

Franklin Graham

He will clothe you in rags if you clothe yourself with idleness.

C. H. Spurgeon

A TIMELY TIP

When you take a disciplined approach to your life and your responsibilities, God will reward your good judgment.

STRENGTH FOR TODAY

I can do all things through Christ which strengtheneth me.

Philippians 4:13 KJV

Have you made God the cornerstone of your life, or is He relegated to a few hours on Sunday morning? Have you genuinely allowed God to reign over every corner of your heart, or have you attempted to place Him in a spiritual compartment? The answer to these questions will determine the direction of your day and your life.

God loves you. In times of trouble, He will comfort you; in times of sorrow, He will dry your tears. When you are weak or sorrowful, God is as near as your next breath. He stands at the door of your heart and waits. Welcome Him in and allow Him to rule. And then, accept the peace, and the strength, and the protection, and the abundance that only God can give.

In my weakness, I have learned, like Moses, to lean hard on God. The weaker I am, the harder I lean on Him. The harder I lean, the stronger I discover Him to be. The stronger I discover God to be, the more resolute I am in this job He's given me to do.

Joni Eareckson Tada

And in truth, if we only knew it, our chief fitness is our utter helplessness. His strength is made perfect, not in our strength, but in our weakness. Our strength is only a hindrance.

Hannah Whitall Smith

A TIMELY TIP

God can handle it. Corrie ten Boom advised, "God's all-sufficiency is a major. Your inability is a minor. Major in majors, not in minors." Enough said.

Day 54

LIGHTING THE PATH

Your word is a lamp to my feet and a light to my path.

Psalm 119:105 NKJV

Are you a woman who trusts God's Word without reservation? Hopefully so, because the Bible is unlike any other book—it is a guidebook for life here on earth and for life eternal. The Psalmist describes God's word as, "a light to my path." Is the Bible your lamp? If not, you are depriving yourself of a priceless gift from the Creator.

Vance Havner observed, "It takes calm, thoughtful, prayerful meditation on the Word to extract its deepest nourishment." How true. God's Word can be a light to guide your steps. Claim it as your light today, tomorrow, and every day of your life—and then walk confidently in the footsteps of God's only begotten Son.

Light is stronger than darkness—darkness cannot "comprehend" or "overcome" it.

Anne Graham Lotz

God's leading will never be contrary to His word.

Vonette Bright

A TIMELY TIP

Trust God's Word: Charles Swindoll writes, "There are four words I wish we would never forget, and they are, 'God keeps his word.'" And remember: When it comes to studying God's Word, school is always in session.

BIG DREAMS

With God's power working in us, God can do much, much more than anything we can ask or imagine.

Ephesians 3:20 NCV

Are you willing to entertain the possibility that God has big plans in store for you? Hopefully so. Yet sometimes, especially if you've recently experienced a life-altering disappointment, you may find it difficult to envision a brighter future for yourself and your family. If so, it's time to reconsider your own capabilities . . . and God's.

Your Heavenly Father created you with unique gifts and untapped talents; your job is to tap them. When you do, you'll begin to feel an increasing sense of confidence in yourself and in your future. So even if you're experiencing difficult days, don't abandon your dreams. Instead, trust that God is preparing you for greater things.

The future lies all before us. Shall it only be a slight advance upon what we usually do? Ought it not to be a bound, a leap forward to altitudes of endeavor and success undreamed of before?

Annie Armstrong

Always stay connected to people and seek out things that bring you joy. Dream with abandon. Pray confidently.

Barbara Johnson

A TIMELY TIP

Making your dreams come true requires work. John Maxwell writes, "The gap between your vision and your present reality can only be filled through a commitment to maximize your potential." Enough said.

Day 56

ENTHUSIASM FOR CHRIST

Therefore, get your minds ready for action, being self-disciplined, and set your hope completely on the grace to be brought to you at the revelation of Jesus Christ. As obedient children, do not be conformed to the desires of your former ignorance but, as the One who called you is holy, you also are to be holy in all your conduct.

1 Peter 1:13-15 HCSB

John Wesley advised, "Catch on fire with enthusiasm and people will come for miles to watch you burn." His words still ring true. When we fan the flames of enthusiasm for Christ, our faith serves as a beacon to others.

Our world desperately needs faithful women who share the Good News of Jesus with joyful exuberance. Be such a woman. The world desperately needs your enthusiasm—and your testimony—now!

We must go out and live among them, manifesting the gentle, loving spirit of our Lord. We need to make friends before we can hope to make converts.

Lottie Moon

One of the great needs in the church today is for every Christian to become enthusiastic about his faith in Jesus Christ.

Billy Graham

A TIMELY TIP

If you become excited about life . . . life will become an exciting adventure.

A WOMAN OF PRAYER

Rejoice always, pray without ceasing, in everything give thanks; for this is the will of God in Christ Jesus for you.

1 Thessalonians 5:16-18 NKJV

On his second missionary journey, Paul started a small church in Thessalonica. A short time later, he penned a letter that was intended to encourage the new believers at that church. Today, almost 2,000 years later, 1 Thessalonians remains a powerful, practical guide for Christian living.

In his letter, Paul advised members of the new church to "pray without ceasing." His advice applies to Christians of every generation. When we consult God on an hourly basis, we avail ourselves of His wisdom, His strength, and His love. As Corrie ten Boom observed, "Any concern that is too small to be turned into a prayer is too small to be made into a burden."

Today, make yourself a woman of prayer. Instead of turning things over in your mind, turn them over to God in prayer. Instead of worrying about your next decision, ask God to lead the way. Don't limit your prayers to meals or bedtime. Become a woman of constant prayer. God is listening, and He wants to hear from you. Now.

The manifold rewards of a serious, consistent prayer life demonstrate clearly that time with our Lord should be our first priority.

Shirley Dobson

A TIMELY TIP

Today, ask yourself if your prayer life is all that it should be. If the answer is yes, keep up the good work. But if the answer is no, set aside a specific time each morning to talk to God. And then, when you've set aside a time for prayer, don't allow yourself to become sidetracked.

QUALITY TIME, QUANTITY TIME

Teach us to number our days carefully so that we may develop wisdom in our hearts.

Psalm 90:12 HCSB

Make no mistake: caring for your family requires time—lots of time. You've probably heard about "quality time" and "quantity time." Your family needs both. So, as a responsible Christian, you should willingly invest large quantities of your time and energy in the care and nurturing of your clan.

While caring for your family, you should do your best to ensure that God remains squarely at the center of your household. When you do, God will bless you and yours in ways that you could have scarcely imagined.

There is so much compassion and understanding that is gained when we've experienced God's grace firsthand within our own families.

Lisa Whelchel

Apart from religious influence, the family is the most important influence on society.

Billy Graham

A TIMELY TIP

Your family is a precious gift from above, a gift that should be treasured, nurtured, and loved.

YOUR BODY, GOD'S TEMPLE

Don't you know that you are God's sanctuary and that the Spirit of God lives in you?

1 Corinthians 3:16 HCSB

Are you shaping up or spreading out? Do you eat sensibly and exercise regularly, or do you spend most of your time on the couch with a Twinkie in one hand and a clicker in the other? Are you choosing to treat your body like a temple or a trash heap? How you answer these questions will help determine how long you live and how well you live.

Physical fitness is a choice, a choice that requires discipline—it's as simple as that. So, do yourself this favor: treat your body like a one-of-a-kind gift from God . . . because that's precisely what your body is.

It is important to set goals because if you do not have a plan, a goal, a direction, a purpose, and a focus, you are not going to accomplish anything for the glory of God.

Bill Bright

You were created to add to life on earth, not just take from it.

Rick Warren

A TIMELY TIP

Fitness 101: Simply put, it's up to you to assume the ultimate responsibility for your health. So if you're fighting the battle of the bulge (the bulging waistline, that is), don't waste your time blaming the fast-food industry—or anybody else, for that matter. It's your body, and it's your responsibility to take care of it.

FINDING FULFILLMENT

For You, O God, have tested us; You have refined us as silver is refined . . . we went through fire and through water; but You brought us out to rich fulfillment.

Psalm 66:10–12 NKJV

Everywhere we turn, or so it seems, the world promises fulfillment, contentment, and happiness. But the contentment that the world offers is fleeting and incomplete. Thankfully, the fulfillment that God offers is all encompassing and everlasting.

Sometimes, amid the inevitable hustle and bustle of life-here-on-earth, we can forfeit—albeit temporarily—the joy of Christ as we wrestle with the challenges of daily living. Yet God's Word is clear: fulfillment through Christ is available to all who seek it and claim it. Count yourself among that number. Seek first a personal, transforming relationship with Jesus, and then claim the joy, the fulfillment, and the spiritual abundance that the Shepherd offers His sheep.

In serving we uncover the greatest fulfillment within and become a stellar example of a woman who knows and loves Jesus.

Vonette Bright

We are never more fulfilled than when our longing for God is met by His presence in our lives.

Billy Graham

A TIMELY TIP

Want to increase your sense of fulfillment? Then strive to find God's path for your life . . . and follow it.

LIVING RIGHTEOUSLY

Flee from youthful passions, and pursue righteousness, faith, love, and peace, along with those who call on the Lord from a pure heart.

2 Timothy 2:22 HCSB

A life of righteousness is lived in accordance with God's commandments. A righteous woman strives to be faithful, honest, generous, disciplined, loving, kind, humble, and grateful, to name only a few of the more obvious qualities which are described in God's Word.

If we seek to follow the steps of Jesus, we must seek to live according to His teachings. In short, we must, to the best of our abilities, live according to the principles contained in the Holy Bible. When we do, we become powerful examples to our families and friends of the blessings that God bestows upon righteous women.

A life lived in God is not lived on the plane of feelings, but of the will.

Elisabeth Elliot

A life growing in its purity and devotion will be a more prayerful life.

E. M. Bounds

A TIMELY TIP

Because God is just, He rewards righteousness just as surely as He punishes sin.

Day 62

GIVE ME PATIENCE . . . NOW!

Rest in the Lord, and wait patiently for Him.

Psalm 37:7 NKJV

Psalm 37:7 commands us to wait patiently for God. But as busy women in a fast-paced world, many of us find that waiting quietly for God is difficult. Why? Because we are fallible human beings seeking to live according to our own timetables, not God's. In our better moments, we realize that patience is not only a virtue, it is also a commandment from God.

We human beings are impatient by nature. We know what we want, and we know exactly when we want it: NOW! But, God knows better. He has created a world that unfolds according to His plans, not our own. As believers, we must trust His wisdom and His goodness.

God instructs us to be patient in all things. We must be patient with our families, our friends, and our associates. We must also be patient with our Creator as He unfolds His plan for our lives. And that's as it should be. After all, think how patient God has been with us.

If you want to hear God's voice clearly and you are uncertain, then remain in His presence until He changes that uncertainty. Often much can happen during this waiting for the Lord. Sometimes he changes pride into humility; doubt into faith and peace . . . .

Corrie ten Boom

A TIMELY TIP

Patience pays. Impatience costs. Behave accordingly.

MAINTAINING PERSPECTIVE

It is important to look at things from God's point of view.

1 Corinthians 4:6 MSG

If a temporary loss of perspective has left you worried, exhausted, or both, it's time to readjust your thought patterns. Negative thoughts are habit-forming; thankfully, so are positive ones. With practice, you can form the habit of focusing on God's priorities and your possibilities. When you do, you'll soon discover that you will spend less time fretting about your challenges and more time praising God for His gifts.

When you call upon the Lord and prayerfully seek His will, He will give you wisdom and perspective. When you make God's priorities your priorities, He will direct your steps and calm your fears. So today and every day hereafter, pray for a sense of balance and perspective. And remember: no problems are too big for God—and that includes yours.

The Bible is a remarkable commentary on perspective. Through its divine message, we are brought face to face with issues and tests in daily living and how, by the power of the Holy Spirit, we are enabled to respond positively to them.

Luci Swindoll

Instead of being frustrated and overwhelmed by all that is going on in our world, go to the Lord and ask Him to give you His eternal perspective.

Kay Arthur

A TIMELY TIP

When you focus on the world, you lose perspective. When you focus on God's promises, you gain clearer perspective.

Day 64

A LIFE OF ABUNDANCE

I have come that they may have life, and that they may have it more abundantly.

John 10:10 NKJV

The 10th chapter of John tells us that Christ came to earth so that our lives might be filled with abundance. But what, exactly, did Jesus mean when He promised "life . . . more abundantly"? Was He referring to material possessions or financial wealth? Hardly. Jesus offers a different kind of abundance: a spiritual richness that extends beyond the temporal boundaries of this world. This everlasting abundance is available to all who seek it and claim it. May we, as believers, claim the riches of Christ Jesus every day that we live, and may we share His blessings with all who cross our path.

The gift of God is eternal life, spiritual life, abundant life through faith in Jesus Christ, the Living Word of God.

Anne Graham Lotz

God loves you and wants you to experience peace and life—abundant and eternal.

Billy Graham

A TIMELY TIP

God offers you His abundance—the rest is up to you.

TODAY'S OPPORTUNITIES

But encourage each other daily, while it is still called today, so that none of you is hardened by sin's deception.

Hebrews 3:13 HCSB

The 118th Psalm reminds us, "This is the day which the Lord hath made; we will rejoice and be glad in it" (v. 24 KJV). As we rejoice in this day that the Lord has given us, let us remember that an important part of today's celebration is the time we spend celebrating others. Each day provides countless opportunities to encourage others and to praise their good works. When we do, we not only spread seeds of joy and happiness, we also follow the commandments of God's Holy Word.

How can we build others up? By celebrating their victories and their accomplishments. So look for the good in others and celebrate the good that you find. When you do, you'll be a powerful force of encouragement in the world . . . and a worthy servant to your God.

Encouragement starts at home, but it should never end there.

Marie T. Freeman

We can never untangle all the woes in other people's lives. We can't produce miracles overnight. But we can bring a cup of cool water to a thirsty soul, or a scoop of laughter to a lonely heart.

Barbara Johnson

A TIMELY TIP

You should seek out encouraging friends who can lift you up, and you should strive to be an encouraging friend to others.

 *Day 66*

HUMBLED BY HIS SACRIFICE

But as for me, I will never boast about anything except the cross of our Lord Jesus Christ, through whom the world has been crucified to me, and I to the world.

Galatians 6:14 HCSB

As we consider Christ's sacrifice on the cross, we should be profoundly humbled. And today, as we come to Christ in prayer, we should do so in a spirit of humble devotion.

Christ humbled Himself on a cross—for you. He shed His blood—for you. He has offered to walk with you through this life and throughout all eternity. As you approach Him today in prayer, think about His sacrifice and His grace. And be humble.

The sacrifice of the Lamb is absolutely sufficient in itself to take away our sin and reconcile us to God.

Anne Graham Lotz

He came all the way from the comfort and beauty of heaven to the blood-stained cross of Palestine, not just for someone like me in the theoretical, but for precisely me in the personal and practical.

Bill Bright

A TIMELY TIP

Christ made incredible sacrifices for mankind. What sacrifices will you make today for Him?

ETERNAL PERSPECTIVE

Our Savior Jesus poured out new life so generously. God's gift has restored our relationship with him and given us back our lives. And there's more life to come—an eternity of life!

Titus 3:6-7 MSG

As mere mortals, our vision for the future, like our lives here on earth, is limited. God's vision is not burdened by such limitations: His plans extend throughout all eternity. Thus, God's plans for you are not limited to the ups and downs of everyday life. Your Heavenly Father has bigger things in mind . . . much bigger things. Christ sacrificed His life on the cross so that we might have eternal life. This gift, freely given by God's only begotten Son, is the priceless possession of everyone who accepts Him as Lord and Savior.

As you struggle with the inevitable hardships and occasional disappointments of everyday life, remember that God has invited you to accept His abundance not only for today but also for all eternity. So keep things in perspective. Although you will inevitably encounter occasional defeats in this world, you'll have all eternity to celebrate the ultimate victory in the next.

Like a shadow declining swiftly . . . away . . . like the dew of the morning gone with the heat of the day; like the wind in the treetops, like a wave of the sea, so are our lives on earth when seen in light of eternity.

Ruth Bell Graham

A TIMELY TIP

God has created heaven and given you a way to get there. The rest is up to you.

Day 68

GOD AND FAMILY

Let the Word of Christ—the Message—have the run of the house. Give it plenty of room in your lives.

Colossians 3:16 MSG

These are difficult days for our nation and for our families. But, thankfully, God is bigger than all of our challenges. God loves us and protects us. In times of trouble, He comforts us; in times of sorrow, He dries our tears. When we are troubled, or weak, or sorrowful, God is as near as our next breath.

Are you concerned for the well-being of your family? You are not alone. We live in a world where temptation and danger seem to lurk on every street corner. Parents and children alike have good reason to be watchful. But, despite the evils of our time, God remains steadfast. Even in these difficult days, no problem is too big for God.

Living life with a consistent spiritual walk deeply influences those we love most.

Vonette Bright

The only true source of meaning in life is found in love for God and his son Jesus Christ, and love for mankind, beginning with our own families.

James Dobson

A TIMELY TIP

Put God first in every aspect of your life. And while you're at it, put Him first in every aspect of your family's life, too.

Day 69

GLORIOUS OPPORTUNITIES

Make the most of every opportunity.

Colossians 4:5 NIV

Are you excited about the opportunities of today and thrilled by the possibilities of tomorrow? Do you confidently expect God to lead you to a place of abundance, peace, and joy? And, when your days on earth are over, do you expect to receive the priceless gift of eternal life? If you trust God's promises, and if you have welcomed God's Son into your heart, then you believe that your future is intensely and eternally bright.

Today, as you prepare to meet the duties of everyday life, pause and consider God's promises. And then think for a moment about the wonderful future that awaits all believers, including you. God has promised that your future is secure. Trust that promise, and celebrate the life of abundance and eternal joy that is now yours through Christ.

Worry is the senseless process of cluttering up tomorrow's opportunities with leftover problems from today.

Barbara Johnson

A TIMELY TIP

God gives us opportunities for a reason . . . to use them. And, God wants you to make the most out of all the opportunities He sends your way. Billy Graham observed, "Life is a glorious opportunity." That's sound advice, so keep looking for your opportunities until you find them, and when you find them, take advantage of them sooner rather than later.

THE POWER OF PERSEVERANCE

I do not consider myself to have taken hold of it. But one thing I do: forgetting what is behind and reaching forward to what is ahead, I pursue as my goal the prize promised by God's heavenly call in Christ Jesus.

Philippians 3:13-14 HCSB

A well-lived life calls for preparation, determination, and, of course, lots of perseverance. As an example of perfect perseverance, we Christians need look no further than our Savior, Jesus Christ. Jesus finished what He began. Despite His suffering, despite the shame of the cross, Jesus was steadfast in His faithfulness to God. We, too, must remain faithful, especially during times of hardship. Sometimes, God may answer our prayers with silence, and when He does, we must patiently persevere.

Are you facing a tough situation? If so, remember this: whatever your problem, God can handle it. Your job is to keep persevering until He does.

Your life is not a boring stretch of highway. It's a straight line to heaven. And just look at the fields ripening along the way. Look at the tenacity and endurance. Look at the grains of righteousness. You'll have quite a crop at harvest . . . so don't give up!

Joni Eareckson Tada

Just remember, every flower that ever bloomed had to go through a whole lot of dirt to get there!

Barbara Johnson

A TIMELY TIP

Life is difficult and success requires effort—so perseverance pays big dividends.

FIRST THINGS FIRST

And I pray this: that your love will keep on growing in knowledge and every kind of discernment, so that you can determine what really matters and can be pure and blameless in the day of Christ.

Philippians 1:9 HCSB

"First things first." These words are easy to speak but hard to put into practice. For busy women living in a demanding world, placing first things first can be difficult indeed. Why? Because so many people are expecting so many things from us!

If you're having trouble prioritizing your day, perhaps you've been trying to organize your life according to your own plans, not God's. A better strategy, of course, is to take your daily obligations and place them in the hands of the One who created you. To do so, you must prioritize your day according to God's commandments, and you must seek His will and His wisdom in all matters. Then, you can face the day with the assurance that the same God who created our universe out of nothingness will help you place first things first in your own life. So, turn the concerns of this day over to God—prayerfully, earnestly, and often. Then listen for His answer . . . and trust the answer He gives.

The work of God is appointed. There is always enough time to do the will of God.

Elisabeth Elliot

With God, it's never "Plan B" or "second best." It's always "Plan A." And, if we let Him, He'll make something beautiful of our lives.

Gloria Gaither

A TIMELY TIP

Prayer changes things and it changes you. So pray.

BEING GENTLE WITH YOURSELF

You're blessed when you're content with just who you are—no more, no less.
That's the moment you find yourselves proud owners of everything that can't
be bought.

Matthew 5:5 MSG

Being patient with other people can be difficult. But sometimes, we find it even more difficult to be patient with ourselves. We have high expectations and lofty goals. We want to receive God's blessings now, not later. And, of course, we want our lives to unfold according to our own wishes and our own timetables—not God's. Yet throughout the Bible, we are instructed that patience is the companion of wisdom. Proverbs 16:32 teaches us that "Patience is better than strength" (NCV). God's message, then, is clear: we must be patient with all people, beginning with that particular woman who stares back at us each time we gaze into the mirror.

The Bible affirms the importance of self-acceptance by exhorting believers to love others as they love themselves (Matthew 22:37-40). Furthermore, the Bible teaches that when we genuinely open our hearts to Him, God accepts us just as we are. And, if He accepts us—faults and all—then who are we to believe otherwise?

I think that if God forgives us we might forgive ourselves. Otherwise it is almost like setting up ourselves as a higher tribunal than Him.

C. S. Lewis

A TIMELY TIP

You were wonderfully made by a loving God who knew exactly what He was doing. Accept it.

IS THE GOLDEN RULE YOUR RULE?

And let us not grow weary while doing good, for in due season we shall reap if we do not lose heart.

Galatians 6:9 NKJV

Would you like to make the world a better place and feel better about yourself at the same time? If so, you can start by practicing the Golden Rule.

The Bible teaches us to treat other people with respect, kindness, courtesy, and love. When we do, we make other people happy, we make God happy, and we feel better about ourselves.

So if you're wondering how to make the world—and your world—a better place, here's a great place to start: let the Golden Rule be your rule. And if you want to know how to treat other people, ask the woman you see every time you glance in the mirror.

Sometimes one little spark of kindness is all it takes to reignite the light of hope in a heart that's blinded by pain.

Barbara Johnson

Our lives, we are told, are but fleeting at best, / Like roses they fade and decay; / Then let us do good while the present is ours, / Be useful as long as we stay.

Fanny Crosby

A TIMELY TIP

The more you help others, the better you'll feel about yourself. So don't delay: somebody needs your help today.

HEALTHY CHOICES

I shall yet praise him, who is the health of my countenance, and my God.

Psalm 42:11 KJV

The journey toward improved health is not only a common-sense exercise in personal discipline, it is also a spiritual journey ordained by our Creator. God does not intend that we abuse our bodies by giving in to excessive appetites or to slothful behavior. To the contrary, God has instructed us to protect our physical bodies to the greatest extent we can. To do otherwise is to disobey Him.

God's plan for you includes provisions for your spiritual, physical, and emotional health. But, He expects you to do your fair share of the work! In a world that is chock-full of tasty temptations, you may find it all too easy to make unhealthy choices. Your challenge, of course, is to resist those unhealthy temptations by every means you can, including prayer. And rest assured: when you ask for God's help, He will give it.

Laughter is the language of the young at heart and the antidote to what ails us.

Barbara Johnson

People are funny. When they are young, they will spend their health to get wealth. Later, they will gladly pay all they have trying to get their health back.

John Maxwell

A TIMELY TIP

Life is a gift—health must be earned. We earn good health by cultivating healthy habits.

THE SELF-FULFILLING PROPHECY

May He grant you according to your heart's desire, and fulfill all your purpose.
Psalm 20:4 NKJV

The self-fulfilling prophecy is alive, well, and living at your house. If you trust God and have faith for the future, your optimistic beliefs will give you direction and motivation. That's one reason that you should never lose hope, but certainly not the only reason. The primary reason that you, as a believer, should never lose hope, is because of God's unfailing promises.

Make no mistake about it: thoughts are powerful things; your thoughts have the power to lift you up or to hold you down. When you acquire the habit of hopeful thinking, you will have acquired a powerful tool for improving your life. So if you fall into the habit of negative thinking, think again. After all, God's Word teaches us that Christ can overcome every difficulty (John 16:33). And when God makes a promise, He keeps it.

Live for today, but hold your hands open to tomorrow. Anticipate the future and its changes with joy. There is a seed of God's love in every event, every circumstance, every unpleasant situation in which you may find yourself.

Barbara Johnson

A TIMELY TIP

As you plan for your future, be aware that attitudes have a way of transforming themselves into reality. In other words, how you think will help determine what you become. So think realistically about yourself and your situation while making a conscious effort to focus on hopes, not fears. When you do, you'll put the self-fulfilling prophecy to work for you.

THE VOICE OF GOD

Be silent before Me.

Isaiah 41:1 HCSB

Sometimes God speaks loudly and clearly. More often, He speaks in a quiet voice—and if you are wise, you will be listening carefully when He does. To do so, you must carve out quiet moments each day to study His Word and sense His direction.

Can you quiet yourself long enough to listen to your conscience? Are you attuned to the subtle guidance of your intuition? Are you willing to pray sincerely and then to wait quietly for God's response. Hopefully so. Usually God refrains from sending His messages on stone tablets or city billboards. More often, He communicates in subtler ways. If you sincerely desire to hear His voice, you must listen carefully, and you must do so in the silent corners of your quiet, willing heart.

When we come to Jesus stripped of pretensions, with a needy spirit, ready to listen, He meets us at the point of need.

Catherine Marshall

In the soul-searching of our lives, we are to stay quiet so we can hear Him say all that He wants to say to us in our hearts.

Charles Swindoll

A TIMELY TIP

Prayer is two-way communication with God. Talking to God isn't enough; you should also listen to Him.

YOUR SPIRITUAL JOURNEY

I pray that you, being rooted and firmly established in love, may be able to comprehend with all the saints what is the breadth and width, height and depth, and to know the Messiah's love that surpasses knowledge, so you may be filled with all the fullness of God.

Ephesians 3:17-19 HCSB

The journey toward spiritual maturity lasts a lifetime. As Christians, we can and should continue to grow in the love and the knowledge of our Savior as long as we live. When we cease to grow, either emotionally or spiritually, we do ourselves a profound disservice. But, if we study God's Word, if we obey His commandments, and if we live in the center of His will, we will not be "stagnant" believers; we will, instead, be healthy, growing Christians.

Life is a series of decisions. Each day, we make countless decisions that can bring us closer to God . . . or not. When we live according to the principles contained in God's Holy Word, we embark upon a journey of spiritual maturity that results in life abundant and life eternal.

We cannot hope to reach Christian maturity in any way other than by yielding ourselves utterly and willingly to His mighty working.

Hannah Whitall Smith

A TIMELY TIP

Today, think about the quality of the choices that you've made recently. Are these choices helping you become a more mature Christian? If so, don't change. If not, think about the quality of your decisions, the consequences of those decisions, and the steps that you can take to make better decisions.

LOVE AND COMMITMENT

If you do nothing in a difficult time, your strength is limited.

Proverbs 24:10 HCSB

In God's program, the words "love" and "commitment" are intertwined. According to God, genuine love is patient, unselfish, and kind, but it goes beyond that—genuine love is committed love, and that means that genuine love is more than a feeling . . . it is a decision to make love endure, no matter what.

Unfortunately, we live in a world where marriage vows are taken far too lightly. Too many couples are far too quick to push the panic button—or the eject button.

If you're a married woman who has vowed to love your partner "till death do you part," then you must take that vow very seriously. And one more thing: you'd better put God right where He belongs: at the absolute center of your marriage.

How committed are you to breaking the ice of prayerlessness so that you and your mate can seek the Lord openly and honestly together, releasing control over your marriage into the capable, trustworthy, but often surprising hands of God?

Stormie Omartian

A TIMELY TIP

Commitment first! The best marriages are built upon an unwavering commitment to God and an unwavering commitment to one's spouse. So, if you're totally committed, congratulations; if you're not, you're building your marriage (and your life) on a very shaky foundation.

THE VOICE INSIDE YOUR HEAD

I always do my best to have a clear conscience toward God and men.

Acts 24:16 HCSB

When you're about to do something that you know is wrong, a little voice inside your head has a way of speaking up. That voice, of course, is your conscience: an early-warning system designed to keep you out of trouble. If you listen to that voice, you'll be okay; if you ignore it, you're asking for headaches, or heartbreaks, or both.

Whenever you're about to make an important decision, you should listen carefully to the quiet voice inside. Sometimes, of course, it's tempting to do otherwise. From time to time you'll be tempted to abandon your better judgement by ignoring your conscience. But remember: a conscience is a terrible thing to waste. So instead of ignoring that quiet little voice, pay careful attention to it. If you do, your conscience will lead you in the right direction—in fact, it's trying to lead you right now. So listen . . . and learn.

If I am walking along the street with a very disfiguring hole in the back of my dress, of which I am in ignorance, it is certainly a very great comfort to me to have a kind friend who will tell me of it. And similarly, it is indeed a comfort to know that there is always abiding with me a divine, all-seeing Comforter, who will reprove me for all my faults and will not let me go on in a fatal unconsciousness of them.

Hannah Whitall Smith

A TIMELY TIP

The more important the decision . . . the more carefully you should listen to your conscience.

Day 80

HIS GENEROSITY . . . AND YOURS

But God proves His own love for us in that while we were still sinners Christ died for us!

Romans 5:8 HCSB

Christ showed His love for us by willingly sacrificing His own life so that we might have eternal life. We, as Christ's followers, are challenged to share His love. And, when we walk each day with Jesus—and obey the commandments found in God's Holy Word—we are worthy ambassadors for Him.

Just as Christ has been—and will always be—the ultimate friend to His flock, so should we be Christlike in our love and generosity to those in need. When we share the love of Christ, we share a priceless gift. As His servants, we must do no less.

The measure of a life, after all, is not its duration but its donation.

Corrie ten Boom

We can't do everything, but can we do anything more valuable than invest ourselves in another?

Elisabeth Elliot

A TIMELY TIP

There is a direct relationship between generosity and joy—the more you give to others, the more joy you will experience for yourself.

PROMISES YOU CAN COUNT ON

God blesses the people who patiently endure testing. Afterward they will receive the crown of life that God has promised to those who love him.

James 1:12 NLT

Throughout the seasons of life, we must all endure life-altering personal losses that leave us breathless. When we do, we may be overwhelmed by fear, by doubt, or by both. Thankfully, God has promised that He will never desert us. And God keeps His promises.

Life is often challenging, but as Christians, we must trust the promises of our Heavenly Father. God loves us, and He will protect us. In times of hardship, He will comfort us; in times of sorrow, He will dry our tears. When we are troubled, or weak, or sorrowful, God is with us. His love endures, not only for today, but also for all of eternity.

Faith is a strong power, mastering any difficulty in the strength of the Lord who made heaven and earth.

Corrie ten Boom

God will never let you sink under your circumstances. He always provides a safety net and His love always encircles.

Barbara Johnson

A TIMELY TIP

Remember that tough times are simply opportunities to trust God completely and to find strength in Him. And remember: Tough times can also be times of intense personal growth.

THE CHAINS OF PERFECTIONISM

Those who wait for perfect weather will never plant seeds; those who look at every cloud will never harvest crops.

Ecclesiastes 11:4 NCV

The media delivers an endless stream of messages that tell you how to look, how to behave, and how to dress. The media's expectations are impossible to meet—God's are not. God doesn't expect perfection . . . and neither should you.

If you find yourself bound up by the chains of perfectionism, it's time to ask yourself who you're trying to impress, and why. If you're trying to impress other people, it's time to reconsider your priorities. Your first responsibility is to the Heavenly Father who created you and to His Son who saved you. Then, you bear a powerful responsibility to your family. But, when it comes to meeting society's unrealistic expectations, forget it! After all, pleasing God is simply a matter of obeying His commandments and accepting His Son. But as for pleasing everybody else? That's impossible!

God is so inconceivably good. He's not looking for perfection. He already saw it in Christ. He's looking for affection.

Beth Moore

The happiest people in the world are not those who have no problems, but the people who have learned to live with those things that are less than perfect.

James Dobson

A TIMELY TIP

Accept your own imperfections: If you're caught up in the modern-day push toward perfection, grow up . . . and then lighten up on yourself.

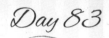
SOLVING PROBLEMS

People who do what is right may have many problems, but the Lord will solve them all.

Psalm 34:19 NCV

L ife is an exercise in problem-solving. The question is not whether we will encounter problems; the real question is how we will choose to address them. When it comes to solving the problems of everyday living, we often know precisely what needs to be done, but we may be slow in doing it—especially if what needs to be done is difficult or uncomfortable for us. So we put off till tomorrow what should be done today.

The words of Psalm 34 remind us that the Lord solves problems for "people who do what is right." And usually, doing "what is right" means doing the uncomfortable work of confronting our problems sooner rather than later. So with no further ado, let the problem-solving begin . . . now.

The great thing, if one can, is to stop regarding all the unpleasant things as interruptions of one's own or real life. The truth is of course that what one calls the interruptions are precisely one's real life—the life God is sending one day by day. What one calls one's real life is a phantom of one's own imagination.

C. S. Lewis

A TIMELY TIP

Everyone has problems, but not everyone deals with their problems in the same way. The way you address your problems—whether you choose to avoid them or address them—determines how successfully—and how quickly—you overcome them.

THE SIMPLE LIFE

Whoever becomes simple and elemental again, like this child, will rank high in God's kingdom.

Matthew 18:4 MSG

You live in a world where simplicity is in short supply. Think for a moment about the complexity of your every-day life and compare it to the lives of your ancestors. Certainly, you are the beneficiary of many technological innovations, but those innovations have a price: in all likelihood, your world is highly complex.

Unless you take firm control of your time and your life, you may be overwhelmed by an ever-increasing tidal wave of complexity that threatens your happiness. But your Heavenly Father understands the joy of living simply, and so should you. So do yourself a favor: keep your life as simple as possible. Simplicity is, indeed, genius. By simplifying your life, you are destined to improve it.

Nobody is going to simplify your life for you. You've got to simplify things for yourself.

Marie T. Freeman

The most powerful life is the most simple life. The most powerful life is the life that knows where it's going, that knows where the source of strength is; it is the life that stays free of clutter and happenstance and hurriedness.

Max Lucado

A TIMELY TIP

Simplicity and peace are two concepts that are closely related. Complexity and peace are not.

A HELPING HAND

The greatest among you will be your servant. Whoever exalts himself will be humbled, and whoever humbles himself will be exalted.

Matthew 23:11-12 HCSB

Jesus has much to teach us about generosity. He teaches that the most esteemed men and women are not the self-congratulatory leaders of society but are, instead, the humblest of servants. If you were being graded on generosity, how would you score? Would you earn "A"s in philanthropy and humility? Hopefully so. But if your grades could stand a little improvement, this is the perfect day to begin.

Today, you may feel the urge to hoard your blessings. Don't do it. Instead, give generously to your neighbors, and do so without fanfare. Find a need and fill it . . . humbly. Lend a helping hand and share a word of kindness . . . anonymously. This is God's way.

When somebody needs a helping hand, he doesn't need it tomorrow or the next day. He needs it now, and that's exactly when you should offer to help. Good deeds, if they are really good, happen sooner rather than later.

Marie T. Freeman

Nothing is really ours until we share it.

C. S. Lewis

A TIMELY TIP

Would you like to be a little happier? Try sharing a few more of the blessings that God has bestowed upon you. In other words, if you want to be happy, be generous. And if you want to be unhappy, be greedy.

WITH GOD'S STRENGTH

Come to Me, all you who are weary and burdened, and I will give you rest. Take My yoke upon you and learn from Me, because I am gentle and humble in heart, and you will find rest for your souls. For My yoke is easy and My burden is light.

Matthew 11:28–30 HCSB

Are you tired? Ask God for strength. Are you discouraged? Believe in His promises. Are you frustrated or fearful? Pray as if everything depended upon God, and work as if everything depended upon you. With God's help, you will find the strength to be the kind of woman who makes your Heavenly Father beam with pride.

Perhaps you are in a hurry for God to reveal His plans for your life. If so, be forewarned: God operates on His own timetable, not yours. Sometimes, God may answer your prayers with silence, and when He does, you must patiently persevere. In times of trouble, you must remain steadfast and trust in the merciful goodness of your Heavenly Father. Whatever your problem, He can handle it. Your job is to keep persevering until He does.

If things are tough, remember that every flower that ever bloomed had to go through a whole lot of dirt to get there.

Barbara Johnson

Failure is one of life's most powerful teachers. How we handle our failures determines whether we're going to simply "get by" in life or "press on."

Beth Moore

A TIMELY TIP

Life is an exercise in perseverance. If you persevere, you win.

YOUR WAY OR GOD'S WAY

A man's heart plans his way, but the Lord determines his steps.

Proverbs 16:9 HCSB

The popular song "My Way" is a perfectly good tune, but it's not a perfect guide for life-here-on-earth. If you're looking for life's perfect prescription, you'd better forget about doing things your way and start doing things God's way. The most important decision of your life is, of course, your commitment to accept Jesus Christ as your personal Lord and Savior. And once your eternal destiny is secured, you will undoubtedly ask yourself the question "What now, Lord?" If you earnestly seek God's will for your life, you will find it . . . in time.

Sometimes, God's plans are crystal clear; sometimes they are not. So be patient, keep searching, and keep praying. If you do, then in time, God will answer your prayers and make His plans known. You'll discover those plans by doing things His way . . . and you'll be eternally grateful that you did.

Ours is an intentional God, brimming over with motive and mission. He never does things capriciously or decides with the flip of a coin.

Joni Eareckson Tada

God cannot lead the individual who is not willing to give Him a blank check with his life.

Catherine Marshall

A TIMELY TIP

God has a wonderful plan for your life. And the time to start looking for that plan—and living it—is now. And remember: Discovering God's plan begins with prayer.

Day 88

TRUSTING HIM COMPLETELY

I will be your God throughout your lifetime—until your hair is white with age. I made you, and I will care for you. I will carry you along and save you.

Isaiah 46:4 NLT

God has promised to lift you up and guide your steps if you let Him do so. God has promised that when you entrust your life to Him completely and without reservation, He will give you the strength to meet any challenge, the courage to face any trial, and the wisdom to live in His righteousness.

God's hand uplifts those who turn their hearts and prayers to Him. Will you count yourself among that number? Will you accept God's peace and wear God's armor against the temptations and distractions of our dangerous world? If you do, you can live courageously and optimistically, knowing that you have been forever touched by the loving, unfailing, uplifting hand of God.

Snuggle in God's arms. When you are hurting, when you feel lonely or left out, let Him cradle you, comfort you, reassure you of His all-sufficient power and love.

Kay Arthur

I feel my weakness and inability to accomplish anything without the aid of the Holy Spirit.

Lottie Moon

A TIMELY TIP

Whatever your weaknesses, God is stronger. And His strength will help you measure up to His tasks.

A FEARLESS WOMAN

Teach me Your way, O Lord; I will walk in Your truth.

Psalm 86:11 NKJV

The Book of Judges (chapters 4 and 5) tells the story of Deborah, the fearless woman who helped lead the army of Israel to victory over the Canaanites. Deborah was a judge and a prophetess, a woman called by God to lead her people. And when she answered God's call, she was rewarded with one of the great victories of Old Testament times. Like Deborah, all of us are called to serve our Creator. And, like Deborah, we may sometimes find ourselves facing trials that can bring trembling to the very depths of our souls. As believers, we must seek God's will and follow it.

As this day unfolds, seek God's will for your own life and obey His Word. He will give you the strength to meet any challenge, the courage to face any trial, and the wisdom to live in His righteousness and in His peace.

We get into trouble when we think we know what to do and we stop asking God if we're doing it.

Stormie Omartian

God has a present will for your life. It is neither chaotic nor utterly exhausting. In the midst of many good choices vying for your time, He will give you the discernment to recognize what is best.

Beth Moore

A TIMELY TIP

When God's will becomes your will, good things happen.

Day 90

DISCOVERING HOPE

These things I have spoken to you, that in Me you may have peace. In the world you will have tribulation; but be of good cheer, I have overcome the world.

John 16:33 NKJV

There are few sadder sights on earth than the sight of a person who has lost all hope. In difficult times, hope can be elusive, but Christians need never lose it. After all, God is good; His love endures; He has promised His children the gift of eternal life.

If you find yourself falling into the spiritual traps of worry and discouragement, consider the words of Jesus. It was Christ who promised, "In the world you will have tribulation; but be of good cheer, I have overcome the world." This world is indeed a place of trials and tribulations, but as believers, we are secure. God has promised us peace, joy, and eternal life. And, of course, God always keeps His promises.

God's Word never said we were not to grieve our losses. It says we are not to grieve as those who have no hope (1 Thessalonians 4:13). Big Difference.

Beth Moore

Hope is faith holding out its hand in the dark.

Barbara Johnson

A TIMELY TIP

Never be afraid to hope—or to ask—for a miracle.

WHEN ANGER IS APPROPRIATE

The face of the Lord is against those who do evil.

Psalm 34:16 NKJV

Sometimes, anger can be a good thing. In the 22nd chapter of Matthew, we see how Christ responded when He confronted the evildoings of those who invaded His Father's house of worship: "And Jesus entered the temple and drove out all those who were buying and selling in the temple, and overturned the tables of the moneychangers and the seats of those who were selling doves" (v. 12 NASB). Thus, Jesus proved that righteous indignation is an appropriate response to evil.

When you come face-to-face with the devil's handiwork, don't be satisfied to remain safely on the sidelines. Instead, follow in the footsteps of your Savior. Jesus never compromised with evil, and neither should you.

When something robs you of your peace of mind, ask yourself if it is worth the energy you are expending on it. If not, then put it out of your mind in an act of discipline. Every time the thought of "it" returns, refuse it.

Kay Arthur

Anger's the anaesthetic of the mind.

C. S. Lewis

A TIMELY TIP

God's Word warns against the folly and the futility of anger. It's a warning you should take seriously.

Day 92

ASKING AND RECEIVING

Ask, and it will be given to you; seek, and you will find; knock, and it will be opened to you. For everyone who asks receives, and he who seeks finds, and to him who knocks it will be opened.

Matthew 7:7-8 NKJV

Are you a woman who asks God for guidance and strength? If so, then you're continually inviting your Creator to reveal Himself in a variety of ways. As a follower of Christ, you must do no less. Jesus made it clear to His disciples: they should petition God to meet their needs. So should we. Genuine, heartfelt prayer produces powerful changes in us and in our world. When we lift our hearts to God, we open ourselves to a never-ending source of divine wisdom and infinite love.

Whatever your need, no matter how great or small, pray about it and never lose hope. God is not just near; He is here, and He's perfectly capable of answering your prayers. Now, it's up to you to ask.

God makes prayer as easy as possible for us. He's completely approachable and available, and He'll never mock or upbraid us for bringing our needs before Him.

Shirley Dobson

God will help us become the people we are meant to be, if only we will ask Him.

Hannah Whitall Smith

A TIMELY TIP

If you want more from life, ask more from God. If you're seeking a worthy goal, ask for God's help—and keep asking—until He answers your prayers.

RIGHTEOUSNESS NOW!

This is how we are sure that we have come to know Him: by keeping His commands.

1 John 2:3 HCSB

When we seek righteousness in our own lives—and when we seek the companionship of those who do likewise—we reap the spiritual rewards that God intends for us to enjoy. When we behave ourselves as godly women, we honor God. When we live righteously and according to God's commandments, He blesses us in ways that we cannot fully understand.

Today, as you fulfill your responsibilities, hold fast that which is good, and associate yourself with believers who behave themselves in like fashion. When you do, your good works will serve as a powerful example for others and as a worthy offering to your Creator.

Let us never suppose that obedience is impossible or that holiness is meant only for a select few. Our Shepherd leads us in paths of righteousness— not for our name's sake but for His.

Elisabeth Elliot

Study the Bible and observe how the persons behaved and how God dealt with them. There is explicit teaching on every condition of life.

Corrie ten Boom

A TIMELY TIP

When it comes to telling the world about your relationship with God . . . your actions speak much more loudly than your words . . . so behave accordingly.

Day 94

ACKNOWLEDGING YOUR BLESSINGS

The Lord bless you and keep you; The Lord make His face shine upon you, And be gracious to you.

Numbers 6:24-25 NKJV

When the demands of life leave us rushing from place to place with scarcely a moment to spare, we may fail to pause and thank our Creator for His gifts. But, whenever we neglect to give proper thanks to the Father, we suffer because of our misplaced priorities.

Today, begin making a list of your blessings. You most certainly will not be able to make a complete list, but take a few moments and jot down as many blessings as you can. Then, give thanks to the Giver of all good things: God. His love for you is eternal, as are His gifts. And it's never too soon—or too late—to offer Him thanks.

Think of the blessings we so easily take for granted: Life itself; preservation from danger; every bit of health we enjoy; every hour of liberty; the ability to see, to hear, to speak, to think, and to imagine all this comes from the hand of God.

Billy Graham

Get rich quick! Count your blessings!

Anonymous

A TIMELY TIP

Don't overlook God's gifts. Every sunrise represents yet another beautifully wrapped gift from God. Unwrap it; treasure it; use it; and give thanks to the Giver.

Day 95

CHEERFUL CHRISTIANITY

Be cheerful. Keep things in good repair. Keep your spirits up. Think in harmony.
Be agreeable. Do all that, and the God of love and peace will be with you for
sure.

2 Corinthians 13:11 MSG

Mrs. Charles E. Cowman, the author of the classic devotional text *Streams in the Desert*, wrote, "Two wings are necessary to lift our souls toward God: prayer and praise. Prayer asks. Praise accepts the answer." That's why we should find the time to lift our concerns to God in prayer, and to praise Him for all that He has done. John Wesley correctly observed, "Sour godliness is the devil's religion." His words remind us that pessimism and doubt are some of the most important tools that Satan uses to achieve his objectives. Our challenge, of course, is to ensure that Satan cannot use these tools on us.

Are you a cheerful Christian? You should be! And what is the best way to attain the joy that is rightfully yours? By giving Christ what is rightfully His: your heart, your soul, and your life.

When we bring sunshine into the lives of others, we're warmed by it ourselves. When we spill a little happiness, it splashes on us.

Barbara Johnson

How changed our lives would be if we could only fly through the days on wings of surrender and trust!

Hannah Whitall Smith

A TIMELY TIP

Cheerfulness is an attitude that is highly contagious. And, remember that cheerfulness starts at the top. A cheerful household usually begins with cheerful adults.

A SERIES OF CHOICES

But seek first the kingdom of God and His righteousness, and all these things will be provided for you.

Matthew 6:33 HCSB

Your life is a series of choices. From the instant you wake up in the morning until the moment you nod off to sleep at night, you make countless decisions—decisions about the things you do, decisions about the words you speak, and decisions about the way that you choose to direct your thoughts.

As a woman who has been transformed by the love of Jesus, you have every reason to make wise choices. But sometimes, when the daily grind threatens to grind you up and spit you out, you may make choices that are displeasing to God. When you do, you'll pay a price because you'll forfeit the happiness and the peace that might otherwise have been yours.

So, as you pause to consider the kind of Christian you are—and the kind of Christian you want to become—ask yourself whether you're sitting on the fence or standing in the light. The choice is yours . . . and so are the consequences.

I do not know how the Spirit of Christ performs it, but He brings us choices through which we constantly change, fresh and new, into His likeness.

Joni Eareckson Tada

A TIMELY TIP

Wise choices bring you happiness; unwise choices don't. So whenever you have a choice to make, choose wisely and prayerfully.

COMPASSIONATE SERVANTS

Finally, all of you be of one mind, having compassion for one another; love as brothers, be tenderhearted, be courteous.

1 Peter 3:8 NKJV

God's Word commands us to be compassionate, generous servants to those who need our support. As believers, we have been richly blessed by our Creator. We, in turn, are called to share our gifts, our possessions, our testimonies, and our talents.

Concentration camp survivor Corrie ten Boom correctly observed, "The measure of a life is not its duration but its donation." These words remind us that the quality of our lives is determined not by what we are able to take from others, but instead by what we are able to share with others.

The thread of compassion is woven into the very fabric of Christ's teachings. If we are to be disciples of Christ, we, too, must be zealous in caring for others. Our Savior expects no less from us. And He deserves no less.

Before you can dry another's tears, you too must weep.

Barbara Johnson

A TIMELY TIP

It's good to feel compassion for others . . . but it's better to do something to ease their suffering. Martin Luther wrote, "Faith never asks whether good works are to be done, but has done them before there is time to ask the question, and it is always doing them." So when in doubt, do something good for somebody.

CONFIDENT CHRISTIANITY

You are my hope; O Lord GOD, You are my confidence.

Psalm 71:5 NASB

We Christians have many reasons to be confident. God is in His heaven; Christ has risen, and we are the sheep of His flock. Yet sometimes, even the most devout Christians can become discouraged. Discouragement, however, is not God's way; He is a God of possibility not negativity.

Are you a confident Christian? You should be. God's grace is eternal and His promises are unambiguous. So count your blessings, not your hardships. And live courageously. God is the Giver of all things good, and He watches over you today and forever.

The Creator has made us each one of a kind. There is nobody else exactly like us, and there never will be. Each of us is his special creation and is alive for a distinctive purpose.

Luci Swindoll

Bible hope is confidence in the future.

Warren Wiersbe

A TIMELY TIP

Increase your confidence by living in God's will for your life.

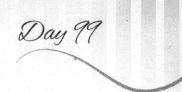

NEIGHBORS IN NEED

Each one of us needs to look after the good of the people around us, asking ourselves, "How can I help?" That's exactly what Jesus did.

Romans 15:2-3 MSG

Neighbors. We know that we are instructed to love them, and yet there's so little time . . . and we're so busy. No matter. As Christians, we are commanded by our Lord and Savior Jesus Christ to love our neighbors just as we love ourselves. Period.

This very day, you will encounter someone who needs a word of encouragement, or a pat on the back, or a helping hand, or a heartfelt prayer. And, if you don't reach out to your friend, who will? If you don't take the time to understand the needs of your neighbors, who will? If you don't love your brothers and sisters, who will? So, today, look for a neighbor in need . . . and then do something to help. Father's orders.

No matter how crazy or nutty your life has seemed, God can make something strong and good out of it. He can help you grow wide branches for others to use as shelter.

Barbara Johnson

When you add value to others, you do not take anything away from yourself.

John Maxwell

A TIMELY TIP

Someone very near you may need a helping hand or a kind word, so keep your eyes open, and look for people who need your help, whether at home, at church, at work, or anywhere in between.

Day 100

SAFE IN GOD'S HANDS

When you pass through the waters, I will be with you; and through the rivers, they shall not overflow you. When you walk through the fire, you shall not be burned, nor shall the flame scorch you. For I am the Lord your God, The Holy One of Israel, your Savior.

Isaiah 43:2-3 NKJV

As a busy woman, you know from firsthand experience that life is not always easy. But as a recipient of God's grace, you also know that you are protected by a loving Heavenly Father.

In times of trouble, God will comfort you; in times of sorrow, He will dry your tears. When you are troubled, or weak, or sorrowful, God is neither distant nor disinterested. To the contrary, God is always present and always vitally engaged in the events of your life. Reach out to Him, and build your future on the rock that cannot be shaken . . . trust in God and rely upon His provisions. He can provide everything you really need . . . and far, far more.

In all the old castles of England, there was a place called the keep. It was always the strongest and best protected place in the castle, and in it were hidden all who were weak and helpless and unable to defend themselves in times of danger. Shall we be afraid to hide ourselves in the keeping power of our Divine Keeper, who neither slumbers nor sleeps, and who has promised to preserve our going out and our coming in, from this time forth and even forever more?

Hannah Whitall Smith

A TIMELY TIP

You are protected by God . . . now and always. The only security that lasts is the security that flows from the loving heart of God.

AN ATTITUDE OF GRATITUDE

And let the peace of God rule in your hearts . . . and be ye thankful.

Colossians 3:15 KJV

For most of us, life is busy and complicated. We have countless responsibilities, some of which begin before sunrise and many of which end long after sunset. Amid the rush and crush of the daily grind, it is easy to lose sight of God and His blessings. But, when we forget to slow down and say "Thank You" to our Maker, we rob ourselves of His presence, His peace, and His joy.

Our task, as believing Christians, is to praise God many times each day. Then, with gratitude in our hearts, we can face our daily duties with the perspective and power that only He can provide.

Let's thank God for allowing us to experience troubles that drive us closer to Him.

Shirley Dobson

If you pause to think—you'll have cause to thank!

Anonymous

A TIMELY TIP

Developing an attitude of gratitude is key to a joyful and satisfying life. So ask yourself this question: "Am I grateful enough?"

DOERS OF THE WORD

But be doers of the word and not hearers only.

James 1:22 HCSB

The old saying is both familiar and true: actions speak louder than words. And as believers, we must beware: our actions should always give credence to the changes that Christ can make in the lives of those who walk with Him.

God calls upon each of us to act in accordance with His will and with respect for His commandments. If we are to be responsible believers, we must realize that it is never enough simply to hear the instructions of God; we must also live by them. And it is never enough to wait idly by while others do God's work here on earth; we, too, must act. Doing God's work is a responsibility that each of us must bear, and when we do, our loving Heavenly Father rewards our efforts with a bountiful harvest.

We spend our lives dreaming of the future, not realizing that a little of it slips away every day.

Barbara Johnson

Never fail to do something because you don't feel like it. Sometimes you just have to do it now, and you'll feel like it later.

Marie T. Freeman

A TIMELY TIP

Because actions do speak louder than words, it's always a good time to let your actions speak for themselves.

CONSIDERING THE CROSS

But God forbid that I should boast except in the cross of our Lord Jesus Christ, by whom the world has been crucified to me, and I to the world.

Galatians 6:14 NKJV

As we consider Christ's sacrifice on the cross, we should be profoundly humbled and profoundly grateful. And today, as we come to Christ in prayer, we should do so in a spirit of quiet, heartfelt devotion to the One who gave His life so that we might have life eternal.

He was the Son of God, but He wore a crown of thorns. He was the Savior of mankind, yet He was put to death on a roughhewn cross made of wood. He offered His healing touch to an unsaved world, and yet the same hands that had healed the sick and raised the dead were pierced with nails.

Christ humbled Himself on a cross—for you. As you approach Him today in prayer, think about His love and His sacrifice. And be grateful.

The cross takes care of the past. The cross takes care of the flesh. The cross takes care of the world.

Kay Arthur

The cross that Jesus commands you and me to carry is the cross of submissive obedience to the will of God, even when His will includes suffering and hardship and things we don't want to do.

Anne Graham Lotz

A TIMELY TIP

The salvation that Jesus provided on the cross is free to us, but it cost Him so much. We must never take His sacrifice for granted.

Day 104

A WORTHY DISCIPLE

He has told you men what is good and what it is the Lord requires of you: Only to act justly, to love faithfulness, and to walk humbly with your God.

Micah 6:8 HCSB

When Jesus addressed His disciples, He warned that each one must, "take up his cross and follow Me." The disciples must have known exactly what the Master meant. In Jesus' day, prisoners were forced to carry their own crosses to the location where they would be put to death. Thus, Christ's message was clear: in order to follow Him, Christ's disciples must deny themselves and, instead, trust Him completely. Nothing has changed since then.

If we are to be disciples of Christ, we must trust Him and place Him at the very center of our beings. Jesus never comes "next." He is always first.

Do you seek to be a worthy disciple of Christ? Then pick up His cross today and every day that you live. When you do, He will bless you now and forever.

I lived with Indians who made pots out of clay which they used for cooking. Nobody was interested in the pot. Everybody was interested in what was inside. The same clay taken out of the same riverbed, always made in the same design, nothing special about it. Well, I'm a clay pot, and let me not forget it. But, the excellency of the power is of God and not us.

Elisabeth Elliot

A TIMELY TIP

If you want to be a disciple of Christ . . . follow in His footsteps, obey His commandments, and share His never-ending love.

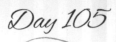

FILLED WITH THE SPIRIT

And don't get drunk with wine, which leads to reckless actions, but be filled with the Spirit.

Ephesians 5:18 HCSB

When you are filled with the Holy Spirit, your words and deeds will reflect a love and devotion to Christ. When you are filled with the Holy Spirit, the steps of your life's journey are guided by the Lord. When you allow God's Spirit to work in you and through you, you will be energized and transformed.

Today, allow yourself to be filled with the Spirit of God. And then stand back in amazement as God begins to work miracles in your own life and in the lives of those you love.

The Holy Spirit is like a living and continually flowing fountain in believers. We have the boundless privilege of tapping into that fountain every time we pray.

Shirley Dobson

God cannot reveal anything to us if we have not His spirit.

Oswald Chambers

A TIMELY TIP

The Holy Spirit is God in us, providing us with all we need to be effective Christians.

Day 106

THE WORLD'S BEST FRIEND

No one has greater love than this, that someone would lay down his life for his friends.

John 15:13 HCSB

Who's the best friend this world has ever had? Jesus, of course. When you invite Him into your heart, Jesus will be your friend, too . . . your friend forever. Jesus has offered to share the gifts of everlasting life and everlasting love with the world . . . and with you. If you make mistakes, He'll still be your friend. If you behave badly, He'll still love you. If you feel sorry or sad, He will help you feel better about your world and yourself.

Jesus wants you to have a happy, meaningful life. He wants you to be generous and kind, and He wants you to follow Him. The rest, of course, is up to you. You can do it! And with a friend like Jesus, you most certainly will.

When we are in a situation where Jesus is all we have, we soon discover he is all we really need.

Gigi Graham Tchividjian

Blessed assurance, Jesus is mine! O what a foretaste of glory divine!

Fanny Crosby

A TIMELY TIP

Jesus is the light of the world. God wants Him to be the light of your life.

TOO MANY POSSESSIONS

Do not love the world or the things that belong to the world. If anyone loves the world, love for the Father is not in him.

1 John 2:15 HCSB

O n the grand stage of a well-lived life, material possessions should play a rather small role. Of course, we all need the basic necessities of life, but once we meet those needs for ourselves and for our families, the piling up of possessions creates more problems than it solves. Our real riches, of course, are not of this world. We are never really rich until we are rich in spirit.

How much stuff is too much stuff? Well, if your desire for stuff is getting in the way of your desire to know God, then you've got too much stuff—it's as simple as that. So, if you find yourself wrapped up in the concerns of the material world, it's time to reorder your priorities. And, it's time to begin storing up riches that will endure throughout eternity—the spiritual kind.

We own too many things that aren't worth owning.

Marie T. Freeman

As faithful stewards of what we have, ought we not to give earnest thought to our staggering surplus?

Elisabeth Elliot

A TIMELY TIP

Materialism Made Simple: The world wants you to believe that "money and stuff" can buy happiness. Don't believe it! Genuine happiness comes not from money, but from the things that money can't buy—starting, of course, with your relationship to God and His only begotten Son.

ON A MISSION

But you are a chosen race, a royal priesthood, a holy nation, a people for His possession, so that you may proclaim the praises of the One who called you out of darkness into His marvelous light.

1 Peter 2:9 HCSB

Whether you realize it or not, you are on a personal mission for God. As a Christian, that mission is straightforward: Honor God, accept Christ as your personal Savior, and serve God's children.

Of course, you will encounter impediments as you attempt to discover the exact nature of God's purpose for your life, but you must never lose sight of the overriding purposes that God has established for all believers. You will encounter these overriding purposes again and again as you worship your Creator and study His Word.

Every day offers countless opportunities to serve God and to worship Him. When you do so, He will bless you in miraculous ways. May you continue to seek God's will, may you trust His word, and may you place Him where He belongs: at the very center of your life.

I am more and more persuaded that all that is required of us is faithful seed-sowing. The harvest is bound to follow.

Annie Armstrong

A TIMELY TIP

God has a plan for your life, a definite purpose that you can fulfill . . . or not. Your challenge is to pray for God's guidance and to follow wherever He leads.

GOD'S GUIDANCE AND YOUR PATH

Trust in the LORD with all your heart; do not depend on your own understanding. Seek his will in all you do, and he will direct your paths.

Proverbs 3:5-6 NLT

Proverbs 3:5-6 makes this promise: if you acknowledge God's sovereignty over every aspect of your life, He will guide your path. And, as you prayerfully consider the path that God intends for you to take, here are things you should do: You should study His Word and be ever-watchful for His signs. You should associate with fellow believers who will encourage your spiritual growth. You should listen carefully to that inner voice that speaks to you in the quiet moments of your daily devotionals. And you should be patient. Your Heavenly Father may not always reveal Himself as quickly as you would like, but rest assured that God intends to use you in wonderful, unexpected ways. Your challenge is to watch, to listen, to learn . . . and to follow.

Let us never suppose that obedience is impossible or that holiness is meant only for a select few. Our Shepherd leads us in paths of righteousness—not for our name's sake but for His.

Elisabeth Elliot

A TIMELY TIP

Following Christ is a daily journey. When you decide to walk in the footsteps of the Master, that means that you're agreeing to be a disciple seven days a week, not just on Sunday. Remember the words of Vance Havner: "We must live in all kinds of days, both high days and low days, in simple dependence upon Christ as the branch on the vine. This is the supreme experience."

THE POWER OF PRAYER

The intense prayer of the righteous is very powerful.

James 5:16 HCSB

"The power of prayer": these words are so familiar, yet sometimes we forget what they mean. Prayer is a powerful tool for communicating with our Creator; it is an opportunity to commune with the Giver of all things good. Prayer helps us find strength for today and hope for the future. Prayer is not a thing to be taken lightly or to be used infrequently.

The quality of your spiritual life will be in direct proportion to the quality of your prayer life. Prayer changes things, and it changes you. Today, instead of turning things over in your mind, turn them over to God in prayer. Instead of worrying about your next decision, ask God to lead the way. Pray constantly about things great and small. God is listening, and He wants to hear from you now.

Always stay connected to people and seek out things that bring you joy. Dream with abandon. Pray confidently.

Barbara Johnson

Prayer is our privilege of constant, unbroken communication with God.

Shirley Dobson

A TIMELY TIP

Pray specifically. If you need something, don't ask for God's help in general terms; ask specifically for the things you need.

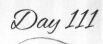
A QUIET PLACE

Now in the morning, having risen a long while before daylight, He went out and departed to a solitary place; and there He prayed.

Mark 1:35 NKJV

In the first chapter of Mark, we read that in the darkness of the early morning hours, Jesus went to a solitary place and prayed. So, too, should we. But sometimes, finding quiet moments of solitude is difficult indeed.

We live in a noisy world, a world filled with distractions, frustrations, and complications. But if we allow the distractions of a clamorous world to separate us from God's peace, we do ourselves a profound disservice. Are you one of those busy women who rushes through the day with scarcely a single moment for quiet contemplation and prayer? If so, it's time to reorder your priorities. Nothing is more important than the time you spend with your Savior. So be still and claim the inner peace that is your spiritual birthright: the peace of Jesus Christ.

The more complicated life becomes, the more we need to quiet our souls before God.

Elisabeth Elliot

In the center of a hurricane there is absolute quiet and peace. There is no safer place than in the center of the will of God.

Corrie ten Boom

A TIMELY TIP

Be still and listen to God. He has something important to say to you.

SO MANY TEMPTATIONS

No temptation has overtaken you except what is common to humanity. God is faithful and He will not allow you to be tempted beyond what you are able, but with the temptation He will also provide a way of escape, so that you are able to bear it.

1 Corinthians 10:13 HCSB

This world is filled to the brim with temptations. Some of these temptations are small; eating a second scoop of ice cream, for example, is tempting, but not very dangerous. Other temptations, however, are not nearly so harmless. The devil is working 24/7, and he's causing pain and heartache in more ways than ever before. Thankfully, in the battle against Satan, we are never alone. God is always with us, and He gives us the power to resist temptation whenever we ask Him for the strength to do so.

In a letter to believers, Peter offered a stern warning: "Your adversary, the devil, prowls around like a roaring lion, seeking someone to devour" (1 Peter 5:8 NASB). As Christians, we must take that warning seriously, and we must behave accordingly.

The only power the devil has is in getting people to believe his lies. If they don't believe his lies, he is powerless to get his work done.

Stormie Omartian

Temptation is not a sin. Even Jesus was tempted. The Lord Jesus gives you the strength needed to resist temptation.

Corrie ten Boom

A TIMELY TIP

Sometimes immorality is obvious and sometimes it's not. So beware: the most subtle forms of sin are often the most dangerous.

THE POWER OF OUR WORDS

No rotten talk should come from your mouth, but only what is good for the building up of someone in need, in order to give grace to those who hear.

Ephesians 4:29 HCSB

The words that we speak have the power to do great good or great harm. If we speak words of encouragement and hope, we can lift others up. And that's exactly what God commands us to do!

Sometimes, when we feel uplifted and secure, it is easy to speak kind words. Other times, when we are discouraged or tired, we can scarcely summon the energy to uplift ourselves, much less anyone else. God intends that we speak words of kindness, wisdom, and truth, no matter our circumstances, no matter our emotions. When we do, we share a priceless gift with the world, and we give glory to the One who gave His life for us. As believers, we must do no less.

Words. Do you fully understand their power? Can any of us really grasp the mighty force behind the things we say? Do we stop and think before we speak, considering the potency of the words we utter?

Joni Eareckson Tada

Overcoming discouragement is simply a matter of taking away the DIS and adding the EN.

Barbara Johnson

A TIMELY TIP

Encouragement is contagious. You can't lift other people up without lifting yourself up, too.

FORGIVENESS STARTS AT HOME

Let all bitterness, wrath, anger, clamor, and evil speaking be put away from you, with all malice. And be kind to one another, tenderhearted, forgiving one another, just as God in Christ forgave you.

Ephesians 4:31-32 NKJV

Sometimes, it's easy to become angry with the people we love most, and sometimes it's hard to forgive them. After all, we know that our family will still love us no matter how angry we become. But while it's easy to become angry at home, it's usually wrong.

The next time you're tempted to lose your temper or to remain angry at a close family member, ask God to help you find the wisdom to forgive. And while you're at it, do your best to calm down sooner rather than later because peace is always beautiful, especially when it's peace at your house.

Anger unresolved will only bring you woe.

Kay Arthur

Anger breeds remorse in the heart, discord in the home, bitterness in the community, and confusion in the state.

Billy Graham

A TIMELY TIP

Angry words are dangerous to your emotional and spiritual health, not to mention your relationships. So treat anger as an uninvited guest, and usher it away as quickly—and as quietly—as possible.

FACING FEARS, LIVING BOLDLY

For God has not given us a spirit of fearfulness, but one of power, love, and sound judgment.

2 Timothy 1:7 HCSB

D o you prefer to face your fears rather than run from them? If so, you will be blessed because of your willingness to live courageously.

When Paul wrote Timothy, he reminded his young protégé that the God they served was a bold God, and God's spirit empowered His children with boldness also. Like Timothy, we face times of uncertainty and fear. God's message is the same to us, today, as it was to Timothy: We can live boldly because the spirit of God resides in us.

So today, as you face the challenges of everyday living, remember that God is with you . . . and you are protected.

The pathway of obedience can sometimes be difficult, but it always leads to a strengthening of our inner woman.

Vonette Bright

Developing a positive attitude means working continually to find what is uplifting and encouraging.

Barbara Johnson

A TIMELY TIP

Today, ask yourself if you're being assertive enough at work, at home, or in between. If the answer is no, decide on at three specific steps you can take to stand up for yourself appropriately, fairly, and often.

THE PURSUIT OF GOD'S TRUTH

But grow in the grace and knowledge of our Lord and Savior Jesus Christ. To Him be the glory both now and forever. Amen.

2 Peter 3:18 NKJV

Have you established a passionate relationship with God's Holy Word? Hopefully so. After all, the Bible is a roadmap for life here on earth and for life eternal. And, as a believer who has been touched by God's grace, you are called upon to study God's Holy Word, to trust His Word, to follow its commandments, and to share its Good News with the world.

The words of Matthew 4:4 remind us that, "Man shall not live by bread alone but by every word that proceedeth out of the mouth of God" (KJV). As believers, we must study the Bible and meditate upon its meaning for our lives. Otherwise, we deprive ourselves of a priceless gift from our Creator. God's Holy Word is, indeed, a transforming gift from the Father in heaven. That's why passionate believers must never live by bread alone . . .

Study the Bible and observe how the persons behaved and how God dealt with them. There is explicit teaching on every condition of life.

Corrie ten Boom

A Bible in the hand is worth two in the bookcase.

Anonymous

A TIMELY TIP

Never stop studying God's Word. Even if you've been studying the Bible for many years, you've still got lots to learn. Bible study should be a lifelong endeavor; make it your lifelong endeavor.

CELEBRATION WITH A SMILE

Jacob said, "For what a relief it is to see your friendly smile. It is like seeing the smile of God!"

Genesis 33:10 NLT

L ife should never be taken for granted. Each day is a priceless gift from God and should be treated as such.

Hannah Whitall Smith observed, "How changed our lives would be if we could only fly through the days on wings of surrender and trust!" How true!

Today, let us celebrate life with smiles on our faces and kind words on our lips. After all, this is God's day, and He has given us clear instructions for its use. We are commanded to rejoice and be glad. So, with no further ado, let the celebration begin . . .

A smile is the light in the window of your face that tells people you're at home.

Barbara Johnson

Our God is so wonderfully good, and lovely, and blessed in every way that the mere fact of belonging to Him is enough for an untellable fullness of joy!

Hannah Whitall Smith

A TIMELY TIP

God has given you the gift of life (here on earth) and the promise of eternal life (in heaven). Now, He wants you to celebrate those gifts.

UNBENDING TRUTH

And put on the new self, which in the likeness of God has been created in righteousness and holiness of the truth. Therefore, laying aside falsehood, speak truth, each one of you, with his neighbor, for we are members of one another.

Ephesians 4:24-25 NASB

We live in a world that presents us with countless temptations to wander far from God's path. These temptations have the potential to destroy us, in part, because they cause us to be dishonest with ourselves and with others. Dishonesty is a habit. Once we start bending the truth, we're likely to keep bending it. A far better strategy, of course, is to acquire the habit of being completely forthright with God, with other people, and with ourselves.

Honesty is also a habit, a habit that pays powerful dividends for those who place character above convenience. So, the next time you're tempted to bend the truth—or to break it—ask yourself this simple question: "What does God want to do?" Then listen carefully to your conscience. When you do, your actions will be honorable, and your character will take care of itself.

God cannot build character without our cooperation. If we resist Him, then He chastens us into submission. But, if we submit to Him, then He can accomplish His work. He is not satisfied with a halfway job. God wants a perfect work; He wants a finished product that is mature and complete.

Warren Wiersbe

A TIMELY TIP

Character matters. Your ability to witness for Christ depends more upon your actions than your words.

CALMNESS IN CHAOS

Thou wilt keep him in perfect peace, whose mind is stayed on thee.

Isaiah 26:3 KJV

The beautiful words of John 14:27 give us hope: "Peace I leave with you, my peace I give unto you . . . ." Jesus offers us peace, not as the world gives, but as He alone gives. We, as believers, can accept His peace or ignore it.

When we accept the peace of Jesus Christ into our hearts, our lives are transformed. And then, because we possess the gift of peace, we can share that gift with fellow Christians, family members, friends, and associates. If, on the other hand, we choose to ignore the gift of peace—for whatever reason—we cannot share what we do not possess.

As every woman knows, peace can be a scarce commodity in a demanding, 21st-century world. How, then, can we find the peace that we so desperately desire? By turning our days and our lives over to God. Elisabeth Elliot writes, "If my life is surrendered to God, all is well. Let me not grab it back, as though it were in peril in His hand but would be safer in mine!" May we give our lives, our hopes, and our prayers to the Lord, and, by doing so, accept His will and His peace.

To know God as He really is—in His essential nature and character—is to arrive at a citadel of peace that circumstances may storm, but can never capture.

Catherine Marshall

A TIMELY TIP

God's peace surpasses human understanding. When you accept His peace, it will revolutionize your life.

COMFORTING OTHERS

Carry one another's burdens; in this way you will fulfill the law of Christ.

Galatians 6:2 HCSB

We live in a world that is, on occasion, a frightening place. Sometimes, we sustain life-altering losses that are so profound and so tragic that it seems we could never recover. But, with God's help and with the help of encouraging family members and friends, we can recover.

In times of need, God's Word is clear: as believers, we must offer comfort to those in need by sharing not only our courage but also our faith. As the revivalist Vance Havner observed, "No journey is complete that does not lead through some dark valleys. We can properly comfort others only with the comfort wherewith we ourselves have been comforted of God." Enough said.

So often we think that to be encouragers we have to produce great words of wisdom when, in fact, a few simple syllables of sympathy and an arm around the shoulder can often provide much needed comfort.

Florence Littauer

God's promises are medicine for the broken heart. Let Him comfort you. And, after He has comforted you, try to share that comfort with somebody else. It will do both of you good.

Warren Wiersbe

A TIMELY TIP

When talking to a person who's enduring obvious pain, don't assume that you know how he or she feels. To say, "I know how you must feel" is to assume that you can know the inner workings of another person's heart. Those words are often better left unsaid.

A LIFE OF INTEGRITY

The godly walk with integrity; blessed are their children after them.

Proverbs 20:7 NLT

Wise women understand that integrity is a crucial building block in the foundation of a well-lived life. Integrity is built slowly over a lifetime. It is the sum of every right decision, every honest word, every noble thought, and every heartfelt prayer. It is forged on the anvil of honorable work and polished by the twin virtues of generosity and humility. Integrity is a precious thing—difficult to build, but easy to tear down; godly women value it and protect it at all costs.

As believers in Christ, we must seek to live each day with discipline, honesty, and faith. When we do, at least two things happen: integrity becomes a habit, and God blesses us because of our obedience to Him.

God never called us to naïveté. He called us to integrity . . . . The biblical concept of integrity emphasizes mature innocence not childlike ignorance.

Beth Moore

Integrity is a sign of maturity.

Charles Swindoll

A TIMELY TIP

The real test of integrity is being willing to tell the truth when it's hard.

Day 122

GOD'S LESSONS

Listen to counsel and receive instruction so that you may be wise in later life.

Proverbs 19:20 HCSB

When it comes to learning life's lessons, we can either do things the easy way or the hard way. The easy way can be summed up as follows: when God teaches us a lesson, we learn it . . . the first time! Unfortunately, too many of us learn much more slowly than that.

When we resist God's instruction, He continues to teach, whether we like it or not. Our challenge, then, is to discern God's lessons from the experiences of everyday life. Hopefully, we learn those lessons sooner rather than later because the sooner we do, the sooner He can move on to the next lesson and the next, and the next . . .

While chastening is always difficult, if we look to God for the lesson we should learn, we will see spiritual fruit.

Vonette Bright

It is pleasing to the dear God whenever you rejoice or laugh from the bottom of your heart.

Martin Luther

A TIMELY TIP

Never stop learning. Think of it like this: when you're through learning, you're through.

THE WISDOM OF MODERATION

Patience is better than power, and controlling one's temper, than capturing a city.

Proverbs 16:32 HCSB

Moderation and wisdom are traveling companions. If we are wise, we must learn to temper our appetites, our desires, and our impulses. When we do, we are blessed, in part, because God has created a world in which temperance is rewarded and intemperance is inevitably punished.

Would you like to improve your life? Then harness your appetites and restrain your impulses. Moderation is difficult, of course; it is especially difficult in a prosperous society such as ours. But the rewards of moderation are numerous and long-lasting. Claim those rewards today. No one can force you to moderate your appetites. The decision to live temperately (and wisely) is yours and yours alone. And so are the consequences.

To many, total abstinence is easier than perfect moderation.

St. Augustine

Virtue—even attempted virtue—brings light; indulgence brings fog.

C. S. Lewis

A TIMELY TIP

God's Word instructs us to be moderate and disciplined as we guard our bodies, our minds, and our hearts.

OPTIMISM 101

I am able to do all things through Him who strengthens me.

Philippians 4:13 HCSB

Pessimism and Christianity don't mix. Why? Because Christians have every reason to be optimistic about life here on earth and life eternal. Mrs. Charles E. Cowman advised, "Never yield to gloomy anticipation. Place your hope and confidence in God. He has no record of failure."

Sometimes, despite our trust in God, we may fall into the spiritual traps of worry, frustration, anxiety, or sheer exhaustion, and our hearts become heavy. What's needed is plenty of rest, a large dose of perspective, and God's healing touch, but not necessarily in that order. So, make this promise to yourself and keep it: vow to be a hope-filled Christian. Think optimistically about your life, your profession, and your future. Trust your hopes, not your fears. Take time to celebrate God's glorious creation. And then, when you've filled your heart with hope and gladness, share your optimism with others. They'll be better for it, and so will you. But not necessarily in that order.

We may run, walk, stumble, drive, or fly, but let us never lose sight of the reason for the journey, or miss a chance to see a rainbow on the way.

Gloria Gaither

A TIMELY TIP

Today (and every day), it's time to count your blessings and to think optimistically about your future.

HIS CALLING

But as God has distributed to each one, as the Lord has called each one, so let him walk.

1 Corinthians 7:17 NKJV

I t is terribly important that you heed God's calling by discovering and developing your talents and your spiritual gifts. If you seek to make a difference—and if you seek to bear eternal fruit—you must discover your gifts and begin using them for the glory of God.

Every believer has at least one gift. In John 15:16, Jesus says, "You did not choose Me, but I chose you and appointed you that you should go and bear fruit, and that your fruit should remain, that whatever you ask the Father in My name He may give you." Have you found your special calling? If not, keep searching and keep praying until you find it. God has important work for you to do, and the time to begin that work is now.

God has given you special talents—now it's your turn to give them back to God.

Marie T. Freeman

If God's Word, your circumstances, and the counsel of others line up, and if you sense his provision, I'd say go for it.

Luci Swindoll

A TIMELY TIP

God calls you to a life that is perfectly suited for you, a life that will bring happiness and satisfaction to yourself and to others.

TODAY'S BIBLE READING
Old Testament: 1 Kings 21-22
New Testament: Luke 24:21-36

NOW, NOT LATER

We can't afford to waste a minute, must not squander these precious daylight hours in frivolity and indulgence . . . . Don't loiter and linger, waiting until the very last minute. Dress yourselves in Christ, and be up and about!

Romans 13:13-14 MSG

The habit of procrastination takes a two-fold toll on its victims. First, important work goes unfinished; second (and more importantly), valuable energy is wasted in the process of putting off the things that remain undone. Procrastination results from an individual's short-sighted attempt to postpone temporary discomfort. What results is a senseless cycle of 1. delay, followed by 2. worry followed by 3. a panicky and often futile attempt to "catch up." Procrastination is, at its core, a struggle against oneself; the only antidote is action.

Once you acquire the habit of doing what needs to be done when it needs to be done, you will avoid untold trouble, worry, and stress. So learn to defeat procrastination by paying less attention to your fears and more attention to your responsibilities. God has created a world that punishes procrastinators and rewards women who "do it now." Life doesn't procrastinate—neither should you.

Never fail to do something because you don't feel like it. Sometimes you just have to do it now, and you'll feel like it later.

Marie T. Freeman

A TIMELY TIP

It's easy to put off unpleasant tasks until "later." A far better strategy is this: Do the unpleasant work first so you can enjoy the rest of the day.

THE POWER OF WORDS

The wise store up knowledge, but the mouth of the fool hastens destruction.

Proverbs 10:14 HCSB

All too often, in the rush to have ourselves heard, we speak first and think next . . . with unfortunate results. God's Word reminds us that, "Reckless words pierce like a sword, but the tongue of the wise brings healing" (Proverbs 12:18 NIV). If we seek to be a source of encouragement to friends and family, then we must measure our words carefully. Words are important: they can hurt or heal. Words can uplift us or discourage us, and reckless words, spoken in haste, cannot be erased.

Today, measure your words carefully. Use words of kindness and praise, not words of anger or derision. Remember that you have the power to heal others or to injure them, to lift others up or to hold them back. When you lift them up, your wisdom will bring healing and comfort to a world that needs both.

The things that we feel most deeply we ought to learn to be silent about, at least until we have talked them over thoroughly with God.

Elisabeth Elliot

When you talk, choose the very same words that you would use if Jesus were looking over your shoulder. Because He is.

Marie T. Freeman

A TIMELY TIP

God understands the importance of the words you speak . . . and so must you.

Day 128

AN INTENSELY BRIGHT FUTURE: YOURS

My purpose is to give life in all its fullness.

John 10:10 HSCB

Are you excited about the opportunities of today and thrilled by the possibilities of tomorrow? Do you confidently expect God to lead you to a place of abundance, peace, and joy? And, when your days on earth are over, do you expect to receive the priceless gift of eternal life? If you trust God's promises, and if you have welcomed God's Son into your heart, then you believe that your future is intensely and eternally bright.

It takes courage to dream big dreams. You will discover that courage when you do three things: accept the past, trust God to handle the future, and make the most of the time He has given you today. No dreams are too big for God—not even yours. So start living—and dreaming—accordingly.

Allow your dreams a place in your prayers and plans. God-given dreams can help you move into the future He is preparing for you.

Barbara Johnson

Set goals so big that unless God helps you, you will be a miserable failure.

Bill Bright

A TIMELY TIP

You can dream big dreams, but you can never out-dream God. His plans for you are even bigger than you can imagine.

WHAT KIND OF EXAMPLE?

Set an example of good works yourself, with integrity and dignity in your teaching.

Titus 2:7 HCSB

What kind of example are you? Are you the kind of woman whose life serves as a powerful example of decency and morality? Are you a woman whose behavior serves as a positive role model for others? Are you the kind of person whose actions, day in and day out, are based upon integrity, fidelity, and a love for the Lord? If so, you are not only blessed by God, you are also a powerful force for good in a world that desperately needs positive influences such as yours. And that's good because your family and friends are watching . . . and so, for that matter, is God.

In serving we uncover the greatest fulfillment within and become a stellar example of a woman who knows and loves Jesus.

Vonette Bright

In your desire to share the gospel, you may be the only Jesus someone else will ever meet. Be real and be involved with people.

Barbara Johnson

A TIMELY TIP

Today, ask yourself this: If every Christian followed your example, what kind of world would we live in? If you like the answer you receive from the person in the mirror, keep doing what you're doing. But if you find room for improvement, start making those improvements today.

TEMPORARY SETBACKS

A time to weep, and a time to laugh; a time to mourn, and a time to dance . . . .

Ecclesiastes 3:4 KJV

The occasional disappointments and failures of life are inevitable. Such setbacks are simply the price that we must occasionally pay for our willingness to take risks as we follow our dreams. But even when we encounter bitter disappointments, we must never lose faith.

When we encounter the inevitable difficulties of life-here-on-earth, God stands ready to protect us. Our responsibility, of course, is to ask Him for protection. When we call upon Him in heartfelt prayer, He will answer—in His own time and according to His own plan—and He will heal us. And, while we are waiting for God's plans to unfold and for His healing touch to restore us, we can be comforted in the knowledge that our Creator can overcome any obstacle, even if we cannot.

Every misfortune, every failure, every loss may be transformed. God has the power to transform all misfortunes into "God-sends."

Mrs. Charles E. Cowman

Failure is one of life's most powerful teachers. How we handle our failures determines whether we're going to simply "get by" in life or "press on."

Beth Moore

A TIMELY TIP

Use your experiences—both good and bad—to learn, to grow, to share, and to teach.

FINANCIAL SECURITY

Honor the Lord with your wealth and the firstfruits from all your crops. Then your barns will be full . . . .

Proverbs 3:9-10 NCV

The quest for financial security is a journey that leads us across many peaks and through a few unexpected valleys. When we reach the mountaintops, we find it easy to praise God and to give thanks. But, when we face disappointment or financial hardship, it seems so much more difficult to trust God's perfect plan. But, trust Him we must.

As you strive to achieve financial security for your family, remember this: The next time you find your courage tested to the limit (and it will be), lean upon God's promises. Trust His Son. Remember that God is always near and that He is your protector and your deliverer. Always.

If the Living Logos of God has the power to create and sustain the universe . . . He is more than able to sustain your marriage and your ministry, your faith and your finances, your hope and your health.

Anne Graham Lotz

Sadly, family problems and even financial problems are seldom the real problem, but often the symptom of a weak or nonexistent value system.

Dave Ramsey

A TIMELY TIP

Don't fall in love with stuff. We live in a society that worships stuff— please don't fall into that trap. Remember this: material possessions are highly overrated. Worship God almighty, not the almighty dollar. (Proverbs 11:28)

Day 132

NOW IS THE TIME

So, my son, throw yourself into this work for Christ.

2 Timothy 1:1 MSG

God's love for you is deeper and more profound than you can imagine. God's love for you is so great that He sent His only Son to this earth to die for your sins and to offer you the priceless gift of eternal life. Now, you must decide whether or not to accept God's gift. Will you ignore it or embrace it? Will you return it or neglect it? Will you accept Christ's love and build a lifelong relationship with Him, or will you turn away from Him and take a different path?

Your decision to allow Christ to reign over your heart is the pivotal decision of your life. It is a decision that you cannot ignore. It is a decision that is yours and yours alone. Accept God's gift now: allow His Son to preside over your heart, your thoughts, and your life, starting this very instant.

I can tell you, from personal experience of walking with God for over fifty years, that He is the Lover of my soul.

Vonette Bright

Peter said, "No, Lord!" But he had to learn that one cannot say "No" while saying "Lord" and that one cannot say "Lord" while saying "No."

Corrie ten Boom

A TIMELY TIP

Think about ways that you can follow Christ—and think about ways you can encourage others to do the same.

FORGIVING AND FORGETTING

But the wisdom from above is first pure, then peace-loving, gentle, compliant, full of mercy and good fruits, without favoritism and hypocrisy.

James 3:17 HCSB

D o you have a tough time forgiving and forgetting? If so, welcome to the club. Most of us find it difficult to forgive the people who have hurt us. And that's too bad because life would be much simpler if we could forgive people "once and for all" and be done with it. Yet forgiveness is seldom that easy. Usually, the decision to forgive is straightforward, but the process of forgiving is more difficult. Forgiveness is a journey that requires time, perseverance, and prayer.

If you sincerely wish to forgive someone, pray for that person. And then pray for yourself by asking God to heal your heart. Don't expect forgiveness to be easy or quick, but rest assured: with God as your partner, you can forgive . . . and you will.

Forgiveness is not an emotion. Forgiveness is an act of the will, and the will can function regardless of the temperature of the heart.

Corrie ten Boom

Grudges are like hand grenades; it is wise to release them before they destroy you.

Barbara Johnson

A TIMELY TIP

Make a list of people whom you have not yet forgiven. Then, challenge yourself to forgive each and every one of them today. And what should you do if you simply cannot find it in your heart to forgive? Ask for God's help. He can give you the wisdom and courage you need to forgive everybody, including yourself.

Day 134

FAR BEYOND ENVY

Therefore, laying aside all malice, all deceit, hypocrisy, envy, and all evil speaking, as newborn babes, desire the pure milk of the word, that you may grow thereby.

1 Peter 2:1-2 NKJV

Because we are frail, imperfect human beings, we are sometimes envious of others. But God's Word warns us that envy is sin. Thus, we must guard ourselves against the natural tendency to feel resentment and jealousy when other people experience good fortune. As believers, we have absolutely no reason to be envious of any people on earth. After all, as Christians we are already recipients of the greatest gift in all creation: God's grace. We have been promised the gift of eternal life through God's only begotten Son, and we must count that gift as our most precious possession.

So here's a simple suggestion that is guaranteed to bring you happiness: fill your heart with God's love, God's promises, and God's Son . . . and when you do so, leave no room for envy, hatred, bitterness, or regret.

What God asks, does, or requires of others is not my business; it is His.

Kay Arthur

Contentment comes when we develop an attitude of gratitude for the important things we do have in our lives that we tend to take for granted if we have our eyes staring longingly at our neighbor's stuff.

Dave Ramsey

A TIMELY TIP

You can be envious, or you can be happy, but you can't be both. Envy and happiness can't live at the same time in the same brain.

FAITH THAT WORKS

In the same way faith, if it doesn't have works, is dead by itself.

James 2:17 HCSB

Corrie ten Boom advised, "Be filled with the Holy Spirit; join a church where the members believe the Bible and know the Lord; seek the fellowship of other Christians; learn and be nourished by God's Word and His many promises. Conversion is not the end of your journey—it is only the beginning."

The work of nourishing your faith can and should be joyful work. The hours that you invest in Bible study, prayer, meditation, and worship should be times of enrichment and celebration. And, as you continue to build your life upon a foundation of faith, you will discover that the journey toward spiritual maturity lasts a lifetime. As a child of God, you are never fully "grown": instead, you can continue "growing up" every day of your life. And that's exactly what God wants you to do.

Faith is an activity. It is something that has to be applied.

Corrie ten Boom

As you walk by faith, you live a righteous life, for righteousness is always by faith.

Kay Arthur

A TIMELY TIP

Faith should be practiced more than studied. Vance Havner said, "Nothing is more disastrous than to study faith, analyze faith, make noble resolves of faith, but never actually to make the leap of faith." How true!

FAITH VERSUS FEAR

Do not fear, for I am with you; do not be afraid, for I am your God. I will strengthen you; I will help you; I will hold on to you with My righteous right hand.

Isaiah 41:10 HCSB

A terrible storm rose quickly on the Sea of Galilee, and the disciples were afraid. Although they had witnessed many miracles, the disciples feared for their lives, so they turned to Jesus, and He calmed the waters and the wind.

The next time you find yourself facing a fear-provoking situation, remember that the One who calmed the wind and the waves is also your personal Savior. Then ask yourself which is stronger: your faith or your fear. The answer should be obvious. So, when the storm clouds form overhead and you find yourself being tossed on the stormy seas of life, remember this: Wherever you are, God is there, too. And, because He cares for you, you are protected.

Only believe, don't fear. Our Master, Jesus, always watches over us, and no matter what the persecution, Jesus will surely overcome it.

Lottie Moon

Our future may look fearfully intimidating, yet we can look up to the Engineer of the Universe, confident that nothing escapes His attention or slips out of the control of those strong hands.

Elisabeth Elliot

A TIMELY TIP

Everybody faces obstacles. Don't overestimate the size of yours.

IN FOCUS

Look straight ahead, and fix your eyes on what lies before you. Mark out a straight path for your feet; then stick to the path and stay safe. Don't get sidetracked; keep your feet from following evil.

Proverbs 4:25-27 NLT

What is your focus today? Are you willing to focus your thoughts and energies on God's blessings and upon His will for your life? Or will you turn your thoughts to other things? This day—and every day hereafter—is a chance to celebrate the life that God has given you. It's also a chance to give thanks to the One who has offered you more blessings than you can possibly count.

Today, why not focus your thoughts on the joy that is rightfully yours in Christ? Why not take time to celebrate God's glorious creation? Why not trust your hopes instead of your fears? When you do, you will think optimistically about yourself and your world . . . and you can then share your optimism with others. They'll be better for it, and so will you. But not necessarily in that order.

Jesus challenges you and me to keep our focus daily on the cross of His will if we want to be His disciples.

Anne Graham Lotz

Whatever we focus on determines what we become.

E. Stanley Jones

A TIMELY TIP

First focus on God . . . and then everything else will come into focus.

A TERRIFIC TOMORROW

"For I know the plans I have for you"—[this is] the Lord's declaration—"plans for [your] welfare, not for disaster, to give you a future and a hope."

Jeremiah 29:11 HCSB

How bright do you believe your future to be? Well, if you're a faithful believer, God has plans for you that are so bright that you'd better pack several pairs of sunglasses and a lifetime supply of sunblock!

The way that you think about your future will play a powerful role in determining how things turn out (it's called the "self-fulfilling prophecy," and it applies to everybody, including you). So here's another question: Are you expecting a terrific tomorrow, or are you dreading a terrible one? The answer to that question will have a powerful impact on the way tomorrow unfolds.

Today, as you live in the present and look to the future, remember that God has an amazing plan for you. Act—and believe—accordingly. And one more thing: don't forget the sunblock.

Do not limit the limitless God! With Him, face the future unafraid because you are never alone.

Mrs. Charles E. Cowman

Like little children on Christmas Eve, we know that lovely surprises are in the making. We can't see them. We have simply been told, and we believe. Tomorrow we shall see.

Elisabeth Elliot

A TIMELY TIP

The future isn't some pie-in-the-sky dream. Hope for the future is simply one aspect of trusting God.

THE THREAD OF GENEROSITY

The one who has two shirts must share with someone who has none, and the one who has food must do the same.

Luke 3:11 HCSB

The thread of generosity is woven—completely and inextricably—into the very fabric of Christ's teachings. As He sent His disciples out to heal the sick and spread God's message of salvation, Jesus offered this guiding principle: "Freely you have received, freely give" (Matthew 10:8 NIV). The principle still applies.

Lisa Whelchel spoke for Christian women everywhere when she observed, "The Lord has abundantly blessed me all of my life. I'm not trying to pay Him back for all of His wonderful gifts; I just realize that He gave them to me to give away." All of us have been blessed, and all of us are called to share those blessings without reservation. So, make this pledge and keep it: Be a cheerful, generous, courageous giver. The world needs your help, and you need the spiritual rewards that will be yours when you share your possessions, your talents, and your time.

What is your focus today? Joy comes when it is Jesus first, others second . . . then you.

Kay Arthur

We are never more like God than when we give.

Charles Swindoll

A TIMELY TIP

Want to admire the person you see in the mirror? Try being a little more generous. The more generous you are, the better you'll feel about yourself.

OBEY AND BE BLESSED

If you obey my commands, you will remain in my love, just as I have obeyed my Father's commands and remain in his love.

John 15:10 NIV

God gave us His commandments for a reason: so that we might obey them and be blessed. Elisabeth Elliot advised, "Obedience to God is our job. The results of that obedience are God's." These words should serve to remind us that obedience is imperative. But, we live in a world that presents us with countless temptations to disobey God's laws.

When we stray from God's path, we suffer. So, whenever we are confronted with sin, we have clear instructions: we must walk—or better yet run—in the opposite direction.

Don't worry about what you do not understand. Worry about what you do understand in the Bible but do not live by.

Corrie ten Boom

God meant that we adjust to the Gospel—not the other way around.

Vance Havner

A TIMELY TIP

If you're wise, you'll allow God to guide you today and every day of your life. When you pray for guidance, God will give it.

ADDITIONAL RESPONSIBILITIES

So he who had received five talents came and brought five other talents, saying, "Lord, you delivered to me five talents; look, I have gained five more talents besides them." His lord said to him, "Well done, good and faithful servant; you were faithful over a few things, I will make you ruler over many things. Enter into the joy of your lord."

Matthew 25:20-21 NKJV

God has promised us this: when we do our duties in small matters, He will give us additional responsibilities. Sometimes, those responsibilities come when God changes the course of our lives so that we may better serve Him. Sometimes, our rewards come in the form of temporary setbacks that lead, in turn, to greater victories. Sometimes, God rewards us by answering "no" to our prayers so that He can say "yes" to a far grander request that we, with our limited understanding, would never have thought to ask for.

If you seek to be God's servant in great matters, be faithful, be patient, and be dutiful in smaller matters. Then step back and watch as God surprises you with the spectacular creativity of His infinite wisdom and His perfect plan.

God has no problems, only plans. There is never panic in heaven.

Corrie ten Boom

A TIMELY TIP

Sometimes, waiting faithfully for God's plan to unfold is more important than understanding God's plan. Ruth Bell Graham once said, "When I am dealing with an all-powerful, all-knowing God, I, as a mere mortal, must offer my petitions not only with persistence, but also with patience. Someday I'll know why." So even when you can't understand God's plans, you must trust Him and never lose faith!

Day 142

CONTENTMENT THAT LASTS

But godliness with contentment is a great gain. For we brought nothing into the world, and we can take nothing out. But if we have food and clothing, we will be content with these. But those who want to be rich fall into temptation, a trap, and many foolish and harmful desires, which plunge people into ruin and destruction.

1 Timothy 6:6-9 HCSB

The preoccupation with happiness and contentment is an ever-present theme in the modern world. We are bombarded with messages that tell us where to find peace and pleasure in a world that worships materialism and wealth. But, lasting contentment is not found in material possessions; genuine contentment is a spiritual gift from God to those who trust in Him and follow His commandments. When God dwells at the center of our lives, peace and contentment will belong to us just as surely as we belong to God.

The key to contentment is to consider. Consider who you are and be satisfied with that. Consider what you have and be satisfied with that. Consider what God's doing and be satisfied with that.

Luci Swindoll

Make God's will the focus of your life day by day. If you seek to please Him and Him alone, you'll find yourself satisfied with life.

Kay Arthur

A TIMELY TIP

Be contented where you are, even if it's not exactly where you want to end up. God has something wonderful in store for you—and remember that God's timing is perfect—so be patient, trust God, do your best, and expect the best.

GOOD THINKING

Guard your heart above all else, for it is the source of life.

Proverbs 4:23 HCSB

Are you an upbeat believer? Are you a woman whose hopes and dreams are alive and well? Do you regularly put a smile on your face? And then, do you share that smile with family and friends? Hopefully so. After all, when you decided to allow Christ to rule over your heart, you entitled yourself to share in His promise of spiritual abundance and eternal joy. But sometimes, when pessimism and doubt invade your thoughts, you won't feel like celebrating. Why? Because thoughts are intensely powerful things.

Are you fearful, angry, bored, or worried? Are you so preoccupied with the concerns of this day that you fail to thank God for the promise of eternity? Are you confused, bitter, or pessimistic? If so, spend more time thinking about your blessings, and less time fretting about your hardships. Then, take time to thank the Giver of all things good for gifts that are, in truth, far too numerous to count.

As we have by faith said no to sin, so we should by faith say yes to God and set our minds on things above, where Christ is seated in the heavenlies.

Vonette Bright

The things we think are the things that feed our souls. If we think on pure and lovely things, we shall grow pure and lovely like them; and the converse is equally true.

Hannah Whitall Smith

A TIMELY TIP

Your thoughts have the power to lift you up or bring you down, so you should guard your thoughts very carefully.

THE LESSONS OF TOUGH TIMES

I waited patiently for the Lord, and He turned to me and heard my cry for help. He brought me up from a desolate pit, out of the muddy clay, and set my feet on a rock, making my steps secure. He put a new song in my mouth, a hymn of praise to our God.

Psalm 40:1-3 HCSB

Have you experienced a recent setback? If so, look for the lesson that God is trying to teach you. Instead of complaining about life's sad state of affairs, learn what needs to be learned, change what needs to be changed, and move on. View failure as an opportunity to reassess God's will for your life. View life's inevitable disappointments as opportunities to learn more about yourself and your world.

Life can be difficult at times. And everybody makes mistakes. Your job is to make them only once.

God is able to take mistakes, when they are committed to Him, and make of them something for our good and for His glory.

Ruth Bell Graham

Mistakes offer the possibility for redemption and a new start in God's kingdom. No matter what you're guilty of, God can restore your innocence.

Barbara Johnson

A TIMELY TIP

When you make a mistake, the time to make things better is now, not later. The sooner you address your problem, the better.

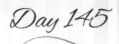

Day 145

GOD'S FORGIVENESS

If we confess our sins, He is faithful and righteous to forgive us our sins and to cleanse us from all unrighteousness.

1 John 1:9 HCSB

The Bible promises you this: When you ask God for forgiveness, He will give it. No questions asked; no explanations required. God's power to forgive, like His love, is infinite. Despite your sins, God offers immediate forgiveness. And it's time to take Him up on His offer.

When it comes to forgiveness, God doesn't play favorites and neither should you. You should forgive all the people who have harmed you (not just the people who have asked for forgiveness or the ones who have made restitution). Complete forgiveness is God's way, and it should be your way, too. Anything less is not enough.

Forgiveness is actually the best revenge because it not only sets us free from the person we forgive, but it frees us to move into all that God has in store for us.

Stormie Omartian

He who cannot forgive others breaks the bridge over which he himself must pass.

Corrie ten Boom

A TIMELY TIP

Forgiveness is its own reward. Bitterness is its own punishment. Guard your words and your thoughts accordingly.

HIS RIGHTFUL PLACE

You shall have no other gods before Me.

Exodus 20:3 NKJV

When Jesus was tempted by Satan, the Master's response was unambiguous. Jesus chose to worship the Lord and serve Him only. We, as followers of Christ, must follow in His footsteps by placing God first.

When we place God in a position of secondary importance, we do ourselves great harm. When we allow temptations or distractions to come between us and our Creator, we suffer. But, when we imitate Jesus and place the Lord in His rightful place—at the center of our lives—then we claim spiritual treasures that will endure forever.

To God be the glory, great things He has done; / So loved He the world that He gave us His Son.

Fanny Crosby

I am of the opinion that we should not be concerned about working for God until we have learned the meaning and delight of worshipping Him.

A. W. Tozer

A TIMELY TIP

God deserves first place in your life . . . and you deserve the experience of putting Him there.

THE SOURCE OF OUR COMFORT

When I am filled with cares, Your comfort brings me joy.

Psalm 94:19 HCSB

In times of adversity, we are wise to remember the words of Jesus, who, when He walked on the waters, reassured His disciples, saying, "Take courage! It is I. Don't be afraid" (Matthew 14:27 NIV). Then, with Christ on His throne—and with trusted friends and loving family members at our sides—we can face our fears with courage and with faith.

Are you facing a difficult challenge? If so, remember that no problem is too big for God . . . not even yours.

In Jesus, the service of God and the service of the least of the brethren were one.

Dietrich Bonhoeffer

As we find that it is not easy to persevere in this being "alone with God," we begin to realize that it is because we are not "wholly for God." God has a right to demand that He should have us completely for Himself.

Andrew Murray

A TIMELY TIP

Never confuse encouragement with pity. Pity parties are best left unattended by you and by your family and friends.

MOVING ON

"You have heard that it was said, 'You shall love your neighbor and hate your enemy.' But I say to you, love your enemies, bless those who curse you, do good to those who hate you, and pray for those who spitefully use you and persecute you, that you may be sons of your Father in heaven."

Matthew 5:43-45 NKJV

Sometimes, people can be discourteous and cruel. Sometimes people can be unfair, unkind, and unappreciative. Sometimes people get angry and frustrated. So what's a Christian to do? God's answer is straightforward: forgive, forget, and move on. In Luke 6:37, Jesus instructs, "Do not judge, and you will not be judged. Do not condemn, and you will not be condemned. Forgive, and you will be forgiven" (HCSB).

Today and every day, make sure that you're quick to forgive others for their shortcomings. And when other people misbehave (as they most certainly will from time to time), don't pay too much attention. Just forgive those people as quickly as you can, and try to move on . . . as quickly as you can.

A keen sense of humor helps us to overlook the unbecoming, understand the unconventional, tolerate the unpleasant, overcome the unexpected, and outlast the unbearable.

Billy Graham

A TIMELY TIP

Unless the person you're trying to change is a young child, and unless you are that child's parent or guardian, don't try to change him or her. Why? Because teenagers and adults change when they want to, not when you want them to.

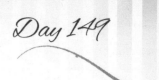
RELYING UPON HIM

Be humble under God's powerful hand so he will lift you up when the right time comes. Give all your worries to him, because he cares about you.

1 Peter 5:6-7 NCV

God is a never-ending source of support and courage for those of us who call upon Him. When we are weary, He gives us strength. When we see no hope, God reminds us of His promises. When we grieve, God wipes away our tears.

Do the demands of this day threaten to overwhelm you? If so, you must rely not only upon your own resources but also upon the promises of your Father in heaven. God will hold your hand and walk with you every day of your life if you let Him. So even if your circumstances are difficult, trust the Father. His love is eternal and His goodness endures forever.

We had plenty of challenges, some of which were tremendously serious, yet God has enabled us to walk, crawl, limp, or leap—whatever way we could progress—toward wholeness.

Beth Moore

God will never lead you where His strength cannot keep you.

Barbara Johnson

A TIMELY TIP

God wants to provide for you and your loved ones. When you trust your life and your future to God, He will provide for your needs.

Day 150

GROWING IN CHRIST

When I was a child, I spoke like a child, I thought like a child, I reasoned like a child. When I became a man, I put aside childish things.

1 Corinthians 13:11 HCSB

The journey toward spiritual maturity lasts a lifetime. As Christians, we can and should continue to grow in the love and the knowledge of our Savior as long as we live. Norman Vincent Peale had the following advice for believers of all ages: "Ask the God who made you to keep remaking you." That advice, of course, is perfectly sound, but often ignored.

When we cease to grow, either emotionally or spiritually, we do ourselves a profound disservice. But, if we study God's Word, if we obey His commandments, and if we live in the center of His will, we will not be "stagnant" believers; we will, instead, be growing Christians . . . and that's exactly what God wants for our lives.

No matter what we are going through, no matter how long the waiting for answers, of one thing we may be sure. God is faithful. He keeps His promises. What He starts, He finishes . . . including His perfect work in us.

Gloria Gaither

Don't be bound by your guilt or your fears any longer, but realize that sin's penalty has already been paid by Christ completely and fully.

Billy Graham

A TIMELY TIP

Your future depends, to a very great extent, upon you. So keep learning and keep growing personally, professionally, and spiritually.

BLESSED BEYOND MEASURE

We always thank God, the Father of our Lord Jesus Christ, when we pray for you.

Colossians 1:3 HCSB

As believing Christians, we are blessed beyond measure. God sent his only Son to die for our sins. And, God has given us the priceless gifts of eternal love and eternal life. We, in turn, are instructed to approach our Heavenly Father with reverence and thanksgiving. But, as busy women caught up in the inevitable demands of everyday life, we sometimes fail to pause and thank our Creator for the countless blessings He has bestowed upon us. When we slow down and express our gratitude to the One who made us, we enrich our own lives and the lives of those around us. Thanksgiving should become a habit, a regular part of our daily routines. Yes, God has blessed us beyond measure, and we owe Him everything, including our eternal praise.

Do we not continually pass by blessings innumerable without notice, and instead fix our eyes on what we feel to be our trials and our losses, and think and talk about these until our whole horizon is filled with them, and we almost begin to think we have no blessings at all?

Hannah Whitall Smith

God is worthy of our praise and is pleased when we come before Him with thanksgiving.

Shirley Dobson

A TIMELY TIP

If you need a little cheering up, start counting your blessings . . . and keep counting until you feel better.

GENTLENESS OF SPIRIT

Your beauty should not be the outer beauty of elaborate hairstyles and the wearing of gold ornaments or of fine clothes; rather, it should be an inner beauty with the imperishability of a gentle and quiet spirit, which is very valuable in God's eyes.

1 Peter 3:3-4 HCSB

In a letter to the Christians at Philippi, Paul instructed his friends to make their gentleness evident to all. But, even for the most dedicated Christians, it is sometimes difficult to be gentle. As fallible human beings, we are subject to the normal frustrations of daily life, and when we are, we are tempted to strike out in anger.

As long as you live here on earth, you will face countless opportunities to lose your temper over small, relatively insignificant events: a traffic jam, a spilled cup of coffee, an inconsiderate comment, a broken promise. When you are tempted to lose your temper over the minor inconveniences of life, don't. Turn away from anger and turn instead to God; when you do, He will fill you with a loving spirit that will help you deal gently and generously with others.

This hard place in which you perhaps find yourself is the very place in which God is giving you opportunity to look only to Him, to spend time in prayer, and to learn long-suffering, gentleness, meekness—in short, to learn the depths of the love that Christ Himself has poured out on all of us.

Elisabeth Elliot

A TIMELY TIP

It's good to feel compassion for others . . . but it's better to do something for them! When in doubt, do the compassionate thing.

THE CHOICE TO FORGIVE

You have heard that it was said, You shall love your neighbor and hate your enemy. But I tell you, love your enemies, and pray for those who persecute you.

Matthew 5:43-44 HCSB

Forgiveness is a choice. We can either choose to forgive those who have injured us, or not. When we obey God by offering forgiveness to His children, we are blessed. But when we allow bitterness and resentment to poison our hearts, we are tortured by our own shortsightedness.

Do you harbor resentment against anyone? If so, you are faced with an important decision: whether or not to forgive the person who has hurt you. God's instructions are clear: He commands you to forgive. And the time to forgive is now because tomorrow may be too late . . . for you.

Forgiveness is actually the best revenge because it not only sets us free from the person we forgive, but it frees us to move into all that God has in store for us.

Stormie Omartian

Forgiveness is the key that unlocks the door of resentment and the handcuffs of hate. It is a power that breaks the chains of bitterness and the shackles of selfishness.

Corrie ten Boom

A TIMELY TIP

God's Word instructs you to forgive others . . . no exceptions.

THE SEEDS OF GENEROSITY

Freely you have received, freely give.

Matthew 10:8 NKJV

Paul reminds us that when we sow the seeds of generosity, we reap bountiful rewards in accordance with God's plan for our lives. Thus, we are instructed to give cheerfully and without reservation: "But this I say, He which soweth sparingly shall reap also sparingly; and he which soweth bountifully shall reap also bountifully. Every man according as he purposeth in his heart, so let him give; not grudgingly, or of necessity: for God loveth a cheerful giver" (2 Corinthians 9:6, 7 KJV).

Today, make this pledge and keep it: Be a cheerful, generous, courageous giver. The world needs your help, and you need the spiritual rewards that will be yours when you give it.

As faithful stewards of what we have, ought we not to give earnest thought to our staggering surplus?

Elisabeth Elliot

Here lies the tremendous mystery—that God should be all-powerful, yet refuse to coerce. He summons us to cooperation. We are honored in being given the opportunity to participate in His good deeds. Remember how He asked for help in performing His miracles: Fill the water pots, stretch out your hand, distribute the loaves.

Elisabeth Elliot

A TIMELY TIP

God has given you countless blessings . . . and He wants you to share them.

Day 155

TRANSCENDENT LOVE

Who can separate us from the love of Christ? Can affliction or anguish or persecution or famine or nakedness or danger or sword? . . . No, in all these things we are more than victorious through Him who loved us.

Romans 8:35,37 HCSB

Where can we find God's love? Everywhere. God's love transcends space and time. It reaches beyond the heavens, and it touches the darkest, smallest corner of every human heart. When we become passionate in our devotion to the Father, when we sincerely open our minds and hearts to Him, His love does not arrive "some day"—it arrives immediately.

Today, take God at His word and welcome His Son into your heart. When you do, God's transcendent love will surround you and transform you, now and forever.

There is no pit so deep that God's love is not deeper still.

Corrie ten Boom

God is my Heavenly Father. He loves me with an everlasting love. The proof of that is the Cross.

Elisabeth Elliot

A TIMELY TIP

God's love makes everything better, including you.

Day 156

TODAY'S BIBLE READING
Old Testament: 2 Chronicles 24-25
New Testament: John 15

A PRESCRIPTION FOR PANIC

Anxiety in the heart of man causes depression, but a good word makes it glad.
Proverbs 12:25 NKJV

We are members of an anxious society, a society in which the changes we face threaten to outpace our abilities to make adjustments. No wonder we sometimes find ourselves beset by feelings of anxiety and panic.

At times, our anxieties may stem from physical causes—chemical imbalances in the brain that result in severe emotional distress or relentless panic attacks. In such cases, modern medicine offers hope to those who suffer. But oftentimes, our anxieties result from spiritual deficits, not physical ones. And when we're spiritually depleted, the best prescription is found not in the medicine cabinet but deep inside the human heart. What we need is a higher daily dose of God's love, God's peace, God's assurance, and God's presence. And how do we acquire these blessings from our Creator? Through prayer, through meditation, through worship, and through trust.

He treats us as sons, and all he asks in return is that we shall treat Him as a Father whom we can trust without anxiety. We must take the son's place of dependence and trust, and we must let Him keep the father's place of care and responsibility.

Hannah Whitall Smith

A TIMELY TIP

No more angry outbursts! If you think you're about to explode in anger, slow down, catch your breath, and walk away if you must. It's better to walk away—and keep walking—than it is to blurt out angry words that can't be un-blurted.

Day 157

FACING UP TO TROUBLE

I will be with you when you pass through the waters . . . when you walk through the fire . . . the flame will not burn you. For I the Lord your God, the Holy One of Israel, and your Savior.

Isaiah 43:2-3 HCSB

As life-here-on-earth unfolds, all of us encounter occasional setbacks: Those occasional visits from Old Man Trouble are simply a fact of life, and none of us are exempt. When tough times arrive, we may be forced to rearrange our plans and our priorities. But even on our darkest days, we must remember that God's love remains constant.

The fact that we encounter adversity is not nearly so important as the way we choose to deal with it. When tough times arrive, we have a clear choice: we can begin the difficult work of tackling our troubles . . . or not. When we summon the courage to look Old Man Trouble squarely in the eye, an amazing thing usually happens: he blinks.

We all go through pain and sorrow, but the presence of God, like a warm, comforting blanket, can shield us and protect us, and allow the deep inner joy to surface, even in the most devastating circumstances.

Barbara Johnson

We're wise to expect times of testing after times of blessing.

Beth Moore

A TIMELY TIP

When tough times arrive, you should work as if everything depended on you and pray as if everything depended on God.

TAKING TIME TO ASK

He granted their request because they trusted in Him.

1 Chronicles 5:20 HCSB

Sometimes, amid the demands and the frustrations of everyday life, we forget to slow ourselves down long enough to talk with God. Instead of turning our thoughts and prayers to Him, we rely upon our own resources. Instead of praying for strength and courage, we seek to manufacture it within ourselves. Instead of asking God for guidance, we depend only upon our own limited wisdom. The results of such behaviors are unfortunate and, on occasion, tragic.

Are you in need? Ask God to sustain you. Are you troubled? Take your worries to Him in prayer. Are you weary? Seek God's strength. In all things great and small, seek God's wisdom and His grace. He hears your prayers, and He will answer. All you must do is ask.

When will we realize that we're not troubling God with our questions and concerns? His heart is open to hear us—his touch nearer than our next thought—as if no one in the world existed but us. Our very personal God wants to hear from us personally.

Gigi Graham Tchividjian

God makes prayer as easy as possible for us. He's completely approachable and available, and He'll never mock or upbraid us for bringing our needs before Him.

Shirley Dobson

A TIMELY TIP

Today, think of a specific need that is weighing heavily on your heart. Then, spend a few quiet moments asking God for His guidance and for His help.

BEYOND OUR REGRETS

All bitterness, anger and wrath, insult and slander must be removed from you, along with all wickedness. And be kind and compassionate to one another, forgiving one another, just as God also forgave you in Christ.

Ephesians 4:31-32 HCSB

A re you mired in the quicksand of bitterness or regret? If so, you are not only disobeying God's Word, you are also wasting your time. The world holds few if any rewards for those who remain angrily focused upon the past. Still, the act of forgiveness is difficult for all but the most saintly men and women.

Being frail, fallible, imperfect human beings, most of us are quick to anger, quick to blame, slow to forgive, and even slower to forget. Yet as Christians, we are commanded to forgive others, just as we, too, have been forgiven.

If there exists even one person—alive or dead—against whom you hold bitter feelings, it's time to forgive. Or, if you are embittered against yourself for some past mistake or shortcoming, it's finally time to forgive yourself and move on. Hatred, bitterness, and regret are not part of God's plan for your life. Forgiveness is.

Grudges are like hand grenades; it is wise to release them before they destroy you.

Barbara Johnson

A TIMELY TIP

You can never fully enjoy the present if you're bitter about the past. Instead of living in the past, make peace with it . . . and move on.

LIMITLESS POWER, LIMITLESS LOVE

I pray that the eyes of your heart may be enlightened so you may know what is the hope of His calling, what are the glorious riches of His inheritance among the saints, and what is the immeasurable greatness of His power to us who believe, according to the working of His vast strength.

Ephesians 1:18-19 HCSB

Because God's power is limitless, it is far beyond the comprehension of mortal minds. Yet even though we cannot fully understand the awesome power of God, we can praise it. When we worship God with faith and assurance, when we place Him at the absolute center of our lives, we invite His love into our hearts. In turn, we grow to love Him more deeply as we sense His love for us. St. Augustine wrote, "I love you, Lord, not doubtingly, but with absolute certainty. Your Word beat upon my heart until I fell in love with you, and now the universe and everything in it tells me to love you."

Let us pray that we, too, will turn our hearts to the Creator, knowing with certainty that His heart has ample room for each of us, and that we, in turn, must make room in our hearts for Him.

The greatness of His power to create and design and form and mold and make and build and arrange defies the limits of our imagination. And since He created everything, there is nothing beyond His power to fix or mend or heal or restore.

Anne Graham Lotz

A TIMELY TIP

God is in control of His world and your world. Rely upon Him. Vance Havner writes, "When we get to a place where it can't be done unless God does it, God will do it!" So teach your children that God can handle anything.

THY WILL BE DONE

"Father, if it is Your will, take this cup away from Me; nevertheless not My will, but Yours, be done."

Luke 22:42 NKJV

As human beings with limited understanding, we can never fully comprehend the will of God. But as believers in a benevolent God, we must always trust the will of our Heavenly Father.

Before His crucifixion, Jesus went to the Mount of Olives and poured out His heart to God. Jesus knew of the agony that He was destined to endure, but He also knew that God's will must be done. We, like our Savior, face trials that bring fear and trembling to the very depths of our souls, but like Christ, we, too, must ultimately seek God's will, not our own. When we entrust our lives to Him completely and without reservation, He gives us the strength to meet any challenge, the courage to face any trial, and the wisdom to live in His righteousness.

The will of God is the most delicious and delightful thing in the universe.

Hannah Whitall Smith

In the center of a hurricane there is absolute quiet and peace. There is no safer place than in the center of the will of God.

Corrie ten Boom

A TIMELY TIP

Even when you cannot understand God's plans, you must trust them. If you place yourself in the center of God's will, He will provide for your needs and direct your path.

HAPPINESS AND HOLINESS

Happy are the people who live at your Temple . . . . Happy are those whose strength comes from you.

Psalm 84:4-5 NCV

D o you seek happiness, abundance, and contentment? If so, here are some things you should do: Love God and His Son; depend upon God for strength; try, to the best of your abilities, to follow God's will; and strive to obey His Holy Word. When you do these things, you'll discover that happiness goes hand-in-hand with righteousness. The happiest people are not those who rebel against God; the happiest people are those who love God and obey His commandments.

What does life have in store for you? A world full of possibilities (of course it's up to you to seize them) and God's promise of abundance (of course it's up to you to accept it). Your Creator has blessed you beyond measure. Honor Him with your prayers, your words, your deeds, and your joy.

Christ is the secret, the source, the substance, the center, and the circumference of all true and lasting gladness.

Mrs. Charles E. Cowman

When we do what is right, we have contentment, peace, and happiness.

Beverly LaHaye

A TIMELY TIP

If you want to find lasting happiness, don't chase it. Instead, do your duty, obey your God, and wait for happiness to find you.

HOPE FOR TODAY, HOPE FOR TOMORROW

We have this hope—like a sure and firm anchor of the soul—that enters the inner sanctuary behind the curtain.

Hebrews 6:19 HCSB

As every woman knows, hope is a perishable commodity. Despite God's promises, despite Christ's love, and despite our countless blessings, we frail human beings can still lose hope from time to time. When we do, we need the encouragement of Christian friends, the life-changing power of prayer, and the healing truth of God's Holy Word.

If we find ourselves falling into the spiritual traps of worry and discouragement, we should seek the healing touch of Jesus and the encouraging words of fellow Christians. Even though this world can be a place of trials and struggles, God has promised us peace, joy, and eternal life if we give ourselves to Him.

Hope looks for the good in people, opens doors for people, discovers what can be done to help, lights a candle, does not yield to cynicism. Hope sets people free.

Barbara Johnson

Troubles we bear trustfully can bring us a fresh vision of God and a new outlook on life, an outlook of peace and hope.

Billy Graham

A TIMELY TIP

Since God has promised to guide and protect you—now and forever—you should never lose hope.

KNOWLEDGE AND WISDOM

A house is built by wisdom, and it is established by understanding; by knowledge the rooms are filled with every precious and beautiful treasure.

Proverbs 24:3-4 HCSB

If we are to grow as Christians and as women, we need both knowledge and wisdom. Knowledge is found in textbooks. Wisdom, on the other hand, is found in God's Holy Word and in the carefully-chosen words of loving parents, family members, and friends. Knowledge is an important building block in a well-lived life, and it pays rich dividends both personally and professionally. But, wisdom is even more important because it refashions not only the mind, but also the heart.

A big difference exists between a head full of knowledge and the words of God literally abiding in us.

Beth Moore

To know the will of God is the greatest knowledge! To do the will of God is the greatest achievement.

George W. Truett

A TIMELY TIP

Need knowledge? Study God's Word and spend time with knowledgeable people.

NO COMPLAINTS

Do everything without grumbling and arguing, so that you may be blameless and pure.

Philippians 2:14-15 HCSB

Because we are imperfect human beings, we often lose sight of our blessings. Ironically, most of us have more blessings than we can count, but we may still find reasons to complain about the minor frustrations of everyday life. To do so, of course, is not only wrong; it is also the pinnacle of shortsightedness and a serious roadblock on the path to spiritual abundance.

Are you tempted to complain about the inevitable minor frustrations of everyday living? Don't do it! Today and every day, make it a practice to count your blessings, not your hardships. It's the truly decent way to live.

Thanksgiving or complaining—these words express two contrastive attitudes of the souls of God's children in regard to His dealings with them. The soul that gives thanks can find comfort in everything; the soul that complains can find comfort in nothing.

Hannah Whitall Smith

He wants us to have a faith that does not complain while waiting, but rejoices because we know our times are in His hands—nail-scarred hands that labor for our highest good.

Kay Arthur

A TIMELY TIP

If you're wise, you'll fill your heart with gratitude. When you do, there's simply no room left for complaints.

THE WISDOM TO OBEY

And the world with its lust is passing away, but the one who does God's will remains forever.

1 John 2:17 HCSB

Since God created Adam and Eve, we human beings have been rebelling against our Creator. Why? Because we are unwilling to trust God's Word, and we are unwilling to follow His commandments. God has given us a guidebook for righteous living called the Holy Bible. It contains thorough instructions which, if followed, lead to fulfillment, righteousness, and salvation. But, if we choose to ignore God's commandments, the results are as predictable as they are tragic.

Talking about God is easy; living by His commandments is considerably harder. But, unless we are willing to abide by God's laws, all of our righteous proclamations ring hollow. How can we best proclaim our love for the Lord? By obeying Him. And, for further instructions, read the manual.

God does not want the forced obedience of slaves. Instead, He covets the voluntary love and obedience of children who love Him for Himself.

Catherine Marshall

The pathway of obedience can sometimes be difficult, but it always leads to a strengthening of our inner woman.

Vonette Bright

A TIMELY TIP

If you're trying to mold your relationship with Jesus into something that fits comfortably into your own schedule and your own personal theology, you may be headed for trouble. A far better strategy is this: conform yourself to Jesus, not vice versa.

GOOD PRESSURES, BAD PRESSURES

For am I now trying to win the favor of people, or God? Or am I striving to please people? If I were still trying to please people, I would not be a slave of Christ.

Galatians 1:10 HCSB

Our world is filled with pressures: some good, some bad. The pressures that we feel to follow God's will and obey His commandments are positive pressures. God places them on our hearts, and He intends that we act in accordance with His leadings. But we also face different pressures, ones that are definitely not from God. When we feel pressured to do things—or even to think thoughts—that lead us away from God, we must beware.

Society seeks to mold us into more worldly beings; God seeks to mold us into new beings that are most certainly not conformed to this world. If we are to please God, we must resist the pressures that society seeks to impose upon us, and we must conform ourselves, instead, to God's will, to His path, and to His Son.

Ambition! We must be careful what we mean by it. If it means the desire to get ahead of other people—which is what I think it does mean—then it is bad. If it simply means wanting to do a thing well, then it is good. It isn't wrong for an actor to want to act his part as well as it can possibly be acted, but the wish to have his name in bigger type than the other actors is a bad one.

C. S. Lewis

A TIMELY TIP

Peer pressure can be good or bad. God wants you to seek out the good and flee from the bad.

WHEN THE ANSWER IS "NO"

For now we see indistinctly, as in a mirror, but then face to face. Now I know in part, but then I will know fully, as I am fully known.

1 Corinthians 13:12 HCSB

God answers our prayers. What God does not do is this: He does not always answer our prayers as soon as we might like, and He does not always answer our prayers by saying "Yes." God isn't an order-taker, and He's not some sort of cosmic vending machine. Sometimes—even when we want something very badly—our loving Heavenly Father responds to our requests by saying "No," and we must accept His answer, even if we don't understand it.

God answers prayers not only according to our wishes but also according to His master plan. We cannot know that plan, but we can know the Planner . . . and we must trust His wisdom, His righteousness, and His love. Always.

Let's never forget that some of God's greatest mercies are His refusals. He says no in order that He may, in some way we cannot imagine, say yes. All His ways with us are merciful. His meaning is always love.

Elisabeth Elliot

I must often be glad that certain past prayers of my own were not granted.

C. S. Lewis

A TIMELY TIP

When God says "No," that's good! Why? Because God knows what's best; God wants what's best; and God is trying to lead you to a place that is best for you. So trust Him . . . especially when He says "No."

SEEKING AND FINDING

Keep asking, and it will be given to you. Keep searching, and you will find. Keep knocking, and the door will be opened to you. For everyone who asks receives, and the one who searches finds, and to the one who knocks, the door will be opened.

Matthew 7:7-8 HCSB

Where is God? He is everywhere you have ever been and everywhere you will ever go. He is with you night and day; He knows your every thought; He hears your every heartbeat.

Sometimes, in the crush of your daily duties, God may seem far away. Or sometimes, when the disappointments and sorrows of life leave you brokenhearted, God may seem distant, but He is not. When you earnestly seek God, you will find Him because He is here, waiting patiently for you to reach out to Him . . . right here . . . right now.

Our souls were made to live in an upper atmosphere, and we stifle and choke if we live on any lower level. Our eyes were made to look off from these heavenly heights, and our vision is distorted by any lower gazing.

Hannah Whitall Smith

You will be able to trust Him only to the extent that you know Him!

Kay Arthur

A TIMELY TIP

God is everywhere you have ever been and everywhere you will ever be. If you seek Him sincerely and often, you will find Him.

TRUST THE SHEPHERD

The Lord is my shepherd; I shall not want. He makes me to lie down in green pastures; He leads me beside the still waters. He restores my soul.

Psalm 23:1-3 NKJV

In the 23rd Psalm, David teaches us that God is like a watchful shepherd caring for His flock. No wonder these verses have provided comfort and hope for generations of believers.

As a busy woman, you know from firsthand experience that life is not always easy. But as a recipient of God's grace, you also know that you are protected by a loving Heavenly Father. On occasion, you will confront circumstances that trouble you to the very core of your soul. When you are afraid, trust in God. When you are worried, turn your concerns over to Him. When you are anxious, be still and listen for the quiet assurance of God's promises. And then, place your life in His hands. He is your shepherd today and throughout eternity. Trust the Shepherd.

The Lord God of heaven and earth, the Almighty Creator of all things, He who holds the universe in His hand as though it were a very little thing, He is your Shepherd, and He has charged Himself with the care and keeping of you, as a shepherd is charged with the care and keeping of his sheep.

Hannah Whitall Smith

A TIMELY TIP

It's simple: Depend upon God: Remember the words of Vance Havner: "We must live in all kinds of days, both high days and low days, in simple dependence upon Christ as the branch on the vine. This is the supreme experience."

OUR ROCK

And he said: "The Lord is my rock and my fortress and my deliverer; the God of my strength, in whom I will trust."

2 Samuel 22:2-3 NKJV

Psalm 145 promises, "The Lord is near to all who call on him, to all who call on him in truth. He fulfills the desires of those who fear him; he hears their cry and saves them" (vv. 18-20 NIV). And the words of Jesus offer us comfort: "These things I have spoken to you, that in Me you may have peace. In the world you will have tribulation; but be of good cheer, I have overcome the world" (John 16:33 NKJV).

As believers, we know that God loves us and that He will protect us. In times of hardship, He will comfort us; in times of sorrow, He will dry our tears. When we are troubled, or weak, or sorrowful, God is always with us. We must build our lives on the rock that cannot be shaken: we must trust in God. And then, we must get on with the hard work of tackling our problems . . . because if we don't, who will? Or should?

If your every human plan and calculation has miscarried, if, one by one, human props have been knocked out . . . take heart. God is trying to get a message through to you, and the message is: "Stop depending on inadequate human resources. Let me handle the matter."

Catherine Marshall

A TIMELY TIP

If you're having tough times, don't hit the panic button and don't keep everything bottled up inside. Find a person you can really trust, and talk things over. A second opinion (or, for that matter, a third, fourth, or fifth opinion) is usually helpful.

Day 172

WHEN MOUNTAINS MOVE

You do not have because you do not ask.

James 4:2 HCSB

God gives the gifts; we, as believers, should accept them—but oftentimes, we don't. Why? Because we fail to trust our Heavenly Father completely, and because we are, at times, surprisingly stubborn. Luke 11 teaches us that God does not withhold spiritual gifts from those who ask. Our obligation, quite simply, is to ask for them.

Are you a woman who asks God to move mountains in your life, or are you expecting Him to stumble over molehills? Whatever the size of your challenges, God is big enough to handle them. Ask for His help today, with faith and with fervor, and then watch in amazement as your mountains begin to move.

God uses our most stumbling, faltering faith-steps as the open door to His doing for us "more than we ask or think."

Catherine Marshall

We honor God by asking for great things when they are a part of His promise. We dishonor Him and cheat ourselves when we ask for molehills where He has promised mountains.

Vance Havner

A TIMELY TIP

If you sincerely want to rise above the stresses and complications of everyday life, ask for God's help many times each day.

BELIEVING MAKES A DIFFERENCE

You love Him, though you have not seen Him. And though not seeing Him now, you believe in Him and rejoice with inexpressible and glorious joy, because you are receiving the goal of your faith, the salvation of your souls.

1 Peter 1:8-9 HCSB

If you'd like to partake in the peace that only God can give, make certain that your actions are guided by His Word. And while you're at it, pay careful attention to the conscience that God, in His infinite wisdom, has placed in your heart. Don't treat your faith as if it were separate from your everyday life. Weave your beliefs into the very fabric of your day. When you do, God will honor your good works, and your good works will honor God.

If you seek to be a responsible believer, you must realize that it is never enough to hear the instructions of God; you must also live by them. And it is never enough to wait idly by while others do God's work here on earth; you, too, must act. Doing God's work is a responsibility that every Christian (including you) should bear. And when you do, your loving Heavenly Father will reward your efforts with a bountiful harvest.

If all things are possible with God, then all things are possible to him who believes in him.

Corrie ten Boom

Jesus taught that the evidence that confirms our leaps of faith comes after we risk believing, not before.

Gloria Gaither

A TIMELY TIP

When you live in accordance with your beliefs, God will guide your steps and protect your heart.

BLESSED BEYOND MEASURE

The Lord bless you and keep you; The Lord make His face shine upon you, And be gracious to you.

Numbers 6:24-25 NKJV

Have you counted your blessings lately? You should. Of course, God's gifts are too numerous to count, but as a grateful Christian, you should attempt to count them nonetheless. Your blessings include life, family, friends, talents, and possessions, for starters. And your greatest gift—a treasure that was paid for on the cross and is yours for the asking—is God's gift of salvation through Christ Jesus.

As believing Christians, we have all been blessed beyond measure. Thus, thanksgiving should become a habit, a regular part of our daily routines. Today, let us pause and thank our Creator for His blessings. And let us demonstrate our gratitude to the Giver of all things good by using His gifts for the glory of His kingdom.

God is always far more willing to give us good things than we are anxious to have them.

Catherine Marshall

It is when we give ourselves to be a blessing that we can specially count on the blessing of God.

Andrew Murray

A TIMELY TIP

Carve out time to thank God for His blessings. Take time out of every day (not just on Sundays) to praise God and thank Him for His gifts.

A PATTERN OF GOOD WORKS

In all things showing yourself to be a pattern of good works; in doctrine showing integrity, reverence, incorruptibility . . . .

Titus 2:7 NKJV

I t has been said that character is what we are when nobody is watching. How true. When we do things that we know aren't right, we try to hide them from our families and friends. But even then, God is watching.

If you sincerely wish to walk with God, you must seek, to the best of your ability, to follow His commandments. When you do, your character will take care of itself . . . and you won't need to look over your shoulder to see who, besides God, is watching.

Often, our character is at greater risk in prosperity than in adversity.

Beth Moore

Learning God's truth and getting it into our heads is one thing, but living God's truth and getting it into our characters is quite something else.

Warren Wiersbe

A TIMELY TIP

Take time to think about your own character, both your strong points and your weaknesses. Then list three aspects of your character—longstanding habits or troublesome behaviors—that you would like to change. Finally, ask God to be your partner as you take steps to improve yourself and your life.

A RELATIONSHIP THAT HONORS GOD

I am always praising you; all day long I honor you.

Psalm 71:8 NCV

As you think about the nature of your relationship with God, remember this: you will always have some type of relationship with Him—it is inevitable that your life must be lived in relationship to God. The question is not if you will have a relationship with Him; the burning question is whether or not that relationship will be one that seeks to honor Him . . . or not.

Are you willing to place God first in your life? And, are you willing to welcome God's Son into your heart? Unless you can honestly answer these questions with a resounding yes, then your relationship with God isn't what it could be or should be. Thankfully, God is always available, He's always ready to forgive, and He's waiting to hear from you now. The rest, of course, is up to you.

The Holy Spirit testifies of Jesus. So when you are filled with the Holy Spirit, you speak about our Lord and really live to His honor.

Corrie ten Boom

This is Christianity as God intended it—a passionate, willful, and fully emotional relationship.

Bill Hybels

A TIMELY TIP

Many people who call themselves Christians don't really invest much time or energy following Jesus. Don't be like them. Instead, make certain that you follow Jesus every day.

A PLACE OF WORSHIP

For where two or three are gathered together in My name, I am there among them.

Matthew 18:20 HCSB

I n the Book of Acts, Luke reminds us to "feed the church of God" (20:28). As Christians who have been saved by a loving, compassionate Creator, we are compelled not only to worship Him in our hearts but also to worship Him in the presence of fellow believers.

We live in a world that is teeming with temptations and distractions—a world where good and evil struggle in a constant battle to win our hearts and souls. Our challenge, of course, is to ensure that we cast our lot on the side of God. One way to ensure that we do so is by the practice of regular, purposeful worship with our families. When we worship God faithfully and fervently, we are blessed.

Our churches are meant to be havens where the caste rules of the world do not apply.

Beth Moore

Be filled with the Holy Spirit; join a church where the members believe the Bible and know the Lord; seek the fellowship of other Christians; learn and be nourished by God's Word and His many promises. Conversion is not the end of your journey—it is only the beginning.

Corrie ten Boom

A TIMELY TIP

God intends for you to be actively involved in His church. Your intentions should be the same.

THE INNER VOICE

Let us draw near with a true heart in full assurance of faith, our hearts sprinkled clean from an evil conscience and our bodies washed in pure water.

Hebrews 10:22 HCSB

American humorist Josh Billings observed, "Reason often makes mistakes, but conscience never does." How true. Even when we deceive our neighbors, and even when we attempt to deceive ourselves, God has given each of us a conscience, a small, quiet voice that tells us right from wrong.

We must listen to that inner voice . . . or else we must accept the consequences that inevitably befall those who choose to rebel against God.

When we learn to listen to Christ's voice for the details of our daily decisions, we begin to know Him personally.

Catherine Marshall

Most of us follow our conscience as we follow a wheelbarrow. We push it in front of us in the direction we want to go.

Billy Graham

A TIMELY TIP

That quiet little voice inside your head will guide you down the right path if you listen carefully. Very often, your conscience will actually tell you what God wants you to do. So listen, learn, and behave accordingly.

Day 179

HOPE FOR THE JOURNEY

Therefore, we may boldly say: The Lord is my helper; I will not be afraid. What can man do to me?

Hebrews 13:6 HCSB

Because we are saved by a risen Christ, we can have hope for the future, no matter how desperate our circumstances may seem. After all, God has promised that we are His throughout eternity. And, He has told us that we must place our hopes in Him.

Today, summon the courage to follow God. Even if the path seems difficult, even if your heart is fearful, trust your Heavenly Father and follow Him. Trust Him with your day and your life. Do His work, care for His children, and share His Good News. Let Him guide your steps. He will not lead you astray.

In all the old castles of England, there was a place called the keep. It was always the strongest and best protected place in the castle, and in it were hidden all who were weak and helpless and unable to defend themselves in times of danger. Shall we be afraid to hide ourselves in the keeping power of our Divine Keeper, who neither slumbers nor sleeps, and who has promised to preserve our going out and our coming in, from this time forth and even forever more?

Hannah Whitall Smith

A TIMELY TIP

If you are a disciple of the risen Christ, you have every reason on earth—and in heaven—to live courageously. And that's precisely what you should do.

DEALING WITH DISAPPOINTMENT

For we do not want you to be ignorant, brethren, of our trouble which came to us in Asia: that we were burdened beyond measure, above strength, so that we despaired even of life. Yes, we had the sentence of death in ourselves, that we should not trust in ourselves but in God who raises the dead, who delivered us from so great a death, and does deliver us; in whom we trust that He will still deliver us.

2 Corinthians 1:8-10 NKJV

From time to time, all of us face life-altering disappointments that leave us breathless. Oftentimes, these disappointments come unexpectedly, leaving us with more questions than answers. But even when we don't have all the answers—or, for that matter, even when we don't seem to have any of the answers—God does. Whatever our circumstances, whether we stand atop the highest mountain or wander through the darkest valley, God is ready to protect us, to comfort us, and to heal us. Our task is to let Him.

The difference between winning and losing is how we choose to react to disappointment.

Barbara Johnson

Recently I've been learning that life comes down to this: God is in everything. Regardless of what difficulties I am experiencing at the moment, or what things aren't as I would like them to be, I look at the circumstances and say, "Lord, what are you trying to teach me?"

Catherine Marshall

A TIMELY TIP

Don't spend too much time asking, "Why me, Lord?" Instead, ask, "What now, Lord?" and then get to work. When you do, you'll feel much better.

BLESSINGS FROM ABOVE

I said to myself, "Relax and rest. God has showered you with blessings."

Psalm 116:7 MSG

Psalm 145 makes this promise: "The LORD is gracious and compassionate, slow to anger and rich in love. The LORD is good to all; he has compassion on all he has made" (vv. 8-9 NIV). As God's children, we are blessed beyond measure, but sometimes, as busy women in a demanding world, we are slow to count our gifts and even slower to give thanks to the Giver. Our blessings include life and health, family and friends, freedom and possessions—for starters. And, the gifts we receive from God are multiplied when we share them with others. May we always give thanks to God for our blessings, and may we always demonstrate our gratitude by sharing them.

Jesus intended for us to be overwhelmed by the blessings of regular days. He said it was the reason he had come: "I am come that they might have life, and that they might have it more abundantly."

Gloria Gaither

We do not need to beg Him to bless us; He simply cannot help it.

Hannah Whitall Smith

A TIMELY TIP

Make your feelings known to God: Of course you are thankful to the Creator for all His blessings. Tell Him so.

OUR PRICELESS TREASURES

For the promise is for you and for your children.

Acts 2:39 HCSB

We are aware that God has entrusted us with priceless treasures from above—our children. Every child is a glorious gift from the Father. And, with the Father's gift comes profound responsibilities. Thoughtful parents understand the critical importance of raising their children with love, with family, with discipline, and with God.

If you're lucky enough to be a mother, give thanks to God for the gift of your child. Whether you're the mother of a newborn or a seasoned grandmother, remember this: your child—like every child—is a child of God. May you, as a responsible parent, behave accordingly.

Children are not so different from kites. Children were created to fly. But, they need wind, the undergirding, and strength that comes from unconditional love, encouragement, and prayer.

Gigi Graham Tchividjian

Our faithfulness, or lack of it, will have an overwhelming impact on the heritage of our children.

Beth Moore

A TIMELY TIP

Raising children is demanding, time-consuming, energy-depleting . . . and profoundly rewarding. Don't ever overlook the rewards.

MEASURING YOUR WORDS

A wise heart instructs its mouth and increases learning with its speech.

Proverbs 16:23 HCSB

God's Word reminds us that "Reckless words pierce like a sword, but the tongue of the wise brings healing" (Proverbs 12:18 NIV). If you seek to be a source of encouragement to friends, to family members and to coworkers, then you must measure your words carefully. And that's exactly what God wants you to do.

Today, make this promise to yourself: vow to be an honest, effective, encouraging communicator at work, at home, and everyplace in between. Speak wisely, not impulsively. Use words of kindness and praise, not words of anger or derision. Learn how to be truthful without being cruel. Remember that you have the power to heal others or to injure them, to lift others up or to hold them back. And when you learn how to lift them up, you'll soon discover that you've lifted yourself up, too.

We should ask ourselves three things before we speak: Is it true? Is it kind? Does it glorify God?

Billy Graham

Attitude and the spirit in which we communicate are as important as the words we say.

Charles Stanley

A TIMELY TIP

Want to be a better communicator? Try being a briefer communicator. Longwinded monologues, although satisfying to the speaker, are usually torture for the listener. So when in doubt, say less and listen more.

GOD'S ASSURANCE

I have told you these things so that in Me you may have peace. In the world you have suffering. But take courage! I have conquered the world.

John 16:33 HCSB

Are you a confident believer, or do you live under a cloud of uncertainty and doubt? As a Christian, you have many reasons to be confident. After all, God is in His heaven; Christ has risen; and you are the recipient of God's grace. Despite these blessings, you may, from time to time, find yourself being tormented by negative emotions—and you are certainly not alone.

Even the most faithful Christians are overcome by occasional bouts of fear and doubt. You are no different.

But even when you feel very distant from God, remember that God is never distant from you. When you sincerely seek His presence, He will touch your heart, calm your fears, and restore your confidence.

If we indulge in any confidence that is not grounded on the Rock of Ages, our confidence is worse than a dream, it will fall on us and cover us with its ruins, causing sorrow and confusion.

C. H. Spurgeon

Jesus gives us the ultimate rest, the confidence we need, to escape the frustration and chaos of the world around us.

Billy Graham

A TIMELY TIP

The more you trust God, the more confident you will become.

THE STORMS OF LIFE

Immediately Jesus spoke to them. "Have courage! It is I. Don't be afraid."

Matthew 14:27 HCSB

A storm rose quickly on the Sea of Galilee, and the disciples were afraid. Although they had seen Jesus perform many miracles, the disciples feared for their lives, so they turned to their Savior, and He calmed the waters and the wind.

Sometimes, we, like the disciples, feel threatened by the inevitable storms of life. And when we are fearful, we, too, can turn to Christ for courage and for comfort.

The next time you're afraid, remember that the One who calmed the wind and the waves is also your personal Savior. And remember that the ultimate battle has already been won at Calvary. We, as believers, can live courageously in the promises of our Lord . . . and we should.

Courage is not simply one of the virtues, but the form of every virtue at the testing point, which means, at the point of highest reality. A chastity or honesty or mercy which yields to danger will be chaste or honest or merciful only on conditions. Pilate was merciful till it became risky.

C. S. Lewis

A TIMELY TIP

If you're a thoughtful believer, you'll make it a habit to praise God many times each day, beginning with your morning devotional.

LETTING GOD DECIDE

We can make our plans, but the LORD determines our steps.

Proverbs 16:9 NLT

Are you facing a difficult decision, a troubling circumstance, or a powerful temptation? If so, it's time to step back, to stop focusing on the world, and to focus, instead, on the will of your Father in heaven. The world will often lead you astray, but God will not. His counsel leads you to Himself, which, of course, is the path He has always intended for you to take.

Everyday living is an exercise in decision-making. Today and every day you must make choices: choices about what you will do, what you will worship, and how you will think. When in doubt, make choices that you sincerely believe will bring you to a closer relationship with God. And if you're uncertain of your next step, pray about it. When you do, answers will come—the right answers for you.

Choices can change our lives profoundly. The choice to mend a broken relationship, to say "yes" to a difficult assignment, to lay aside some important work to play with a child, to visit some forgotten person—these small choices may affect many lives eternally.

Gloria Gaither

A TIMELY TIP

Never take on a major obligation of any kind without first taking sufficient time to carefully consider whether or not you should commit to it. The bigger the obligation, the more days you should take to decide. If someone presses you for an answer before you are ready, your automatic answer should always be "No."

OUR FAITH, HIS PROMISES

Let us hold on to the confession of our hope without wavering, for He who promised is faithful.

Hebrews 10:23 HCSB

The Christian faith is founded upon promises that are contained in a unique book. That book is the Holy Bible. The Bible is a roadmap for life here on earth and for life eternal. As Christians, we are called upon to study its meaning, to trust its promises, to follow its commandments, and to share its Good News. God's Holy Word is, indeed, a transforming, one-of-a-kind treasure, and must be treated that way.

God has made promises to you, and He intends to keep them. So take God at His word: trust His promises and share them with your family, with your friends, and with the world.

Shake the dust from your past, and move forward in His promises.

Kay Arthur

Claim all of God's promises in the Bible. Your sins, your worries, your life—you may cast them all on Him.

Corrie ten Boom

A TIMELY TIP

Today, think about the role that God's Word plays in your life, and think about ways that you can worry less and trust God more.

TRUSTING HIS TIMING

He told them, "You don't get to know the time. Timing is the Father's business."

Acts 1:7 MSG

I f you sincerely seek to be a woman of faith, then you must learn to trust God's timing. You will be sorely tempted, however, to do otherwise. Because you are a fallible human being, you are impatient for things to happen. But, God knows better.

God has created a world that unfolds according to His own timetable, not ours . . . thank goodness! We mortals might make a terrible mess of things. God does not.

God's plan does not always happen in the way that we would like or at the time of our own choosing. Our task—as believing Christians who trust in a benevolent, all-knowing Father—is to wait patiently for God to reveal Himself. And reveal Himself He will. Always. But until God's perfect plan is made known, we must walk in faith and never lose hope. And we must continue to trust Him. Always.

We must leave it to God to answer our prayers in His own wisest way. Sometimes, we are so impatient and think that God does not answer. God always answers! He never fails! Be still. Abide in Him.

Mrs. Charles E. Cowman

A TIMELY TIP

God has very big plans in store for your life, so trust Him and wait patiently for those plans to unfold. And remember: God's timing is best, so don't allow yourself to become discouraged if things don't work out exactly as you wish. Instead of worrying about your future, entrust it to God.

HOW TO TREAT OTHERS

Therefore, whatever you want others to do for you, do also the same for them—this is the Law and the Prophets.

Matthew 7:12 HCSB

Would you like to make the world a better place? If so, you can start by practicing the Golden Rule.

Is the Golden Rule your rule, or is it just another Bible verse that goes in one ear and out the other? Jesus made Himself perfectly clear: He instructed you to treat other people in the same way that you want to be treated. But sometimes, especially when you're feeling pressures of everyday living, obeying the Golden Rule can seem like an impossible task—but it's not. So if you want to know how to treat other people, ask the person you see every time you look into the mirror. The answer you receive will tell you exactly what to do.

It is one of the most beautiful compensations of life that no one can sincerely try to help another without helping herself.

Barbara Johnson

Here lies the tremendous mystery—that God should be all-powerful, yet refuse to coerce. He summons us to cooperation. We are honored in being given the opportunity to participate in His good deeds. Remember how He asked for help in performing His miracles: Fill the water pots, stretch out your hand, distribute the loaves.

Elisabeth Elliot

A TIMELY TIP

When you become a living, breathing example of the Golden Rule in action, other people will notice, and the results will be better than gold.

TODAY'S BIBLE READING
Old Testament: Job 39-40
New Testament: Acts 17:1-15

HIS JOY . . . AND OURS

Rejoice in the Lord always. I will say it again: Rejoice!

Philippians 4:4 HCSB

Christ made it clear: He intends that His joy should become our joy. Yet sometimes, amid the inevitable hustle and bustle of life-here-on-earth, we can forfeit—albeit temporarily—the joy of Christ as we wrestle with the challenges of daily living.

Corrie ten Boom correctly observed, "Jesus did not promise to change the circumstances around us. He promised great peace and pure joy to those who would learn to believe that God actually controls all things." So here's a prescription for better spiritual health: Learn to trust God, and open the door of your soul to Christ. When you do, He will most certainly give you the peace and pure joy He has promised.

If you're a thinking Christian, you will be a joyful Christian.

Marie T. Freeman

Joy is the keynote of the Christian life. It is not something that happens. It is a gift, given to us in the coming of Christ.

Elisabeth Elliot

A TIMELY TIP

Joy begins with a choice—the choice to establish a genuine relationship with God and His Son. Joy does not depend upon your circumstances, but upon your relationship with God.

CHOOSING KINDNESS

Talk and act like a person expecting to be judged by the Rule that sets us free. For if you refuse to act kindly, you can hardly expect to be treated kindly. Kind mercy wins over harsh judgment every time.

James 2:12-13 MSG

If we believe the words of Proverbs 11:17—and we should—then we understand that kindness is its own reward. And, if we obey the commandments of our Savior—and we should—we must sow seeds of kindness wherever we go.

Kindness is a choice. Sometimes, when we feel happy or generous, we find it easy to be kind. Other times, when we are discouraged or tired, we can scarcely summon the energy to utter a single kind word. But, God's commandment is clear: He intends that we make the conscious choice to treat others with kindness and respect, no matter our circumstances, no matter our emotions. Kindness, therefore, is a choice that we, as Christians must make many times each day.

There are many timid souls whom we jostle morning and evening as we pass them by; but if only the kind word were spoken they might become fully persuaded.

Fanny Crosby

The attitude of kindness is everyday stuff like a great pair of sneakers. Not frilly. Not fancy. Just plain and comfortable.

Barbara Johnson

A TIMELY TIP

Kindness is contagious—make sure that your family and friends catch it from you!

Day 192

GOD'S ALLY

Be sober! Be on the alert! Your adversary the Devil is prowling around like a roaring lion, looking for anyone he can devour.

1 Peter 5:8 HCSB

Nineteenth-century clergyman Edwin Hubbel Chapin warned, "Neutral people are the devil's allies." His words were true then, and they're true now. Neutrality in the face of evil is a sin. Yet all too often, we fail to fight evil, not because we are neutral, but because we are shortsighted: we don't fight the devil because we don't recognize his handiwork.

If we are to recognize evil and fight it, we must pay careful attention. We must pay attention to God's Word, and we must pay attention to the realities of everyday life. When we observe life objectively, and when we do so with eyes and hearts that are attuned to God's Holy Word, we can no longer be neutral believers. And when we are no longer neutral, God rejoices while the devil despairs.

We are in a continual battle with the spiritual forces of evil, but we will triumph when we yield to God's leading and call on His powerful presence in prayer.

Shirley Dobson

Holiness has never been the driving force of the majority. It is, however, mandatory for anyone who wants to enter the kingdom.

Elisabeth Elliot

A TIMELY TIP

Evil exists, and it exists someplace not too far from you. You must guard your steps and your heart accordingly.

NEW BEGINNINGS

I will give you a new heart and put a new spirit within you.

Ezekiel 36:26 HCSB

I f we sincerely want to change ourselves for the better, we must start on the inside and work our way out from there. Lasting change doesn't occur "out there"; it occurs "in here." It occurs, not in the shifting sands of our own particular circumstances, but in quiet depths of our own hearts.

Are you in search of a new beginning or, for that matter, a new you? If so, don't expect changing circumstances to miraculously transform you into the person you want to become. Transformation starts with God, and it starts in the silent center of a humble human heart—like yours.

In those desperate times when we feel like we don't have an ounce of strength, He will gently pick up our heads so that our eyes can behold something—something that will keep His hope alive in us.

Kathy Troccoli

No matter how badly we have failed, we can always get up and begin again. Our God is the God of new beginnings.

Warren Wiersbe

A TIMELY TIP

If you're graduating into a new phase of life, be sure to make God your partner. If you do, He'll guide your steps, He'll help carry your burdens, and He'll help you focus on the things that really matter.

SAYING YES TO GOD

Fear thou not; for I am with thee.

Isaiah 41:10 KJV

Your decision to seek a deeper relationship with God will not remove all problems from your life; to the contrary, it will bring about a series of personal crises as you constantly seek to say "yes" to God although the world encourages you to do otherwise. Each time you are tempted to distance yourself from the Creator, you will face a spiritual crisis. A few of these crises may be monumental in scope, but most will be the small, everyday decisions of life. In fact, life here on earth can be seen as one test after another—and with each crisis comes yet another opportunity to grow closer to God . . . or to distance yourself from His plan for your life.

Today, you will face many opportunities to say "yes" to your Creator—and you will also encounter many opportunities to say "no" to Him. Your answers will determine the quality of your day and the direction of your life, so answer carefully . . . very carefully.

The Christian lifestyle is not one of legalistic do's and don'ts, but one that is positive, attractive, and joyful.

Vonette Bright

Christians, like pianos, need frequent tuning!

Anonymous

A TIMELY TIP

If you want to be more like Jesus . . . follow in His footsteps every day, obey His commandments every day, and share His never-ending love—every day.

PRAISE HIM

Give thanks to the Lord, for He is good; His faithful love endures forever.

Psalm 106:1 HCSB

Sometimes, in our rush "to get things done," we simply don't stop long enough to pause and thank our Creator for the countless blessings He has bestowed upon us. But when we slow down and express our gratitude to the One who made us, we enrich our own lives and the lives of those around us.

Thanksgiving should become a habit, a regular part of our daily routines. God has blessed us beyond measure, and we owe Him everything, including our eternal praise. Let us praise Him today, tomorrow, and throughout eternity.

Praise Him! Praise Him! / Tell of His excellent greatness. / Praise Him! Praise Him! / Ever in joyful song!

Fanny Crosby

This is my story, this is my song, praising my Savior all the day long; this is my story, this is my song, praising my Savior all the day long.

Fanny Crosby

A TIMELY TIP

Thoughtful believers (like you) make it a habit to carve out quiet moments throughout the day to praise God.

TODAY'S BIBLE READING
Old Testament: Psalms 12-14
New Testament: Acts 21:18-40

TAKING RISKS

Is anything too hard for the Lord?

Genesis 18:14 NKJV

As we consider the uncertainties of the future, we are confronted with a powerful temptation: the temptation to "play it safe." Unwilling to move mountains, we fret over molehills. Unwilling to entertain great hopes for the tomorrow, we focus on the unfairness of the today. Unwilling to trust God completely, we take timid half-steps when God intends that we make giant leaps.

Today, ask God for the courage to step beyond the boundaries of your doubts. Ask Him to guide you to a place where you can realize your full potential—a place where you are freed from the fear of failure. Ask Him to do His part, and promise Him that you will do your part. Don't ask Him to lead you to a "safe" place; ask Him to lead you to the "right" place . . . and remember: those two places are seldom the same.

God is teaching me to become more and more "teachable": To keep evolving. To keep taking the risk of learning something new . . . or unlearning something old and off base.

Beth Moore

The really committed leave the safety of the harbor, accept the risk of the open seas of faith, and set their compasses for the place of total devotion to God and whatever life adventures He plans for them.

Bill Hybels

A TIMELY TIP

If you're about to make a big decision or take a significant risk, always pray about it first. And the bigger the decision, the more you should pray about it.

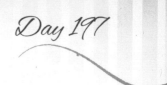

DURING DARK DAYS

I have heard your prayer, I have seen your tears; surely I will heal you.

2 Kings 20:5 NKJV

The sadness that accompanies any significant loss is an inevitable fact of life. In time, sadness runs its course and gradually abates. Depression, on the other hand, is a physical and emotional condition that is highly treatable.

If you find yourself feeling "blue," perhaps it's a logical reaction to the ups and downs of daily life. But if you or someone close to you have become dangerously depressed, it's time to seek professional help.

Some days are light and happy, and some days are not. When we face the inevitable dark days of life, we must choose how we will respond. Will we allow ourselves to sink even more deeply into our own sadness, or will we do the difficult work of pulling ourselves out? We bring light to the dark days of life by turning first to God, and then to trusted family members, friends, and medical professionals. When we do, the clouds will eventually part, and the sun will shine once more upon our souls.

Emotions we have not poured out in the safe hands of God can turn into feelings of hopelessness and depression. God is safe.

Beth Moore

Self blame over the past leads to depression in the present and poor decisions for the future.

Barbara Johnson

A TIMELY TIP

Depression is serious business, and it's a highly treatable disease . . . treat it that way.

OUR ULTIMATE SAVIOR

And we have seen and testify that the Father has sent the Son as Savior of the world.

1 John 4:14 NKJV

Hannah Whitall Smith spoke to believers of every generation when she advised, "Keep your face upturned to Christ as the flowers do to the sun. Look, and your soul shall live and grow." How true. When we turn our hearts to Jesus, we receive His blessings, His peace, and His grace.

Christ is the ultimate Savior of mankind and the personal Savior of those who believe in Him. As His servants, we should place Him at the very center of our lives. And, every day that God gives us breath, we should share Christ's love and His message with a world that needs both.

I now know the power of the risen Lord! He lives! The dawn of Easter has broken in my own soul! My night is gone!

Mrs. Charles E. Cowman

Keep your face upturned to Christ as the flowers do to the sun. Look, and your soul shall live and grow.

Hannah Whitall Smith

A TIMELY TIP

Make Christ the cornerstone: Every family is built upon something; let the foundation of your family be the love of God and the salvation of Christ.

CONTAGIOUS FAITH

Whatever you do, do it enthusiastically, as something done for the Lord and not for men.

Colossians 3:23 HCSB

Genuine, heartfelt Christianity is contagious. If you enjoy a life-altering relationship with God, that relationship will have an impact on others—perhaps a profound impact.

Are you genuinely excited about your faith? And do you make your enthusiasm known to those around you? Or are you a "silent ambassador" for Christ? God's preference is clear: He intends that you stand before others and proclaim your faith.

Does Christ reign over your life? Then share your testimony and your excitement. The world needs both.

Enthusiasm, like the flu, is contagious—we get it from one another.

Barbara Johnson

We act as though comfort and luxury were the chief requirements of life, when all we need to make us really happy is something to be enthusiastic about.

Charles Kingsley

A TIMELY TIP

When you become genuinely enthused about your life and your faith, you'll guard your heart and improve your life.

GOD'S VOICE

For this is commendable, if because of conscience toward God one endures grief, suffering wrongfully.

1 Peter 2:19 NKJV

Billy Graham correctly observed, "Most of us follow our conscience as we follow a wheelbarrow. We push it in front of us in the direction we want to go." To do so, of course, is a profound mistake. Yet all of us, on occasion, have failed to listen to the voice that God planted in our hearts, and all of us have suffered the consequences.

God gave you a conscience for a very good reason: to make your path conform to His will. Wise believers make it a practice to listen carefully to that quiet internal voice. Count yourself among that number. When your conscience speaks, listen and learn. In all likelihood, God is trying to get His message through. And in all likelihood, it is a message that you desperately need to hear.

God desires that we become spiritually healthy enough through faith to have a conscience that rightly interprets the work of the Holy Spirit.

Beth Moore

God has revealed Himself in man's conscience. Conscience has been described as the light of the soul.

Billy Graham

A TIMELY TIP

Trust the quiet inner voice of your conscience: Treat your conscience as you would a trusted advisor.

GOD CAN HANDLE IT

Fear not, for I have redeemed you; I have called you by your name; You are Mine.

Isaiah 43:1 NKJV

Life-here-on-earth can be difficult and discouraging at times. During our darkest moments, God offers us strength and courage if we turn our hearts and our prayers to Him.

As believing Christians, we have every reason to live courageously. After all, the ultimate battle has already been fought and won on the cross at Calvary. But sometimes, because we are imperfect human beings who possess imperfect faith, we fall prey to fear and doubt. The answer to our fears, of course, is God.

The next time you find your courage tested to the limit, remember that God is as near as your next breath. He is your shield and your strength; He is your protector and your deliverer. Call upon Him in your hour of need and then be comforted. Whatever your challenge, whatever your trouble, God can handle it . . . and will!

When once we are assured that God is good, then there can be nothing left to fear.

Hannah Whitall Smith

If a person fears God, he or she has no reason to fear anything else. On the other hand, if a person does not fear God, then fear becomes a way of life.

Beth Moore

A TIMELY TIP

Is your courage being tested? Cling tightly to God's promises, and pray. God can give you the strength to meet any challenge, and that's exactly what you should ask Him to do.

BEYOND NEGATIVITY

Do not be afraid or discouraged, for the LORD is the one who goes before you.
He will be with you; he will neither fail you nor forsake you.

Deuteronomy 31:8 NLT

We Christians have many reasons to celebrate. God is in His heaven; Christ has risen, and we are the sheep of His flock. Yet sometimes, even the most devout Christian women can become discouraged. After all, we live in a world where expectations can be high and demands can be even higher.

If you become discouraged with the direction of your day or your life, turn your thoughts and prayers to God. He is a God of possibility, not negativity. He will help you count your blessings instead of your hardships. And then, with a renewed spirit of optimism and hope, you can properly thank your Father in heaven for His blessings, for His love, and for His Son.

I was learning something important: we are most vulnerable to the piercing winds of doubt when we distance ourselves from the mission and fellowship to which Christ has called us. Our night of discouragement will seem endless and our task impossible, unless we recognize that He stands in our midst.

Joni Eareckson Tada

A TIMELY TIP

If you're feeling discouraged, try to redirect your thoughts away from the troubles that plague you—focus, instead, upon the opportunities that surround you.

GETTING IT ALL DONE

Everyone was trying to touch him—so much energy surging from him, so many people healed!

Luke 6:19 MSG

All of us have moments when we feel drained. All of us suffer through difficult days, trying times, and perplexing periods of our lives. During times of hardship, we are tempted to burn the candle at both ends, but we should resist this temptation. Instead, we should strive to place first things first by saying no to the things that we simply don't have the time or the energy to do.

If you're a woman with too many demands and too few hours in which to meet them, don't fret. Instead, focus upon God and upon His love for you. Then, ask Him for the wisdom to prioritize your life and the strength to fulfill your responsibilities. God will give you the energy to do the most important things on today's to-do list . . . if you ask Him. So ask Him.

When the dream of our heart is one that God has planted there, a strange happiness flows into us. At that moment, all of the spiritual resources of the universe are released to help us. Our praying is then at one with the will of God and becomes a channel for the Creator's purposes for us and our world.

Catherine Marshall

A TIMELY TIP

Feeling exhausted? Try this: Start getting more sleep each night; begin a program of regular, sensible exercise; avoid harmful food and drink; and turn your problems over to God . . . and the greatest of these is "turn your problems over to God."

TODAY'S BIBLE READING
Old Testament: Psalms 30-33
New Testament: Acts 27:1-18

WE ARE ALL ROLE MODELS

Therefore, we are ambassadors for Christ; certain that God is appealing through us, we plead on Christ's behalf, "Be reconciled to God."

2 Corinthians 5:20 HCSB

Whether we like it or not, all of us are role models. Our friends and family members watch our actions and, as followers of Christ, we are obliged to act accordingly.

What kind of example are you? Are you the kind of woman whose life serves as a genuine example of righteousness? Are you a woman whose behavior serves as a positive role model for young people? Are you the kind of woman whose actions, day in and day out, are based upon kindness, faithfulness, and a love for the Lord? If so, you are not only blessed by God, you are also a powerful force for good in a world that desperately needs positive influences such as yours.

Corrie ten Boom advised, "Don't worry about what you do not understand. Worry about what you do understand in the Bible but do not live by." And that's sound advice because our families and friends are watching . . . and so, for that matter, is God.

We must mirror God's love in the midst of a world full of hatred. We are the mirrors of God's love, so we may show Jesus by our lives.

Corrie ten Boom

A TIMELY TIP

Your life is a sermon. What kind of sermon will you preach? The words you choose to speak may have some impact on others, but not nearly as much impact as the life you choose to live. Today, pause to consider the tone, the theme, and the context of your particular sermon, and ask yourself if it's a message that you're proud to deliver.

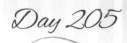
ALL IN THE FAMILY

Let the message about the Messiah dwell richly among you, teaching and admonishing one another in all wisdom, and singing psalms, hymns, and spiritual songs, with gratitude in your hearts to God.

Colossians 3:16 HCSB

As every woman knows, family life is a mixture of conversations, mediations, irritations, deliberations, commiserations, frustrations, negotiations, and celebrations. In other words, the life of the typical mom is incredibly varied.

Certainly, in the life of every family, there are moments of frustration and disappointment. Lots of them. But, for those who are lucky enough to live in the presence of a close-knit, caring clan, the rewards far outweigh the frustrations. That's why we pray fervently for our family members, and that's why we love them despite their faults.

No family is perfect, and neither is yours. But, despite the inevitable challenges and occasional hurt feelings of family life, your clan is God's gift to you. That little band of men, women, kids, and babies is a priceless treasure on temporary loan from the Father above. Give thanks to the Giver for the gift of family . . . and act accordingly.

I think the greatest benefit to having a big family, especially a family with five or more children, is that it's harder to be selfish. In today's prosperous world, it's hard to teach our children sacrifice.

Lisa Whelchel

A TIMELY TIP

Don't give up on God. And remember: He will never give up on you or your family.

THE FINANCIAL GUIDE

The blessing of the Lord makes one rich . . . .

Proverbs 10:22 NKJV

God's Word is not only a roadmap to eternal life, it is also an indispensable guidebook for life here on earth. As such, the Bible has much to say about your life and your finances.

God's Word can be a roadmap to a place of righteous and abundance. Make it your roadmap. God's wisdom can be a light to guide your steps. Claim it as your light. God's Word can be an invaluable tool for crafting a better day and a better life. Make it your tool. And finally, God's Word can help you organize your financial life in such a way that you have less need to worry and more time to celebrate His glorious creation. If that sounds appealing, open your Bible, read its instructions, and follow them.

Here's a good recipe for managing your money: Never make a big financial decision without first talking it over with God.

Marie T. Freeman

The first discipline of finances is to maximize your earning potential.

John Maxwell

A TIMELY TIP

Live within your means and save money from every paycheck. Never spend more than you make.

LOVE THAT FORGIVES

And whenever you stand praying, if you have anything against anyone, forgive him, so that your Father in heaven may also forgive you your wrongdoing.

Mark 11:25 HCSB

Genuine love is an exercise in forgiveness. If we wish to build lasting relationships, we must learn how to forgive. Why? Because our loved ones are imperfect (as are we). How often must we forgive our family and friends? More times than we can count. Why? Because that's what God wants us to do.

Perhaps granting forgiveness is hard for you. If so, you are not alone. Genuine, lasting forgiveness is often difficult to achieve—difficult but not impossible. Thankfully, with God's help, all things are possible, and that includes forgiveness. But, even though God is willing to help, He expects you to do some of the work. And make no mistake: forgiveness is work, which is okay with God. He knows that the payoffs are worth the effort.

God calls upon the loved not just to love but to be loving. God calls upon the forgiven not just to forgive but to be forgiving.

Beth Moore

It is better to forgive and forget than to resent and remember.

Barbara Johnson

A TIMELY TIP

Forgive . . . and keep forgiving! Sometimes, you may forgive someone once and then, at a later time, become angry at the very same person again. If so, you must forgive that person again and again . . . until it sticks!

IN HIS HANDS

Don't brashly announce what you're going to do tomorrow; you don't know the first thing about tomorrow.

Proverbs 27:1 MSG

The old saying is both familiar and true: "Man proposes and God disposes." Our world unfolds according to God's plans, not our wishes. Thus, boasting about future events is to be avoided by those who acknowledge God's sovereignty over all things.

Are you planning for a better tomorrow for yourself and your family? If so, you are to be congratulated: God rewards forethought in the same way that He often punishes impulsiveness. But as you make your plans, do so with humility, with gratitude, and with trust in your Heavenly Father. His hand directs the future; to think otherwise is both arrogant and naïve.

No matter how heavy the burden, daily strength is given, so I expect we need not give ourselves any concern as to what the outcome will be. We must simply go forward.

Annie Armstrong

The Christian believes in a fabulous future.

Billy Graham

A TIMELY TIP

Even when the world seems dark, the future is bright for those who look to the Son.

GOD IS LOVE

God is love, and the one who remains in love remains in God, and God remains in him.

1 John 4:16 HCSB

The Bible makes this promise: God is love. It's a sweeping statement, a profoundly important description of what God is and how God works. God's love is perfect. When we open our hearts to His perfect love, we are touched by the Creator's hand, and we are transformed.

Today, even if you can only carve out a few quiet moments, offer sincere prayers of thanksgiving to your Creator. He loves you now and throughout all eternity. Open your heart to His presence and His love.

Let's never forget that some of God's greatest mercies are His refusals. He says no in order that He may, in some way we cannot imagine, say yes. All His ways with us are merciful. His meaning is always love.

Elisabeth Elliot

Knowing God's sovereignty and unconditional love imparts a beauty to life . . . and to you.

Kay Arthur

A TIMELY TIP

When all else fails, God's love does not. You can always depend upon God's love . . . and He is always your ultimate protection.

TRUST HIM TO GUIDE YOU

Trust in the Lord with all your heart, and do not rely on your own understanding; think about Him in all your ways, and He will guide you on the right paths.

Proverbs 3:5-6 HCSB

A s Christians whose salvation has been purchased by the blood of Christ, we have every reason to live joyously and courageously. After all, Christ has already fought and won our battle for us—He did so on the cross at Calvary. But despite Christ's sacrifice, and despite God's promises, we may become confused or disoriented by the endless complications and countless distractions of life-here-in-the-21st-century.

If you're unsure of your next step, lean upon God's promises and lift your prayers to Him. Remember that God is your protector. Open yourself to His heart, and trust Him to guide you. When you do, God will direct your steps, and you will receive His blessings today, tomorrow, and throughout eternity.

It is a joy that God never abandons His children. He guides faithfully all who listen to His directions.

Corrie ten Boom

Are you serious about wanting God's guidance to become a personal reality in your life? The first step is to tell God that you know you can't manage your own life; that you need his help.

Catherine Marshall

A TIMELY TIP

Pray for guidance. When you seek it, He will give it. (Luke 11:9)

ULTIMATE PROTECTION

What time I am afraid, I will trust in thee.

Psalm 56:3 KJV

God has promised to protect us, and He intends to fulfill His promise. In a world filled with dangers and temptations, God is the ultimate armor. In a world filled with misleading messages, God's Word is the ultimate truth. In a world filled with more frustrations than we can count, God's Son offers the ultimate peace.

Will you accept God's peace and wear God's armor against the dangers of our world? Hopefully so, because when you do, you can live courageously, knowing that you possess the ultimate protection: God's unfailing love for you.

Who is it that is your Shepherd? The Lord! Oh, my friends, what a wonderful announcement! The Lord God of heaven and earth, and Almighty Creator of all things, He who holds the universe in His hand as though it were a very little thing. He is your shepherd and has charged himself with the care and keeping of you, as a shepherd is charged with the care and keeping of his sheep. If your hearts could really take in this thought, you would never have a fear or a care again, for with such a Shepherd how could it be possible for you ever to want for any good thing?

Hannah Whitall Smith

A TIMELY TIP

Earthly security is an illusion. Your only real security comes from the loving heart of God.

Day 212

SEEKING GOD AND FINDING HAPPINESS

Happy is the one whose help is the God of Jacob, whose hope is in the Lord his God.

Psalm 146:5 HCSB

Happiness depends less upon our circumstances than upon our thoughts. When we turn our thoughts to God, to His gifts, and to His glorious creation, we experience the joy that God intends for His children. But, when we focus on the negative aspects of life, we suffer needlessly.

Do you sincerely want to be a happy Christian? Then set your mind and your heart upon God's love and His grace. The fullness of life in Christ is available to all who seek it and claim it. Count yourself among that number. Seek first the salvation that is available through a personal relationship with Jesus Christ, and then claim the joy, the peace, and the spiritual abundance that the Shepherd offers His sheep.

We will never be happy until we make God the source of our fulfillment and the answer to our longings.

Stormie Omartian

Those who have had to wait and work for happiness seem to enjoy it more, because they never take it for granted.

Barbara Johnson

A TIMELY TIP

Happiness is a positive interpretation of the world and its events. Happiness requires that you train yourself to see the good in everything, no matter what happens.

HIS HEALING TOUCH

I am the Lord that healeth thee.

Exodus 15:26 KJV

Are you concerned about your spiritual, physical, or emotional health? If so, there is a timeless source of comfort and assurance that is as near as your bookshelf. That source is the Holy Bible.

God's Word has much to say about every aspect of your life, including your health. And, when you face concerns of any sort—including health-related challenges—God is with you. So trust your medical doctor to do his or her part, but place your ultimate trust in your benevolent Heavenly Father. His healing touch, like His love, endures forever.

Jesus Christ is the One by Whom, for Whom, through Whom everything was made. Therefore, He knows what's wrong in your life and how to fix it.

Anne Graham Lotz

Ultimate healing and the glorification of the body are certainly among the blessings of Calvary for the believing Christian. Immediate healing is not guaranteed.

Warren Wiersbe

A TIMELY TIP

God has given you a body, and He's placed you in charge of caring for it. Your body is a temple that should be treated with respect. So be proactive about your health: Don't sit around and wait for things to get worse; seek the best help you can find for your health problems.

SELF-MADE?

Respecting the Lord and not being proud will bring you wealth, honor, and life.

Proverbs 22:4 NCV

We have heard it said on countless occasions: "He's a self-made man," or "She's a self-made woman." In truth, none of us are self-made. We all owe countless debts that we can never repay. Our first debt, of course, is to our Father in heaven—who has given us everything that we are and will ever be—and to His Son who sacrificed His own life so that we might live eternally. We are also indebted to ancestors, parents, teachers, friends, spouses, family members, coworkers, fellow believers . . . and the list, of course, goes on.

Most of us, it seems, are more than willing to stick out our chests and say, "Look at me; I did that!" But in our better moments, in the quiet moments when we search the depths of our own hearts, we know better. Whatever "it" is, God did that. And He deserves the credit.

That some of my hymns have been dictated by the blessed Holy Spirit I have no doubt; and that others have been the result of deep meditation I know to be true; but that the poet has any right to claim special merit for himself is certainly presumptuous.

Fanny Crosby

A TIMELY TIP

Humility leads to happiness; pride doesn't. Max Lucado writes, "God exalts humility. When God works in our lives, helping us to become humble, he gives us a permanent joy. Humility gives us a joy that cannot be taken away." Enough said.

LOVE IS A CHOICE

Dear friends, if God loved us in this way, we also must love one another.

1 John 4:11 HCSB

Love is always a choice. Sometimes, of course, we may "fall in love," but it takes work to stay there. Sometimes, we may be "swept off our feet," but the "sweeping" is only temporary; sooner or later, if love is to endure, one must plant one's feet firmly on the ground. The decision to love another person for a lifetime is much more than the simple process of "falling in" or "being swept up." It requires "reaching out," "holding firm," and "lifting up." Love, then, becomes a decision to honor and care for the other person, come what may.

Charity says, "I grant you your rights. I do not insist on mine. I give myself to you; I do not insist that you give yourself to me."

Elisabeth Elliot

It is important to know that you have to work to keep love alive; you have to protect it and maintain it, just like you would a delicate flower.

James Dobson

A TIMELY TIP

God loves you, and He wants you to reflect His love to those around you.

BEYOND MATERIALISM

For what does it benefit a man to gain the whole world yet lose his life? What can a man give in exchange for his life?

Mark 8:36-37 HCSB

In our modern society, we need money to live. But as Christians, we must never make the acquisition of money the central focus of our lives. Money is a tool, but it should never overwhelm our sensibilities. The focus of life must be squarely on things spiritual, not things material.

Whenever we place our love for material possessions above our love for God—or when we yield to the countless other temptations of everyday living—we find ourselves engaged in a struggle between good and evil. Let us respond to this struggle by freeing ourselves from that subtle yet powerful temptation: the temptation to love the world more than we love God.

Why is love of gold more potent than love of souls?

Lottie Moon

Greed is enslaving. The more you have, the more you want—until eventually avarice consumes you.

Kay Arthur

A TIMELY TIP

God's Word warns against the spiritual trap of materialism. Material possessions may seem appealing at first, but they pale in comparison to the spiritual gifts that God gives to those who put Him first. Count yourself among that number.

BLESSED OBEDIENCE

When you and your children return to the LORD your God and obey him with all your heart and with all your soul according to everything I command you today, then the LORD your God will restore your fortunes and have compassion on you and gather you again from all the nations where he scattered you.

Deuteronomy 30:2-3 NIV

We live in a world filled with temptations, distractions, and countless opportunities to disobey God. But as women who seek to be godly role models for our families, we must turn our thoughts and our hearts away from the evils of this world. We must turn instead to God.

Talking about God is easy; living by His laws is considerably harder. But unless we are willing to live obediently, all our righteous words ring hollow.

How can we best proclaim our love for the Lord? By obeying Him. We must seek God's counsel and trust the counsel He gives. And, when we invite God into our hearts and live according to His commandments, we are blessed today, and tomorrow, and forever.

God is God. Because He is God, He is worthy of my trust and obedience. I will find rest nowhere but in His holy will, a will that is unspeakably beyond my largest notions of what He is up to.

Elisabeth Elliot

A TIMELY TIP

Obey God or face the consequences. God rewards obedience and punishes disobedience. It's not enough to understand God's rules; you must also live by them . . . or else.

LOST IN THE CROWD

The fear of man is a snare, but the one who trusts in the Lord is protected.

Proverbs 29:25 HCSB

Rick Warren observed, "Those who follow the crowd usually get lost in it." We know these words to be true, but oftentimes we fail to live by them. Instead of trusting God for guidance, we imitate our neighbors and suffer the consequences. Instead of seeking to please our Father in heaven, we strive to please our peers, with decidedly mixed results.

Whom will you try to please today: your God or your associates? Your obligation is most certainly not to neighbors, to friends, or even to family members. Your obligation is to an all-knowing, all-powerful God. You must seek to please Him first and always. No exceptions.

It is comfortable to know that we are responsible to God and not to man. It is a small matter to be judged of man's judgement.

Lottie Moon

When we are set free from the bondage of pleasing others, when we are free from currying others' favor and others' approval—then no one will be able to make us miserable or dissatisfied. And then, if we know we have pleased God, contentment will be our consolation.

Kay Arthur

A TIMELY TIP

If you are burdened with a "people-pleasing" personality, outgrow it. Realize that you can't please all of the people all of the time, nor should you attempt to.

FOOLISH PRIDE

Do nothing out of rivalry or conceit, but in humility consider others as more important than yourselves.

Philippians 2:3 HCSB

Sometimes our faith is tested more by prosperity than by adversity. Why? Because in times of plenty, we are tempted to stick out our chests and say, "I did that." But nothing could be further from the truth. All of our blessings start and end with God, and whatever "it" is, He did it. And He deserves the credit.

Who are the greatest among us? Are they the proud and the powerful? Hardly. The greatest among us are the humble servants who care less for their own glory and more for God's glory. If we seek greatness in God's eyes, we must forever praise God's good works, not our own.

We cannot be filled until we are empty. We have to be poor in spirit of ourselves in order to be filled with the Holy Spirit.

Corrie ten Boom

All kindness and good deeds, we must keep silent. The result will be an inner reservoir of personality power.

Catherine Marshall

A TIMELY TIP

Give God your full attention by putting prayer at the very top of your daily to-do list.

THE MORNING WATCH

Every morning he wakes me. He teaches me to listen like a student. The Lord God helps me learn . . .

Isaiah 50:4-5 NCV

Each new day is a gift from God, and if you are wise, you will spend a few quiet moments each morning thanking the Giver. When you begin each day with your head bowed and your heart lifted, you are reminded of God's love, His protection, and His commandments. Then, you can align your priorities for the coming day with the teachings and commandments that God has placed upon your heart.

So, if you've acquired the unfortunate habit of trying to "squeeze" God into the corners of your life, it's time to reshuffle the items on your to-do list by placing God first. And if you haven't already done so, form the habit of spending quality time with your Father in heaven. He deserves it . . . and so do you.

Think of this—we may live together with Him here and now, a daily walking with Him who loved us and gave Himself for us.

Elisabeth Elliot

We all need to make time for God. Even Jesus made time to be alone with the Father.

Kay Arthur

A TIMELY TIP

How much time can you spare? Decide how much of your time God deserves, and then give it to Him. Don't organize your day so that God gets "what's left." Give Him what you honestly believe He deserves.

WHEN PEOPLE MISBEHAVE

Bad temper is contagious—don't get infected.

Proverbs 22:25 MSG

Face it: sometimes people can be rude . . . very rude. When other people are unkind to you, you may be tempted to strike back, either verbally or in some other way. Don't do it! Instead, remember that God corrects other people's behaviors in His own way, and He doesn't need your help (even if you're totally convinced that He does).

So, when other people behave cruelly, foolishly, or impulsively—as they will from time to time—don't be hotheaded. Instead, speak up for yourself as politely as you can, and walk away. Then, forgive everybody as quickly as you can, and leave the rest up to God.

You can be sure you are abiding in Christ if you are able to have a Christlike love toward the people that irritate you the most.

Vonette Bright

A pessimist is someone who believes that when her cup runneth over she'll need a mop.

Barbara Johnson

A TIMELY TIP

If you can't find it in your heart to forgive those who have hurt you, you're hurting yourself more than you're hurting anyone else. But remember: forgiveness should not be confused with enabling. Even after you've forgiven the difficult person in your life, you are not compelled to accept continued mistreatment from him or her.

TEACHING DISCIPLINE

The one who follows instruction is on the path to life, but the one who rejects correction goes astray.

Proverbs 10:17 HCSB

Wise women understand the importance of discipline. In Proverbs 28:19, God's message is clear: "He who works his land will have abundant food, but the one who chases fantasies will have his fill of poverty" (NIV). When we work diligently and consistently, we can expect a bountiful harvest. But we must never expect the harvest to precede the labor.

Thoughtful Christians understand that God doesn't reward laziness or misbehavior. To the contrary, God expects His children (of all ages) to lead disciplined lives . . . very disciplined lives.

The Bible calls for discipline and a recognition of authority. Children must learn this at home.

Billy Graham

The alternative to discipline is disaster.

Vance Havner

A TIMELY TIP

If you choose to lead a disciplined lifestyle, your steps will be protected. If you choose to lead an undisciplined lifestyle, your steps will be misdirected.

A HELPING HAND

Then a Samaritan traveling down the road came to where the hurt man was.
When he saw the man, he felt very sorry for him. The Samaritan went to him,
poured olive oil and wine on his wounds, and bandaged them. Then he put the
hurt man on his own donkey and took him to an inn where he cared for him.

Luke 10:33-34 NCV

Sometimes we would like to help make the world a better place, but we're not sure how to do it. Jesus told the story of the "Good Samaritan," a man who helped a fellow traveler when no one else would. We, too, should be good Samaritans when we find people who need our help.

When bad things happen in our world, there's always something we can do. So what can you do to make God's world a better place? You can start by making your own corner of the world a little nicer place to live (by sharing kind words and good deeds). And then, you can take your concerns to God in prayer. Whether you've offered a helping hand or a heartfelt prayer, you've done a lot.

We can never untangle all the woes in other people's lives. We can't produce miracles overnight. But we can bring a cup of cool water to a thirsty soul, or a scoop of laughter to a lonely heart.

Barbara Johnson

A TIMELY TIP

It's good to feel compassion for others . . . but it's better to do something to ease their suffering. Martin Luther wrote, "Faith never asks whether good works are to be done, but has done them before there is time to ask the question, and it is always doing them." So when in doubt, do something good!

CHOICES, CHOICES, CHOICES

Therefore, whether we are at home or away, we make it our aim to be pleasing to Him.

2 Corinthians 5:9 HCSB

Your life is a series of choices. From the instant you wake up in the morning until the moment you nod off to sleep at night, you make lots of decisions: decisions about the things you do, decisions about the words you speak, and decisions about the thoughts you choose to think. Simply put, the quality of those decisions determines the quality of your life.

So, if you sincerely want to lead a life that is pleasing to God, you must make choices that are pleasing to Him. He deserves no less . . . and neither, for that matter, do you.

No matter how many books you read, no matter how many schools you attend, you're never really wise until you start making wise choices.

Marie T. Freeman

Good and evil both increase at compound interest. That is why the little decisions you and I make every day are of such infinite importance.

C. S. Lewis

A TIMELY TIP

Every step of your life's journey is a choice . . . and the quality of those choices determines the quality of the journey.

OBEDIENCE NOW

And hereby we do know that we know him, if we keep his commandments.

1 John 2:3 KJV

In order to enjoy a deeper relationship with God, you must strive diligently to live in accordance with His commandments. But there's a problem—you live in a world that seeks to snare your attention and lead you away from God.

Because you are an imperfect mortal being, you cannot be perfectly obedient, nor does God expect you to be. What is required, however, is a sincere desire to be obedient coupled with an awareness of sin and a willingness to distance yourself from it as soon as you encounter it.

Are you willing to conform your behavior to God's rules? Hopefully, you can answer that question with a resounding yes. Otherwise, you'll never experience a full measure of the blessings that the Creator gives to those who obey Him.

In the very place where God has put us, whatever its limitations, whatever kind of work it may be, we may indeed serve the Lord Christ.

Elisabeth Elliot

Here is our opportunity: we cannot see God, but we can see Christ. Christ was not only the Son of God, but He was the Father. Whatever Christ was, that God is.

Hannah Whitall Smith

A TIMELY TIP

When Jesus endured His sacrifice on the cross, He paid a terrible price for you. What price are you willing to pay for Him?

FEEDING THE CHURCH

The church, you see, is not peripheral to the world; the world is peripheral to the church. The church is Christ's body, in which he speaks and acts, by which he fills everything with his presence.

Ephesians 1:23 MSG

One way that we come to know God is by involving ourselves in His church.

In the Book of Acts, Luke reminds us to "feed the church of God" (20:28). As Christians who have been saved by a loving, compassionate Creator, we are compelled not only to worship Him in our hearts but also to worship Him in the presence of fellow believers.

Do you feed the church of God? Do you attend regularly, and are you an active participant? The answer to these questions will have a profound impact on the quality and direction of your spiritual journey.

So do yourself a favor: become actively involved in your church. Don't just go to church out of habit. Go to church out of a sincere desire to know and worship God. When you do, you'll be blessed by the One who sent His Son to die so that you might have everlasting life.

Every time a new person comes to God, every time someone's gifts find expression in the fellowship of believers, every time a family in need is surrounded by the caring church, the truth is affirmed anew: the Church triumphant is alive and well!

Gloria Gaither

A TIMELY TIP

Jesus promised that the church would be triumphant. So, you simply can't go wrong investing your life in His church. The church is eternal.

OLD YOU, NEW YOU

Therefore if anyone is in Christ, he is a new creature; the old things passed away; behold, new things have come.

2 Corinthians 5:17 HCSB

Think, for a moment, about the "old" you, the person you were before you invited Christ to reign over your heart. Now, think about the "new" you, the person you have become since then. Is there a difference between the "old" you and the "new and improved" version? There should be! And that difference should be noticeable not only to you but also to others.

The Bible clearly teaches that when we welcome Christ into our hearts, we become new creations through Him. Our challenge, of course, is to behave ourselves like new creations. When we do, God fills our hearts, He blesses our endeavors, and transforms our lives . . . forever.

The amazing thing about Jesus is that He doesn't just patch up our lives, He gives us a brand new sheet, a clean slate to start over, all new.

Gloria Gaither

Conversion is not a blind leap into the darkness. It is a joyous leap into the light that is the love of God.

Corrie ten Boom

A TIMELY TIP

All of your talents and opportunities come from God. Give Him thanks, and give Him the glory.

LIFE'S MOUNTAINTOPS, LIFE'S VALLEYS

I sought the Lord, and He heard me, and delivered me from all my fears.

Psalm 34:4 NKJV

Every life (including yours) is an unfolding series of events: some fabulous, some not-so-fabulous, and some downright disheartening. When you reach the mountaintops of life, praising God is easy. But, when the storm clouds form overhead, your faith will be tested, sometimes to the breaking point. As a believer, you can take comfort in this fact: Wherever you find yourself, whether at the top of the mountain or the depths of the valley, God is there, and because He cares for you, you can live courageously.

The next time you find your courage tested to the limit, remember that God is your shield and your strength; He is your protector and your deliverer. Call upon Him in your hour of need and He will protect you.

Just as courage is faith in good, so discouragement is faith in evil, and, while courage opens the door to good, discouragement opens it to evil.

Hannah Whitall Smith

The great paralysis of our heart is unbelief.

Oswald Chambers

A TIMELY TIP

If you trust God completely and without reservation, you have every reason on earth—and in heaven—to live courageously. And that's precisely what you should do.

EXPECTING THE BEST

Set your minds on what is above, not on what is on the earth.

Colossians 3:2 HCSB

What do you expect from the day ahead? Are you expecting God to do wonderful things, or are you living beneath a cloud of apprehension and doubt? The familiar words of Psalm 118:24 remind us of a profound yet simple truth: "This is the day which the LORD hath made; we will rejoice and be glad in it" (KJV). For believers, every day begins and ends with God's Son and God's promises. When we accept Christ into our hearts, God promises us the opportunity for earthly peace and spiritual abundance. But more importantly, God promises us the priceless gift of eternal life.

As we face the inevitable challenges of life-here-on-earth, we must arm ourselves with the promises of God's Holy Word. When we do, we can expect the best, not only for the day ahead, but also for all eternity.

Make the least of all that goes and the most of all that comes. Don't regret what is past. Cherish what you have. Look forward to all that is to come. And most important of all, rely moment by moment on Jesus Christ.

Gigi Graham Tchividjian

We honor God by asking for great things when they are a part of His promise. We dishonor Him and cheat ourselves when we ask for molehills where He has promised mountains.

Vance Havner

A TIMELY TIP

God has made many promises to you, and He will keep every single one of them. Your job is to trust God's promises and live accordingly.

TODAY'S BIBLE READING

Old Testament: Psalms 101-103

New Testament: 1 Corinthians 2

THE REMEDY FOR UNCERTAINTY

But He said to them, "Why are you fearful, you of little faith?" Then He got up and rebuked the winds and the sea. And there was a great calm.

Matthew 8:26 HCSB

Sometimes, like Jesus' disciples, we feel threatened by the storms of life. During these moments, when our hearts are flooded with uncertainty, we must remember that God is not simply near, He is here.

Have you ever felt your faith in God slipping away? If so, you are in good company. Even the most faithful Christians are, at times, beset by occasional bouts of discouragement and doubt. But even when you feel far removed from God, God never leaves your side. He is always with you, always willing to calm the storms of life. When you sincerely seek His presence—and when you genuinely seek to establish a deeper, more meaningful relationship with His Son—God will calm your fears, answer your prayers, and restore our soul.

I was learning something important: we are most vulnerable to the piercing winds of doubt when we distance ourselves from the mission and fellowship to which Christ has called us. Our night of discouragement will seem endless and our task impossible, unless we recognize that He stands in our midst.

Joni Eareckson Tada

Unconfessed sin in your life will cause you to doubt.

Anne Graham Lotz

A TIMELY TIP

Are you sincerely looking for a way to address your doubts? Try Bible Study, prayer, and worship.

SERENITY

Do not remember the past events, pay no attention to things of old. Look, I am about to do something new; even now it is coming. Do you not see it? Indeed, I will make a way in the wilderness, rivers in the desert.

Isaiah 43:18-19 HCSB

The American theologian Reinhold Niebuhr composed a profoundly simple verse that came to be known as the Serenity Prayer: "God, grant me the serenity to accept the things I cannot change, the courage to change the things I can, and the wisdom to know the difference." Niebuhr's words are far easier to recite than they are to live by. Why? Because most of us want life to unfold in accordance with our own wishes and timetables. But sometimes God has other plans.

If you've encountered unfortunate circumstances that are beyond your power to control, accept those circumstances . . . and trust God. When you do, you can be comforted in the knowledge that your Creator is both loving and wise, and that He understands His plans perfectly, even when you do not.

We must meet our disappointments, our persecutions, our malicious enemies, our provoking friends, our trials and temptations of every sort, with an attitude of surrender and trust. We must spread our wings and "mount up" to the "heavenly places in Christ" above them all, where they will lose their power to harm or distress us.

Hannah Whitall Smith

A TIMELY TIP

When you encounter situations that you cannot change, you must learn the wisdom of acceptance . . . and you must learn to trust God.

THANKSGIVING YES . . . ENVY NO!

Stop your anger! Turn from your rage! Do not envy others—it only leads to harm.

Psalm 37:8 NLT

As the recipient of God's grace, you have every reason to celebrate life. After all, God has promised you the opportunity to receive His abundance and His joy—in fact, you have the opportunity to receive those gifts right now. But if you allow envy to gnaw away at the fabric of your soul, you'll find that joy remains elusive. So do yourself an enormous favor: Rather than succumbing to the sin of envy, focus on the marvelous things that God has done for you—starting with Christ's sacrifice. Thank the Giver of all good gifts, and keep thanking Him for the wonders of His love and the miracles of His creation. Count your own blessings and let your neighbors count theirs. It's the godly way to live.

Discontent dries up the soul.

Elisabeth Elliot

How can you possess the miseries of envy when you possess in Christ the best of all portions?

C. H. Spurgeon

A TIMELY TIP

Envy is a sin. Plus, it's a major-league waste of time and energy. So get over it.

COMPETENCE, YES. EXCUSES, NO!

Do you see people skilled in their work? They will work for kings, not for ordinary people.

Proverbs 22:29 NCV

E xcuses are everywhere . . . excellence is not. If you seek excellence (and the rewards that accompany it), you must avoid the bad habit of making excuses.

Whatever your job description, it's up to you, and no one else, to become a master of your craft. It's up to you to do your job right—and to do it right now. When you do, you'll discover that excellence is its own reward . . . but not its only reward.

We need to stop focusing on our lacks and stop giving out excuses and start looking at and listening to Jesus.

Anne Graham Lotz

Jesus knows one of the greatest barriers to our faith is often our unwillingness to be made whole—our unwillingness to accept responsibility—our unwillingness to live without excuse for our spiritual smallness and immaturity.

Anne Graham Lotz

A TIMELY TIP

Today, think of something important that you've been putting off. Then think of the excuses you've used to avoid that responsibility. Finally, ask yourself what you can do today to finish the work you've been avoiding.

GOD'S PLAN FOR YOUR FAMILY

Unless the Lord builds a house, its builders labor over it in vain; unless the Lord watches over a city, the watchman stays alert in vain.

Psalm 127:1 HCSB

A s you consider God's purpose for your own life, you must also consider how your plans will effect the most important people that God has entrusted to your care: your loved ones.

A loving family is a treasure from God. If you happen to be a member of a close knit, supportive clan, offer a word of thanks to your Creator. He has blessed you with one of His most precious earthly possessions. Your obligation, in response to God's gift, is to treat your family in ways that are consistent with His commandments. So, as you prayerfully seek God's direction, remember that He has important plans for your home life as well as your professional life. It's up to you to act—and to plan—accordingly.

The Golden Rule begins at home.

Marie T. Freeman

The first essential for a happy home is love.

Billy Graham

A TIMELY TIP

If you're lucky enough to be a member of a loving, supportive family, then you owe it to yourself—and to them—to share your thoughts, your hopes, your encouragement, and your love.

OUR FEAR-BASED WORLD

They do not fear bad news; they confidently trust the Lord to care for them.
They are confident and fearless and can face their foes triumphantly.

Psalm 112:7-8 NLT

We live in a fear-based world, a world where bad new travels at light speed and good news doesn't. These are troubled times, times when we have legitimate fears for the future of our nation, our world, and our families. But as Christians, we have every reason to live courageously. After all, the ultimate battle has already been fought and won on that faraway cross at Calvary.

Perhaps you, like countless other believers, have found your courage tested by the anxieties and fears that are an inevitable part of 21st-century life. If so, God wants to have a little chat with you. The next time you find your courage tested to the limit, God wants to remind you that He is not just near, He is here. So remember this: your Heavenly Father is your Protector and your Deliverer. Call upon Him in your hour of need, and be comforted. Whatever your challenge, whatever your trouble, God can handle it. And will.

You needn't worry about not feeling brave. Our Lord didn't—see the scene in Gethsemane. How thankful I am that when God became man He did not choose to become a man of iron nerves; that would not have helped weaklings like you and me nearly so much.

C. S. Lewis

A TIMELY TIP

If you're too afraid of failure, you may not live up to your potential. Remember that failing isn't nearly as bad as failing to try.

A WILLINGNESS TO FORGIVE

And be kind and compassionate to one another, forgiving one another, just as God also forgave you in Christ.

Ephesians 4:32 HCSB

To forgive others is difficult. Being frail, fallible, imperfect human beings, we are quick to anger, quick to blame, slow to forgive, and even slower to forget. No matter. Forgiveness, no matter how difficult, is God's way, and it must be our way, too.

God's commandments are not intended to be customized for the particular whims of particular believers. God's Word is not a menu from which each of us may select items à la carte, according to our own desires. Far from it. God's Holy Word is a book that must be taken in its entirety; all of God's commandments are to be taken seriously. And, so it is with forgiveness. So, if you hold bitterness against even a single person, forgive. Then, to the best of your abilities, forget. It's God's way for you to live.

There is nothing, absolutely nothing, that God will not forgive. You cannot "out-sin" His forgiveness. You cannot "out-sin" the love of God.

Kathy Troccoli

Forgiveness enables you to bury your grudge in icy earth. To put the past behind you. To flush resentment away by being the first to forgive. Forgiveness fashions your future. It is a brave and brash thing to do.

Barbara Johnson

A TIMELY TIP

If you're having trouble forgiving someone else . . . think how many times other people have forgiven you!

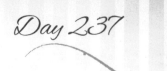
OFFERING THANKS

In everything give thanks; for this is the will of God in Christ Jesus for you.

1 Thessalonians 5:18 NKJV

Sometimes, life-here-on-earth can be complicated, demanding, and frustrating. When the demands of life leave us rushing from place to place with scarcely a moment to spare, we may fail to pause and thank our Creator for His gifts. But, whenever we neglect to give proper thanks to the Father, we suffer because of our misplaced priorities.

Today, begin making a list of your blessings. You most certainly will not be able to make a complete list, but take a few moments and jot down as many blessings as you can. Then, give thanks to the Giver of all good things: God. His love for you is eternal, as are His gifts. And it's never too soon—or too late—to offer Him thanks.

When you and I are related to Jesus Christ, our strength and wisdom and peace and joy and love and hope may run out, but His life rushes in to keep us filled to the brim. We are showered with blessings, not because of anything we have or have not done, but simply because of Him.

Anne Graham Lotz

We prevent God from giving us the great spiritual gifts He has in store for us, because we do not give thanks for daily gifts.

Dietrich Bonhoeffer

A TIMELY TIP

God wants to bless you abundantly and eternally. When you trust God completely and obey Him faithfully, you will be blessed.

Day 238

HIS AWESOME CREATION

Then God saw everything that He had made, and indeed it was very good.

Genesis 1:31 NKJV

When we consider God's glorious universe, we marvel at the miracle of nature. The smallest seedlings and grandest stars are all part of God's infinite creation. God has placed His handiwork on display for all to see, and if we are wise, we will make time each day to celebrate the world that surrounds us.

Today, as you fulfill the demands of everyday life, pause to consider the majesty of heaven and earth. It is as miraculous as it is beautiful, as incomprehensible as it is breathtaking.

The Psalmist reminds us that the heavens are a declaration of God's glory (Psalm 19:1). May we never cease to praise the Father for a universe that stands as an awesome testimony to His presence and His power.

How awesome that the "Word" that was in the beginning, by which and through which God created everything, was—and is—a living Person with a mind, will, emotions, and intellect.

Anne Graham Lotz

Today you will encounter God's creation. When you see the beauty around you, let each detail remind you to lift your head in praise.

Max Lucado

A TIMELY TIP

Every day can be a celebration of God's creation. And every day should be.

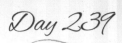

Day 239

HIS INTIMATE LOVE

As the Father loved Me, I also have loved you; abide in My love.

John 15:9 NKJV

St. Augustine observed, "God loves each of us as if there were only one of us." Do you believe those words? Do you seek an intimate, one-on-one relationship with your Heavenly Father, or are you satisfied to keep Him at a "safe" distance?

Sometimes, in the crush of our daily duties, God may seem far away, but He is not. God is everywhere we have ever been and everywhere we will ever go. He is with us night and day; He knows our thoughts and our prayers. And, when we earnestly seek Him, we will find Him because He is here, waiting patiently for us to reach out to Him. May we reach out to Him today and always. And may we praise Him for the glorious gifts that have transformed us today and forever.

Behold, behold the wondrous love, That ever flows from God above / Through Christ His only Son, Who gave / His precious blood our souls to save.

Fanny Crosby

When you agree to let God love the unlovely through you, He never fails to make the unlovely lovely to you.

Beth Moore

A TIMELY TIP

When you invite the love of God into your heart, everything changes . . . including you.

TODAY'S BIBLE READING
Old Testament: Psalms 128-132
New Testament: 1 Corinthians 11:1-18

HE REIGNS

In all your ways acknowledge Him, and He shall direct your paths.

Proverbs 3:6 NKJV

God is sovereign. He reigns over the entire universe and He reigns over your little corner of that universe. Your challenge is to recognize God's sovereignty and live in accordance with His commandments. Sometimes, of course, this is easier said than done.

Your Heavenly Father may not always reveal Himself as quickly (or as clearly) as you would like. But rest assured: God is in control, God is here, and God intends to use you in wonderful, unexpected ways. He desires to lead you along a path of His choosing. Your challenge is to watch, to listen, to learn . . . and to follow.

As you place yourself under the sovereign lordship of Jesus Christ, each mistake or failure can lead you right back to the throne.

Barbara Johnson

Either we are adrift in chaos or we are individuals, created, loved, upheld and placed purposefully, exactly where we are. Can you believe that? Can you trust God for that?

Elisabeth Elliot

A TIMELY TIP

God is in control of our world . . . and your world.

SERVING OTHERS WITH LOVE

Whoever wants to become great among you must be your servant, and whoever wants to be first among you must be your slave; just as the Son of Man did not come to be served, but to serve, and to give His life—a ransom for many.

Matthew 20:26-28 HCSB

Jesus came to earth as a servant of man and the Savior of mankind. One way that we can demonstrate our love for the Savior is by obeying His commandment to serve one another.

Whom will you choose to serve today? Will you be a woman who cheerfully meets the needs of family and friends? And, will you meet those needs with love in your heart and encouragement on your lips? As you plan for the day ahead, remember that the needs are great and the workers are few. And remember that God is doing His very best to enlist able-bodied believers—like you.

Jesus never asks us to give Him what we don't have. But He does demand that we give Him all we do have if we want to be a part of what He wishes to do in the lives of those around us!

Anne Graham Lotz

God wants us to serve Him with a willing spirit, one that would choose no other way.

Beth Moore

A TIMELY TIP

The direction of your steps and the quality of your life will be determined by the level of your service.

Day 242

SETBACKS

And my God shall supply all your need according to His riches in glory by Christ Jesus.

Philippians 4:19 NKJV

All of us experience adversity, disappointments, and hardship. Sometimes we bring these hardships upon ourselves, and sometimes we are victimized by circumstances that we cannot control and cannot fully understand. As human beings with limited insight, we can never completely comprehend the will of our Father in heaven. But as believers in a benevolent God, we must always trust His providence.

Have you been touched by personal tragedy that you did not deserve and cannot understand? If so, it's time to make peace with life. It's time to forgive others, and, if necessary, to forgive yourself. It's time to accept the unchangeable past, to embrace the priceless present, and to have faith in the promise of tomorrow. It's time to trust God completely. And it's time to reclaim the peace—His peace—that can and should be yours.

Jesus loved the will of His Father. He embraced the limitations, the necessities, the conditions, the very chains of his humanity as he walked and worked here on earth, fulfilling moment by moment His divine commission and the stern demands of His incarnation. Never was there a word or even a look of complaint.

Elisabeth Elliot

A TIMELY TIP

You should learn from the past, but you should never allow ourself to become stuck there. Once you have made peace with the past, you are then free to live more fully in the present . . . and that's precisely what you should do.

HOPE IS CONTAGIOUS

Finally, all of you be of one mind, having compassion for one another; love as brothers, be tenderhearted, be courteous.

1 Peter 3:8 NKJV

One of the reasons that God placed you here on earth is so that you might become a beacon of encouragement to the world. As a faithful follower of the One from Galilee, you have every reason to be hopeful, and you have every reason to share your hopes with others. When you do, you will discover that hope, like other human emotions, is contagious.

As a follower of Christ, you are instructed to choose your words carefully so as to build others up through wholesome, honest encouragement (Ephesians 4:29). So look for the good in others and celebrate the good that you find. As the old saying goes, "When someone does something good, applaud—you'll make two people happy."

One of the ways God refills us after failure is through the blessing of Christian fellowship. Just experiencing the joy of simple activities shared with other children of God can have a healing effect on us.

Anne Graham Lotz

A TIMELY TIP

Today, challenge your faith by finding at least three people who need your encouragement, and then give them as much encouragement as you can. Be generous with your words, with pats on the back, and with your prayers. And remember: encouragement is contagious. You can't lift other people up without lifting yourself up, too.

A POSITIVE INFLUENCE

Be an example to the believers in word, in conduct, in love, in spirit, in faith, in purity.

1 Timothy 4:12 NKJV

As followers of Christ, we must each ask ourselves an important question: "What kind of example am I?" The answer to that question determines, in large part, whether or not we are positive influences on our own little corners of the world.

Are you the kind of woman whose life serves as a powerful example of righteousness? Are you a person whose behavior serves as a positive role model for young people? Are you the kind of Christian whose actions, day in and day out, are based upon integrity, fidelity, and a love for the Lord? If so, you are not only blessed by God, you are also a powerful force for good in a world that desperately needs positive influences such as yours.

Among the most joyful people I have known have been some who seem to have had no human reason for joy. The sweet fragrance of Christ has shown through their lives.

Elisabeth Elliot

There is nothing anybody else can do that can stop God from using us. We can turn everything into a testimony.

Corrie ten Boom

A TIMELY TIP

As a Christian, the most important light you shine is the light that your own life shines on the lives of others. May your light shine brightly, righteously, obediently, and eternally!

CARING FOR YOUR FAMILY

Now if anyone does not provide for his own relatives, and especially for his household, he has denied the faith and is worse than an unbeliever.

1 Timothy 5:8 HCSB

The words of 1 Timothy 5:8 are unambiguous: if God has blessed us with families, then He expects us to care for them. Sometimes, this profound responsibility seems daunting. And sometimes, even for the most dedicated Christian women, family life holds moments of frustration and disappointment. But, for those who are lucky enough to live in the presence of a close-knit, caring clan, the rewards far outweigh the demands.

No family is perfect, and neither is yours. Despite the inevitable challenges of providing for your family, and despite the occasional hurt feelings of family life, your clan is God's gift to you. Give thanks to the Giver for the gift of family . . . and act accordingly.

When God asks someone to do something for Him entailing sacrifice, He makes up for it in surprising ways. Though He has led Bill all over the world to preach the gospel, He has not forgotten the little family in the mountains of North Carolina.

Ruth Bell Graham

There is always room for more loving forgiveness within our homes.

James Dobson

A TIMELY TIP

Let your family and friends know that you love them by the things you say and the things you do. And, never take your family for granted; they deserve your very best treatment!

PASS IT ON

Do not neglect the gift that is in you.

1 Timothy 4:14 HCSB

God has given you an array of talents, and He has given you unique opportunities to share those talents with the world. Your Creator intends for you to use your talents for the glory of His kingdom in the service of His children. Will you honor Him by sharing His gifts? And, will you share His gifts humbly and lovingly? Hopefully you will.

The old saying is both familiar and true: "What you are is God's gift to you; what you become is your gift to God." As a woman who has been touched by the transforming love of Jesus Christ, your obligation is clear: You must strive to make the most of your own God-given talents, and you must encourage your family and friends to do likewise. So, make this promise to yourself and to God: Promise to use your talents to minister to your family, to your friends, and to the world. And remember: The best way to say "Thank You" for God's gifts is to use them.

Not everyone possesses boundless energy or a conspicuous talent. We are not equally blessed with great intellect or physical beauty or emotional strength. But we have all been given the same ability to be faithful.

Gigi Graham Tchividjian

A TIMELY TIP

Each person possesses special abilities that can be nurtured carefully or ignored totally. The challenge, of course, is to do the former and to avoid the latter.

LETTING GO

Blessed are the merciful, because they will be shown mercy.

Matthew 5:7 HCSB

Even the most mild-mannered women will, on occasion, have reason to become angry with the inevitable shortcomings of family members and friends. But wise women are quick to forgive others, just as God has forgiven them. The commandment to forgive others is clearly a part of God's Word, but oh how difficult a commandment it can be to follow. Because we are imperfect beings, we are quick to anger, quick to blame, slow to forgive, and even slower to forget. No matter. Even when forgiveness is difficult, God's instructions are straightforward: As Christians who have received the gift of forgiveness, we must now share that gift with others.

Bitterness and regret are not part of God's plan for your life. Forgiveness is. And once you've forgiven others, you can then turn your thoughts to a far more pleasant subject: the incredibly bright future that God has promised.

God expects us to forgive others as He has forgiven us; we are to follow His example by having a forgiving heart.

Vonette Bright

When God tells us to love our enemies, he gives, along with the command, the love itself.

Corrie ten Boom

A TIMELY TIP

Holding a grudge? Drop it. Never expect other people to be more forgiving than you are. And remember: the best time to forgive is now.

RICHLY BLESSED

Each person should do as he has decided in his heart—not out of regret or out of necessity, for God loves a cheerful giver.

2 Corinthians 9:7 HCSB

God's Word commands us to be generous, compassionate servants to those who need our support. As believers, we have been richly blessed by our Creator. We, in turn, are called to share our gifts, our possessions, our testimonies, and our talents.

The theme of generosity is one of the cornerstones of Christ's teachings. If we are to be disciples of Christ, we, too, must be cheerful, generous, courageous givers. Our Savior expects no less from us. And He deserves no less.

We do not need to beg Him to bless us; He simply cannot help it.

Hannah Whitall Smith

A happy spirit takes the grind out of giving. The grease of gusto frees the gears of generosity.

Charles Swindoll

A TIMELY TIP

Today, challenge your faith by thinking of at least one small, practical step you can take to help someone in need.

HEARING THE CALL

One thing I do, forgetting those things which are behind and reaching forward to those things which are ahead, I press toward the goal for the prize of the upward call of God in Christ Jesus.

Philippians 3:13-14 NKJV

It is vitally important that you heed God's call. In John 15:16, Jesus says, "You did not choose me, but I chose you and appointed you to go and bear fruit—fruit that will last" (NIV). In other words, you have been called by Christ, and now, it is up to you to decide precisely how you will answer.

Have you already found your special calling? If so, you're a very lucky man. If not, keep searching and keep praying until you discover it. And remember this: God has important work for you to do—work that no one else on earth can accomplish but you.

If God has called you, do not spend time looking over your shoulder to see who is following you.

Corrie ten Boom

God never calls without enabling us. In other words, if he calls you to do something, he makes it possible for you to do it.

Luci Swindoll

A TIMELY TIP

God has a plan for your life, a divine calling that you can either answer or ignore. How you choose to respond to God's calling will determine the direction you take and the contributions you make.

GOD IS LOVE

He who does not love does not know God, for God is love.

1 John 4:8 NKJV

God loves you. He loves you more than you can imagine; His affection is deeper than you can fathom. God made you in His own image and gave you salvation through the person of His Son Jesus Christ. And as a result, you have an important decision to make. You must decide what to do about God's love: you can return it . . . or not.

When you accept the love that flows from the heart of God, you are transformed. When you embrace God's love, you feel differently about yourself, your neighbors, your community, your church, and your world. When you open your heart to God's love, you will feel compelled to share God's message—and His compassion—with others. God's heart is overflowing—accept His love; return His love; and share His love. Today.

Life in God is a great big hug that lasts forever!

Barbara Johnson

The unfolding of our friendship with the Father will be a never-ending revelation stretching on into eternity.

Catherine Marshall

A TIMELY TIP

When all else fails, God's love does not. You can always depend upon God's love . . . and He is always your ultimate protection.

CONQUERING OUR FRUSTRATIONS

People with quick tempers cause trouble, but those who control their tempers stop a quarrel.

Proverbs 15:18 NCV

Life is full of frustrations: some great and some small. On occasion, you, like Jesus, will confront evil, and when you do, you may respond as He did: vigorously and without reservation. But, more often your frustrations will be of the more mundane variety. As long as you live here on earth, you will face countless opportunities to lose your temper over small, relatively insignificant events: a traffic jam, a spilled cup of coffee, an inconsiderate comment, a broken promise.

When you are tempted to lose your temper over the minor inconveniences of life, don't. Turn away from anger, hatred, bitterness, and regret. Turn instead to God. When you do, you'll be following His commandments and giving yourself a priceless gift . . . the gift of peace.

Life is too short to spend it being angry, bored, or dull.

Barbara Johnson

Bitterness and anger, usually over trivial things, make havoc of homes, churches, and friendships.

Warren Wiersbe

A TIMELY TIP

Avoid angry outbursts: Sweet words usually work better than sour ones. (Proverbs 19:11)

THE RIGHT KIND OF ATTITUDE

May the words of my mouth and the meditation of my heart be acceptable to You, Lord, my rock and my Redeemer.

Psalm 19:14 HCSB

What is your attitude today? Are you fearful or worried? Are you more concerned about pleasing your friends than about pleasing your God? Are you bitter, confused, cynical, or pessimistic? If so, it's time to have a little chat with your Father in heaven.

God intends that your life be filled with spiritual abundance and joy—but God will not force His joy upon you—you must claim it for yourself. So do yourself this favor: accept God's gifts with a smile on your face, a song on your lips, and joy in your heart. Think optimistically about yourself and your future. Give thanks to the One who has given you everything, and trust in your heart that He wants to give you so much more.

The Reference Point for the Christian is the Bible. All values, judgments, and attitudes must be gauged in relationship to this Reference Point.

Ruth Bell Graham

A positive attitude will have positive results because attitudes are contagious.

Zig Ziglar

A TIMELY TIP

Attitudes are contagious, so it's important to associate with people who are upbeat, optimistic, and encouraging.

THE GUIDEBOOK

There's nothing like the written Word of God for showing you the way to salvation through faith in Christ Jesus. Every part of Scripture is God-breathed and useful one way or another, showing us truth, exposing our rebellion, correcting our mistakes, training us to live God's way. Through the Word we are put together and shaped up for the tasks God has for us.

2 Timothy 3:15-17 MSG

God has given us a guidebook for righteous living called the Holy Bible. It contains thorough instructions which, if followed, lead to fulfillment, righteousness, and salvation. But, if we choose to ignore God's commandments, the results are as predictable as they are tragic.

God has given us the Bible for the purpose of knowing His promises, His power, His commandments, His wisdom, His love, and His Son. As we study God's teachings and apply them to our lives, we live by the Word that shall never pass away. Today, let us follow God's commandments, and let us conduct our lives in such a way that we might be shining examples to our families, and, most importantly, to those who have not yet found Christ.

Don't worry about what you do not understand of the Bible. Worry about what you do understand and do not live by.

Corrie ten Boom

A TIMELY TIP

If you have a choice to make, the Bible can help you make it. If you've got questions, the Bible has answers.

BEYOND WORRY

Your heart must not be troubled. Believe in God; believe also in Me.

John 14:1 HCSB

B ecause we are fallible human beings, we worry. Even though we, as Christians, have the promise of God's love and protection, we find ourselves fretting over the countless details of everyday life.

If you are like most women, you may, on occasion, find yourself worrying about health, about finances, about safety, about relationships, about family, and about countless other challenges of life, some great and some small. Where is the best place to take your worries? Take them to God. Take your troubles to Him, and your fears, and your sorrows. And remember: God is trustworthy . . . and you are protected.

Worry is a cycle of inefficient thoughts whirling around a center of fear.

Corrie ten Boom

This life of faith, then, consists in just this—being a child in the Father's house. Let the ways of childish confidence and freedom from care, which so please you and win your heart when you observe your own little ones, teach you what you should be in your attitude toward God.

Hannah Whitall Smith

A TIMELY TIP

An important part of becoming a more mature Christian is learning to worry less and to trust God more.

IT'S UP TO YOU TO ASK

Now if any of you lacks wisdom, he should ask God, who gives to all generously and without criticizing, and it will be given to him.

James 1:5 HCSB

Jesus made it clear to His disciples: they should petition God to meet their needs. So should we. Genuine, heartfelt prayer produces powerful changes in us and in our world. When we lift our hearts to God, we open ourselves to a never-ending source of divine wisdom and infinite love.

Do you have questions about your future that you simply can't answer? Do you have needs that you simply can't meet by yourself? Do you sincerely seek to know God's unfolding plans for your life? If so, ask Him for direction, for protection, and for strength—and then keep asking Him every day that you live. Whatever your need, no matter how great or small, pray about it and never lose hope. God is not just near; He is here, and He's perfectly capable of answering your prayers. Now, it's up to you to ask.

When trials come your way—as inevitably they will—do not run away. Run to your God and Father.

Kay Arthur

We get into trouble when we think we know what to do, and we stop asking God if we're doing it right.

Stormie Omartian

A TIMELY TIP

If you're searching for peace and abundance, ask for God's help—and keep asking—until He answers your prayers.

A PRICELESS GIFT

Man shall not live by bread alone, but by every word that proceeds from the mouth of God.

Matthew 4:4 NKJV

The Bible is a priceless gift, a tool for Christians to use as they share the Good News of their Savior, Christ Jesus. Too many Christians, however, keep their spiritual tool kits tightly closed and out of sight.

Jonathan Edwards advised, "Be assiduous in reading the Holy Scriptures. This is the fountain whence all knowledge in divinity must be derived. Therefore let not this treasure lie by you neglected."

God's Holy Word is, indeed, a priceless, one-of-a-kind treasure. Handle it with care, but more importantly, handle it every day . . . starting today.

Either God's Word keeps you from sin, or sin keeps you from God's Word.

Corrie ten Boom

Decisions which are made in the light of God's Word are stable and show wisdom.

Vonette Bright

A TIMELY TIP

Take a Bible with you wherever you go. You never know when you may need a midday spiritual pick-me-up.

BORN AGAIN

You have been born again—not of perishable seed but of imperishable—through the living and enduring word of God.

1 Peter 1:23 HCSB

Why did Christ die on the cross? Christ sacrificed His life so that we might be born again. This gift, freely given from God's only begotten Son, is the priceless possession of everyone who accepts Him as Lord and Savior. Let us claim Christ's gift today. Let us walk with the Savior, let us love Him, let us praise Him, and let us share His message of salvation with all those who cross our paths.

The comforting words of Ephesians 2:8 make God's promise clear: "For by grace you have been saved through faith, and that not of yourselves; it is the gift of God" (NKJV). Thus, we are saved not because of our good deeds but because of our faith in Christ. May we, who have been given so much, praise our Savior for the gift of salvation, and may we share the joyous news of our Master's limitless love with our families, with our friends, and with the world.

Being born again is God's solution to our need for love and life and light.

Anne Graham Lotz

Jesus divided people—everyone—into two classes—the once-born and the twice-born, the unconverted and the converted. No other distinction mattered.

E. Stanley Jones

A TIMELY TIP

A true conversion experience results in a life transformed by Christ and a commitment to following in His footsteps.

Day 258

LIFE'S FOUNDATION

The one who lives with integrity will be helped, but one who distorts right and wrong will suddenly fall.

Proverbs 28:18 HCSB

Wise women understand that character is a crucial building block in the foundation of a well-lived life. Character is built slowly over a lifetime. It is the sum of every right decision, every honest word, every noble thought, and every heartfelt prayer. It is forged on the anvil of honorable work and polished by the twin virtues of generosity and humility. Character is a precious thing—difficult to build, but easy to tear down; godly women value it and protect it at all costs.

Each one of us is God's special work of art. Through us, He teaches and inspires, delights and encourages, informs and uplifts all those who view our lives. God, the master artist, is most concerned about expressing Himself—His thoughts and His intentions—through what He paints in our characters.

Joni Eareckson Tada

The single most important element in any human relationship is honesty—with oneself, with God, and with others.

Catherine Marshall

A TIMELY TIP

Remember: Character is more important than popularity.

ENDURING DIFFICULT DAYS

I have heard your prayer, I have seen your tears; surely I will heal you.

2 Kings 20:5 NKJV

From time to time, all of us must endure discouragement. And, we sometimes experience life-changing personal losses that leave us reeling. When we do, God stands ready to protect us. When we are troubled, we must call upon God, and, in His own time and according to His own plan, He will heal us.

Are you anxious? Take those anxieties to God. Are you troubled? Take your troubles to Him. Does your world seem to be trembling beneath your feet? Seek protection from the One who cannot be moved. The same God who created the universe will protect you if you ask Him . . . so ask Him.

Often, in the midst of great problems, we stop short of the real blessing God has for us, which is a fresh vision of who He is.

Anne Graham Lotz

Failure is one of life's most powerful teachers. How we handle our failures determines whether we're going to simply "get by" in life or "press on."

Beth Moore

A TIMELY TIP

When times are tough, you should guard your heart by turning it over to God.

SUPPORTING HIS CHURCH

For we are God's fellow workers; you are God's field, you are God's building.

1 Corinthians 3:9 NKJV

The church belongs to God; it is His just as certainly as we are His. When we help build God's church, we bear witness to the changes that He has made in our lives.

Today and every day, let us worship God with grateful hearts and helping hands as we support the church that He has created. Let us witness to our friends, to our families, and to the world. When we do so, we bless others—and we are blessed by the One who sent His Son to die so that we might have eternal life.

The church needs the power and the gifts of the Holy Spirit more now than ever before.

Corrie ten Boom

Churches do not lack great scholars and great minds. They lack men and women who can and will be channels of the power of God.

Corrie ten Boom

A TIMELY TIP

Make church a celebration, not an obligation. Your attitude towards church is important, in part, because it is contagious . . . so celebrate accordingly!

A CLEAR CONSCIENCE

If then you were raised with Christ, seek those things which are above, where Christ is, sitting at the right hand of God. Set your mind on things above, not on things on the earth.

Colossians 3:1-2 NKJV

Few things in life torment us more than a guilty conscience. And, few things in life provide more contentment than the knowledge that we are obeying God's commandments.

A clear conscience is one of the rewards we earn when we obey God's Word and follow His will. When we follow God's will and accept His gift of salvation, our earthly rewards are never-ceasing, and our heavenly rewards are everlasting.

Whatever weakens your reason, impairs the tenderness of your conscience, obscures your sense of God, or removes your relish for spiritual things— that is sin to you.

Susanna Wesley

One of the ways God has revealed Himself to us is in the conscience. Conscience is God's lamp within the human breast.

Billy Graham

A TIMELY TIP

If you're not sure what to do . . . slow down and listen to your conscience. That little voice inside your head is remarkably dependable, but you can't depend upon it if you never listen to it. So stop, listen, and learn—your conscience is almost always right!

SUFFICIENT FOR YOUR NEEDS

And God is able to make all grace abound toward you, that you, always having all sufficiency in all things, may have an abundance for every good work.

2 Corinthians 9:8 NKJV

O f this you can be sure: the love of God is sufficient to meet your needs. Whatever dangers you may face, whatever heartbreaks you must endure, God is with you, and He stands ready to comfort you and to heal you.

The Psalmist writes, "Weeping may endure for a night, but joy comes in the morning" (Psalm 30:5 NKJV). But when we are suffering, the morning may seem very far away. It is not. God promises that He is "near to those who have a broken heart" (Psalm 34:18 NKJV).

If you are experiencing the intense pain of a recent loss, or if you are still mourning a loss from long ago, perhaps you are now ready to begin the next stage of your journey with God. If so, be mindful of this fact: the loving heart of God is sufficient to meet any challenge, including yours.

God's all-sufficiency is a major. Your inability is a minor. Major in majors, not in minors.

Corrie ten Boom

God walks with us. He scoops us up in His arms or simply sits with us in silent strength until we cannot avoid the awesome recognition that yes, even now, He is here.

Gloria Gaither

A TIMELY TIP

Whatever you need, God can provide. He is always sufficient to meet your needs.

WHEN IT'S HARD TO BE KIND

Don't be obsessed with getting your own advantage. Forget yourselves long enough to lend a helping hand.

Philippians 2:4 MSG

Sometimes, when we feel happy or generous, we find it easy to be kind. Other times, when we are discouraged or tired, we can scarcely summon the energy to utter a single kind word. But, God's commandment is clear: He intends that we make the conscious choice to treat others with kindness and respect, no matter our circumstances, no matter our emotions.

Today, as you consider all the things that Christ has done in your life, honor Him by following His commandment and obeying the Golden Rule. He expects no less, and He deserves no less.

The Golden Rule starts at home, but it should never stop there.

Marie T. Freeman

Doing something positive toward another person is a practical approach to feeling good about yourself.

Barbara Johnson

A TIMELY TIP

Don't wait. The best time to do a good deed is as soon as you can do it.

PRIORITIES . . .
MOMENT BY MOMENT

You can't go wrong when you love others. When you add up everything in the law code, the sum total is love. But make sure that you don't get so absorbed and exhausted in taking care of all your day-by-day obligations that you lose track of the time and doze off, oblivious to God.

Romans 13:10-11 MSG

Each waking moment holds the potential to think a creative thought or offer a heartfelt prayer. So even if you're a person with too many demands and too few hours in which to meet them, don't panic. Instead, be comforted in the knowledge that when you sincerely seek to discover God's priorities for your life, He will provide answers in marvelous and surprising ways.

Remember: this is the day that God has made and that He has filled it with countless opportunities to love, to serve, and to seek His guidance. Seize those opportunities. And as a gift to yourself, to your family, and to the world, slow down and claim the inner peace that is your spiritual birthright: the peace of Jesus Christ. It is yours for the asking. So ask . . . and be thankful.

In our tense, uptight society where folks are rushing to make appointments they have already missed, a good laugh can be as refreshing as a cup of cold water in the desert.

Barbara Johnson

A TIMELY TIP

The world wants to grab every spare minute of your time, but God wants some of your time, too. When in doubt, trust God.

THE WISDOM TO BE HUMBLE

Do nothing out of rivalry or conceit, but in humility consider others as more important than yourselves.

Philippians 2:3 HCSB

God's Word clearly instructs us to be humble. And that's good because, as fallible human beings, we have so very much to be humble about! Yet some of us continue to puff ourselves up, seeming to say, "Look at me!" To do so is wrong.

As Christians, we have been refashioned and saved by Jesus Christ, and that salvation came not because of our own good works but because of God's grace. How, then, can we be prideful? The answer, of course, is that, if we are honest with ourselves and with our God, we simply can't be boastful . . . we must, instead, be eternally grateful and exceedingly humble. The good things in our lives, including our loved ones, come from God. He deserves the credit—and we deserve the glorious experience of giving it to Him.

If you know who you are in Christ, your personal ego is not an issue.

Beth Moore

Because Christ Jesus came to the world clothed in humility, he will always be found among those who are clothed with humility. He will be found among the humble people.

A. W. Tozer

A TIMELY TIP

You must remain humble or face the consequences. Pride does go before the fall, but humility often prevents the fall.

TODAY'S BIBLE READING
Old Testament: Ecclesiastes 7-8
New Testament: Galatians 3

BEING PATIENT WITH OURSELVES

Knowing God leads to self-control. Self-control leads to patient endurance, and patient endurance leads to godliness.

2 Peter 1:6 NLT

Being patient with other people can be difficult. But sometimes, we find it even more difficult to be patient with ourselves. We have high expectations and lofty goals. We want to accomplish things now, not later. And, of course, we want our lives to unfold according to our own timetables, not God's.

Throughout the Bible, we are instructed that patience is the companion of wisdom. God's message, then, is clear: we must be patient with all people, beginning with that particular person who stares back at us each time we gaze into the mirror.

In times of uncertainty, wait. Always, if you have any doubt, wait. Do not force yourself to any action. If you have a restraint in your spirit, wait until all is clear, and do not go against it.

Mrs. Charles E. Cowman

He makes us wait. He keeps us in the dark on purpose. He makes us walk when we want to run, sit still when we want to walk, for he has things to do in our souls that we are not interested in.

Elisabeth Elliot

A TIMELY TIP

When you learn to be more patient with yourself and with others, you'll make your world—and your heart—a more peaceful and less stressful place.

THE LOVE OF MONEY

For the love of money is a root of all kinds of evil, and by craving it, some have wandered away from the faith and pierced themselves with many pains.

1 Timothy 6:10 HCSB

Our society is in love with money and the things that money can buy. God is not. God cares about people, not possessions, and so must we. We must, to the best of our abilities, love our neighbors as ourselves, and we must, to the best of our abilities, resist the mighty temptation to place possessions ahead of people.

Money, in and of itself, is not evil; worshipping money is. So today, as you prioritize matters of importance for you and yours, remember that God is almighty, but the dollar is not. If we worship God, we are blessed. But if we worship "the almighty dollar," we are inevitably punished because of our misplaced priorities—and our punishment inevitably comes sooner rather than later.

Have you prayed about your resources lately? Find out how God wants you to use your time and your money. No matter what it costs, forsake all that is not of God.

Kay Arthur

There is nothing wrong with people possessing riches. The wrong comes when riches possess people.

Billy Graham

A TIMELY TIP

When you realize that this world is not your home, that realization changes the way you think about money . . . and the way you spend it.

RELATIONSHIPS BUILT UPON HONESTY

The one who lives with integrity lives securely, but whoever perverts his ways will be found out.

Proverbs 10:9 HCSB

Lasting relationships are built upon a foundation of honesty and trust. It has been said on many occasions that honesty is the best policy. For believers, it is far more important to note that honesty is God's policy. And if we are to be servants worthy of our Savior, Jesus Christ, we must be honest and forthright in all our communications with others.

Sometimes, honesty is difficult; sometimes, honesty is painful; sometimes, honesty makes us feel uncomfortable. Despite these temporary feelings of discomfort, we must make honesty the hallmark of all our relationships; otherwise, we invite needless suffering into our own lives and into the lives of those we love.

The single most important element in any human relationship is honesty—with oneself, with God, and with others.

Catherine Marshall

God doesn't expect you to be perfect, but he does insist on complete honesty.

Rick Warren

A TIMELY TIP

Beware of "white" lies. Sometimes, we're tempted to "shade" the truth. Unfortunately, little white lies have a tendency to turn black . . . and they grow. The best strategy is to avoid untruths of all sizes and colors.

TO GOD BE THE GLORY

Clothe yourselves with humility toward one another, because God resists the proud, but gives grace to the humble.

1 Peter 5:5 HCSB

As Christians, we have a profound reason to be humble: We have been refashioned and saved by Jesus Christ, and that salvation came not because of our own good works but because of God's grace. Thus, we are not "self-made"; we are "God-made" and "Christ-saved." How, then, can we be boastful?

Dietrich Bonhoeffer observed, "It is very easy to overestimate the importance of our own achievements in comparison with what we owe others." In other words, reality breeds humility. So, instead of puffing out your chest and saying, "Look at me!", give credit where credit is due, starting with God. And, rest assured: There is no such thing as a self-made woman. All of us are made by God . . . and He deserves the glory, not us.

Our God is so wonderfully good, and lovely, and blessed in every way that the mere fact of belonging to Him is enough for an untellable fullness of joy!

Hannah Whitall Smith

We can never have more of true faith than we have of true humility.

Andrew Murray

A TIMELY TIP

God favors the humble just as surely as He disciplines the proud.

Day 270

MISTAKES HAPPEN

Have mercy on me, O God, according to your unfailing love; according to your great compassion blot out my transgressions. Wash away all my iniquity and cleanse me from my sin.

Psalm 51:1-2 NIV

We are imperfect women living in an imperfect world; mistakes are simply part of the price we pay for being here. But, even though mistakes are an inevitable part of life's journey, repeated mistakes should not be. When we commit the inevitable blunders of life, we must correct them, learn from them, and pray to God for the wisdom not to repeat them. And then, if we are successful, our mistakes become lessons, and our lives become adventures in growth, not stagnation.

Mistakes offer the possibility for redemption and a new start in God's kingdom. No matter what you're guilty of, God can restore your innocence.

Barbara Johnson

Lord, when we are wrong, make us willing to change; and when we are right, make us easy to live with.

Peter Marshall

A TIMELY TIP

When it comes to repairing mistakes, sooner beats later. So ask yourself, "If not now, when?"

ENOUGH HOURS IN THE DAY?

It is good to give thanks to the Lord, to sing praises to the Most High. It is good to proclaim your unfailing love in the morning, your faithfulness in the evening.

Psalm 92:1-2 NLT

Each day has 1,440 minutes—do you value your relationship with God enough to spend a few of those minutes with Him? He deserves that much of your time and more—is He receiving it from you? Hopefully so. But if you find that you're simply "too busy" for a daily chat with your Father in heaven, it's time to take a long, hard look at your priorities and your values.

As you consider your plans for the day ahead, here's a tip: organize your life around this simple principle: "God first." When you place your Creator where He belongs—at the very center of your day and your life—the rest of your priorities will fall into place.

Knowing God involves an intimate, personal relationship that is developed over time through prayer and getting answers to prayer, through Bible study and applying its teaching to our lives, through obedience and experiencing the power of God, through moment-by-moment submission to Him that results in a moment-by-moment filling of the Holy Spirit.

Anne Graham Lotz

A TIMELY TIP

Find the best time of the day to spend with God: Hudson Taylor, an English missionary, wrote, "Whatever is your best time in the day, give that to communion with God." That's powerful advice that leads to a powerful faith.

DOUBT AND BELIEF

Immediately the father of the child cried out and said with tears, "Lord, I believe; help my unbelief!"

Mark 9:24 NKJV

Even the most faithful Christians are overcome by occasional bouts of fear and doubt. You are no different. When you feel that your faith is being tested to its limits, seek the comfort and assurance of the One who sent His Son as a sacrifice for you.

Have you ever felt your faith in God slipping away? If so, you are not alone. Every life—including yours—is a series of successes and failures, celebrations and disappointments, joys and sorrows, hopes and doubts. But even when you feel very distant from God, God is never distant from you. When you sincerely seek His presence, He will touch your heart, calm your fears, and restore your faith in the future . . . and your faith in Him.

Resisting His will for your life will cause you to doubt.

Anne Graham Lotz

Fear and doubt are conquered by a faith that rejoices. And faith can rejoice because the promises of God are as certain as God Himself.

Kay Arthur

A TIMELY TIP

Doubts creeping in? Increase the amount of time you spend in Bible Study, prayer, and worship.

THE BEST POLICY

The righteousness of the blameless clears his path, but the wicked person will fall because of his wickedness.

Proverbs 11:5 HCSB

From the time we are children, we are taught that honesty is the best policy, but sometimes, being honest is hard. So, we convince ourselves that it's alright to tell "little white lies." But there's a problem: Little white lies tend to grow up, and when they do, they cause havoc and pain in our lives.

For Christians, the issue of honesty is not a topic for debate. Honesty is not just the best policy, it is God's policy, pure and simple. And if we are to be servants worthy of our Savior, Jesus Christ, we must avoid all lies, white or otherwise. So, if you're tempted to sow the seeds of deception (perhaps in the form of a "harmless" white lie), resist that temptation. Truth is God's way, and a lie—of whatever color—is not.

Much guilt arises in the life of the believer from practicing the chameleon life of environmental adaptation.

Beth Moore

You cannot glorify Christ and practice deception at the same time.

Warren Wiersbe

A TIMELY TIP

One of your greatest possessions is integrity . . . don't lose it. Billy Graham was right when he said: "Integrity is the glue that holds our way of life together. We must constantly strive to keep our integrity intact. When wealth is lost, nothing is lost; when health is lost, something is lost; when character is lost, all is lost."

IMPERFECT BEINGS,
IMPERFECT FAITH

The one who trusts in the Lord will be happy.

Proverbs 16:20 HCSB

Why are we humans plagued by worry? Because we are imperfect beings with imperfect faith. Even though we are Christians who have been given the assurance of salvation—even though we are Christians who have received the promise of God's love and protection—we find ourselves fretting over the countless details of everyday life. Jesus understood our concerns when He spoke the reassuring words found in Matthew 6: "Therefore I tell you, do not worry about your life . . ."

As you consider the promises of Jesus, remember that God still sits in His heaven and you are His beloved child. Then, perhaps, you will worry a little less and trust God a little more, and that's as it should be because God is trustworthy . . . and you are protected.

Remember always that there are two things which are more utterly incompatible even than oil and water, and these two are trust and worry.

Hannah Whitall Smith

Submit each day to God, knowing that He is God over all your tomorrows.

Kay Arthur

A TIMELY TIP

Focus on your work, not your worries. Worry is never a valid substitute for work, so get out there, do your best, and turn your worries over to God.

SO LAUGH!

A joyful heart makes a face cheerful.

Proverbs 15:13 HCSB

Laughter is God's gift, and He intends that we enjoy it. Yet sometimes, because of the inevitable stresses of everyday life, laughter seems only a distant memory. As Christians we have every reason to be cheerful and to be thankful. Our blessings from God are beyond measure, starting, of course, with a gift that is ours for the asking, God's gift of salvation through Christ Jesus.

Few things in life are more absurd than the sight of a grumpy Christian. So today, as you go about your daily activities, approach life with a grin and a chuckle. After all, God created laughter for a reason . . . to use it. So laugh!

Laughter dulls the sharpest pain and flattens out the greatest stress. To share it is to give a gift of health.

Barbara Johnson

A keen sense of humor helps us to overlook the unbecoming, understand the unconventional, tolerate the unpleasant, overcome the unexpected, and outlast the unbearable.

Billy Graham

A TIMELY TIP

If you can't see the joy and humor in everyday life . . . you're not paying attention to the right things. Remember the donut-maker's creed: "As you travel through life brother, whatever be your goal, keep your eye upon the donut, and not upon the hole."

SHARING THE GOOD NEWS

As you go, announce this: "The kingdom of heaven has come near."

Matthew 10:7 HCSB

The Good News of Jesus Christ should be shouted from the rooftops by believers the world over. But all too often, it is not. For a variety of reasons, many Christians keep their beliefs to themselves, and when they do, the world suffers because of their failure to speak up.

As believers, we are called to share the transforming message of Jesus with our families, with our neighbors, and with the world. Jesus commands us to become fishers of men. And, the time to go fishing is now. We must share the Good News of Jesus Christ today—tomorrow may indeed be too late.

There is no thrill quite as wonderful as seeing someone else come to trust Christ because I have been faithful in sharing the story of my own faith.

Vonette Bright

Ministry is not something we do for God; it is something God does in and through us.

Warren Wiersbe

A TIMELY TIP

God's Word clearly instructs you to share His Good News with the world. If you're willing, God will empower you to share your faith

WISDOM IN A DONUT SHOP

My cup runs over. Surely goodness and mercy shall follow me all the days of my life; and I will dwell in the house of the Lord Forever.

Psalm 23:5-6 NKJV

Many years ago, this rhyme was posted on the wall of a small donut shop:

As you travel through life brother,
Whatever be your goal,
Keep your eye upon the donut,
And not upon the hole.

These simple words remind us of a profound truth: we should spend more time looking at the things we have, not worrying about the things we don't have.

When you think about it, you've got more blessings than you can count. So make it a habit to thank God for the gifts He's given you, not the gifts you wish He'd given you.

Make the least of all that goes and the most of all that comes. Don't regret what is past. Cherish what you have. Look forward to all that is to come. And most important of all, rely moment by moment on Jesus Christ.

Gigi Graham Tchividjian

A TIMELY TIP

Be a realistic optimist. Your attitude toward the future will help create your future. So think realistically about yourself and your situation while making a conscious effort to focus on hopes, not fears. When you do, you'll put the self-fulfilling prophecy to work for you.

PLEASING GOD

Therefore, whether we are at home or away, we make it our aim to be pleasing to Him.

2 Corinthians 5:9 HCSB

When God made you, He equipped you with an array of talents and abilities that are uniquely yours. It's up to you to discover those talents and to use them, but sometimes the world will encourage you to do otherwise. At times, society will attempt to cubbyhole you, to standardize you, and to make you fit into a particular, preformed mold. Perhaps God has other plans.

Sometimes, because you're an imperfect human being, you may become so wrapped up in meeting society's expectations that you fail to focus on God's expectations. To do so is a mistake of major proportions—don't make it. Instead, seek God's guidance as you focus your energies on becoming the best "you" that you can possibly be. And, when it comes to matters of conscience, seek approval not from your peers, but from your Creator.

You will get untold flak for prioritizing God's revealed and present will for your life over man's . . . but, boy, is it worth it.

Beth Moore

Make God's will the focus of your life day by day. If you seek to please Him and Him alone, you'll find yourself satisfied with life.

Kay Arthur

A TIMELY TIP

First, focus on your relationship with God. Then, you'll find that every other relationship and every other aspect of your life will be more fulfilling.

COMMUNITY LIFE

Regarding life together and getting along with each other, you don't need me to tell you what to do. You're God-taught in these matters. Just love one another!

1 Thessalonians 4:9 MSG

A s we travel along life's road, we build lifelong relationships with a small, dear circle of family and friends. And how best do we build and maintain these relationships? By following the Word of God. Healthy relationships are built upon honesty, compassion, responsible behavior, trust, and optimism. Healthy relationships are built upon the Golden Rule. Healthy relationships are built upon sharing and caring. All of these principles are found time and time again in God's Holy Word. When we read God's Word and follow His commandments, we enrich our own lives and the lives of those who are closest to us.

Line by line, moment by moment, special times are etched into our memories in the permanent ink of everlasting love in our relationships.

Gloria Gaither

The love life of the Christian is a crucial battleground. There, if nowhere else, it will be determined who is Lord: the world, the self, and the devil— or the Lord Christ.

Elisabeth Elliot

A TIMELY TIP

When you understand that Christianity is about servanthood, other people become your focus and your ministry.

SHARING THE GOOD NEWS

Christ did not send me to baptize people but to preach the Good News. And he sent me to preach the Good News without using words of human wisdom so that the cross of Christ would not lose its power.

1 Corinthians 1:17 NCV

In his second letter to Timothy, Paul offers a message to believers of every generation when he writes, "God has not given us a spirit of timidity" (1:7 NASB). Paul's meaning is crystal clear: When sharing our testimonies, we, as Christians, must be courageous, forthright, and unashamed.

We live in a world that desperately needs the healing message of Christ Jesus. Every believer, each in his or her own way, bears a personal responsibility for sharing that message.

You know how Christ has touched your heart and changed your life. Now it's your turn to share the Good News with others. And remember: today is the perfect time to share your testimony because tomorrow may quite simply be too late.

Claim the joy that is yours. Pray. And know that your joy is used by God to reach others.

Kay Arthur

There is nothing anybody else can do that can stop God from using us. We can turn everything into a testimony.

Corrie ten Boom

A TIMELY TIP

Whether you realize it or not, you have a profound responsibility to tell as many people as you can about the eternal life that Christ offers to those who believe in Him.

STANDING UP FOR OUR FAITH

Be alert, stand firm in the faith, be brave and strong.

1 Corinthians 16:13 HCSB

Are you a woman whose faith is obvious to your family and to the world, or are you a spiritual shrinking violet? God needs more women who are willing to stand up and be counted for Him.

Genuine faith is never meant to be locked up in the heart of a believer; to the contrary, it is meant to be shared. And a woman who wishes to share God's Good News with the world should begin by sharing that message with his own family.

Through every triumph and tragedy, God will stand by your side and strengthen you . . . if you have faith in Him. Jesus taught His disciples that if they had faith, they could move mountains. You can, too, and so can your family . . . if you have faith.

If God chooses to remain silent, faith is content.

Ruth Bell Graham

Faith is like a radar that sees like the fog—the reality of things at a distance that the human eye cannot see.

Corrie ten Boom

A TIMELY TIP

Today, dare to place your hopes, your dreams, and your future in God's hands.

THE GIFT OF THE SHEPHERD

My cup runs over. Surely goodness and mercy shall follow me all the days of my life; and I will dwell in the house of the Lord forever.

Psalm 23:5-6 NKJV

The Word of God is clear: Christ came in order that we might have life abundant and life eternal. Eternal life is priceless possession of all who invite Christ into their hearts, but God's abundance is optional: He does not force it upon us.

Do you sincerely seek the riches that our Savior offers to those who give themselves to Him? Then follow Him completely and obey Him without reservation. When you do, you will receive the love and the abundance that He has promised. Seek first the salvation that is available through a personal relationship with Jesus Christ, and then claim His joy, His peace, and His abundance.

Jesus intended for us to be overwhelmed by the blessings of regular days. He said it was the reason he had come: "I am come that they might have life, and that they might have it more abundantly."

Gloria Gaither

God's riches are beyond anything we could ask or even dare to imagine! If my life gets gooey and stale, I have no excuse.

Barbara Johnson

A TIMELY TIP

God wants to shower you with abundance—your job is to let Him.

WHY DO BAD THINGS HAPPEN?

They won't be afraid of bad news; their hearts are steady because they trust the Lord.

Psalm 112:7 NCV

If God is good, and if He made the world, why do bad things happen? Part of that question is easy to answer, and part of it isn't. Let's get to the easy part first: Sometimes, bad things happen because people disobey God's commandments and invite sadness and heartache into God's beautiful world.

But on other occasions, bad things happen, and it's nobody's fault. So who is to blame? Sometimes, nobody is to blame. Sometimes, things just happen and we simply cannot know why. Thankfully, all our questions will be answered . . . some day. The Bible promises that in heaven we will understand all the reasons behind God's plans. But until then, we must simply trust that God is good, and that, in the end, He will make things right.

On the darkest day of your life, God is still in charge. Take comfort in that.

Marie T. Freeman

The difference between winning and losing is how we choose to react to disappointment.

Barbara Johnson

A TIMELY TIP

The grieving process takes time. God does not promise instantaneous healing, but He does promise healing: "I have heard your prayer, I have seen your tears; surely I will heal you" (2 Kings 20:5 NKJV).

PRACTICING WHAT WE PREACH

If the way you live isn't consistent with what you believe, then it's wrong.

Romans 14:23 MSG

In describing our beliefs, our actions are far better descriptors than our words. Yet far too many of us spend more energy talking about our beliefs than living by them—with predictably poor results.

As believers, we must beware: Our actions should always give credence to the changes that Christ can make in the lives of those who walk with Him.

Your beliefs shape your values, and your values shape your life. Is your life a clearly-crafted picture book of your creed? Are your actions always consistent with your beliefs? Are you willing to practice the philosophies that you preach? Hopefully so; otherwise, you'll be tormented by inconsistencies between your beliefs and your behaviors.

Faith sees the invisible, believes the unbelievable, and receives the impossible.

Corrie ten Boom

What you do reveals what you believe about God, regardless of what you say. When God reveals what He has purposed to do, you face a crisis—a decision time. God and the world can tell from your response what you really believe about God.

Henry Blackaby

A TIMELY TIP

When you stand up for your beliefs—and when you follow your conscience—you'll feel better about yourself. When you don't, you won't.

ALWAYS WITH US

For unto us a Child is born, Unto us a Son is given; And the government will be upon His shoulder. And His name will be called Wonderful, Counselor, Mighty God, Everlasting Father, Prince of Peace.

Isaiah 9:6 NKJV

Are you facing difficult circumstances or unwelcome changes? If so, please remember that God is far bigger than any problem you may face. So, instead of worrying about life's inevitable challenges, put your faith in the Father and His only begotten Son: "Jesus Christ is the same yesterday, today, and forever" (Hebrews 13:8 NKJV). And remember: it is precisely because your Savior does not change that you can face your challenges with courage for today and hope for tomorrow.

Life is often challenging, but as Christians, we should not be afraid. God loves us, and He will protect us. In times of hardship, He will comfort us; in times of change, He will guide our steps. When we are troubled, or weak, or sorrowful, God is always with us. We must build our lives on the rock that cannot be moved . . . we must trust in God. Always.

With God, it isn't who you were that matters; it's who you are becoming.

Liz Curtis Higgs

When we are young, change is a treat, but as we grow older, change becomes a threat. But when Jesus Christ is in control of your life, you need never fear change or decay.

Warren Wiersbe

A TIMELY TIP

If a big change is called for . . . don't be afraid to make a big change— sometimes, one big leap is better than a thousand baby steps.

CRITICS BEWARE

Don't pick on people, jump on their failures, criticize their faults—unless, of course, you want the same treatment. Don't condemn those who are down; that hardness can boomerang. Be easy on people; you'll find life a lot easier.

Luke 6:37 MSG

From experience, we know that it is easier to criticize than to correct. And we know that it is easier to find faults than solutions. Yet the urge to criticize others remains a powerful temptation for most of us. Our task, as obedient believers, is to break the twin habits of negative thinking and critical speech.

Negativity is highly contagious: we give it to others who, in turn, give it back to us. This cycle can be broken by positive thoughts, heartfelt prayers, and encouraging words. As thoughtful servants of a loving God, we can use the transforming power of Christ's love to break the chains of negativity. And we should.

Never be afraid of the world's censure; it's praise is much more to be dreaded.

C. H. Spurgeon

The scrutiny we give other people should be for ourselves.

Oswald Chambers

A TIMELY TIP

If you're tempted to be critical of others, remember that your ability to judge others requires a level of insight that you simply don't have. So do everybody (including yourself) a favor: don't criticize.

Day 287

A SACRIFICIAL LOVE

I am the good shepherd. The good shepherd lays down his life for the sheep.

John 10:11 HCSB

How much does Christ love us? More than we, as mere mortals, can comprehend. His love is perfect and steadfast. Even though we are fallible and wayward, the Shepherd cares for us still. Even though we have fallen far short of the Father's commandments, Christ loves us with a power and depth that is beyond our understanding. The sacrifice that Jesus made upon the cross was made for each of us, and His love endures to the edge of eternity and beyond.

Christ's love changes everything. When you accept His gift of grace, you are transformed, not only for today, but also for all eternity. If you haven't already done so, accept Jesus Christ as your Savior. He's waiting patiently for you to invite Him into your heart. Please don't make Him wait a single minute longer.

God is my Heavenly Father. He loves me with an everlasting love. The proof of that is the Cross.

Elisabeth Elliot

Behold, behold the wondrous love, That ever flows from God above / Through Christ His only Son, Who gave / His precious blood our souls to save.

Fanny Crosby

A TIMELY TIP

Jesus loves you. His love can—and should—be the cornerstone and the touchstone of your life.

GOD'S GUIDANCE

Those who are blessed by Him will inherit the land.

Psalm 37:22 HCSB

God is intensely interested in each of us, and He will guide our steps if we serve Him obediently.

When we sincerely offer heartfelt prayers to our Heavenly Father, He will give direction and meaning to our lives—but He won't force us to follow Him. To the contrary, God has given us the free will to follow His commandments . . . or not.

When we stray from God's commandments, we invite bitter consequences. But, when we follow His commandments, and when we genuinely and humbly seek His will, He touches our hearts and leads us on the path of His choosing.

Will you trust God to guide your steps? You should. When you entrust your life to Him completely and without reservation, God will give you the strength to meet any challenge, the courage to face any trial, and the wisdom to live in His righteousness and in His peace. So trust Him today and seek His guidance. When you do, your next step will be the right one.

God's leading will never be contrary to His word.

Vonette Bright

God's guidance is even more important than common sense. I can declare that the deepest darkness is outshone by the light of Jesus.

Corrie ten Boom

A TIMELY TIP

If you want God's guidance, ask for it. When you pray for guidance, God will give it.

CONTENTMENT THROUGH CHRIST

The LORD will give strength to His people; The LORD will bless His people with peace.

Psalm 29:11 NKJV

Everywhere we turn, or so it seems, the world promises us contentment and happiness. But the contentment that the world offers is fleeting and incomplete. Thankfully, the contentment that God offers is all encompassing and everlasting. Happiness, of course, depends less upon our circumstances than upon our thoughts. When we turn our thoughts to God, to His gifts, and to His glorious creation, we experience the joy that God intends for His children. But, when we focus on the negative aspects of life—or when we disobey God's commandments—we cause ourselves needless suffering.

Do you sincerely want to be a contented Christian? Then set your mind and your heart upon God's love and His grace. Seek first the salvation that is available through a personal relationship with Jesus Christ, and then claim the joy, the contentment, and the spiritual abundance that the Shepherd offers His sheep.

When we are set free from the bondage of pleasing others, when we are free from currying others' favor and others' approval—then no one will be able to make us miserable or dissatisfied. And then, if we know we have pleased God, contentment will be our consolation.

Kay Arthur

A TIMELY TIP

Because you are loved and protected by God, you should be contented, whatever your circumstances.

Day 290

FOR ALL ETERNITY

"I assure you: Anyone who hears My word and believes Him who sent Me has eternal life and will not come under judgment, but has passed from death to life."

John 5:24–25 HCSB

As mere mortals, our vision for the future, like our lives here on earth, is limited. God's vision is not burdened by such limitations: His plans extend throughout all eternity. Thus, God's plans for you are not limited to the ups and downs of everyday life. Your Heavenly Father has bigger things in mind . . . much bigger things.

Let us praise the Creator for His priceless gift, and let us share the Good News with all who cross our paths. We return our Father's love by accepting His grace and by sharing His message and His love. When we do, we are blessed here on earth and throughout all eternity.

Your choice to either receive or reject the Lord Jesus Christ will determine where you spend eternity.

Anne Graham Lotz

The damage done to us on this earth will never find its way into that safe city. We can relax, we can rest, and though some of us can hardly imagine it, we can prepare to feel safe and secure for all of eternity.

Bill Hybels

A TIMELY TIP

God offers you a priceless gift: the gift of eternal life. If you have not already done so, accept God's gift today—tomorrow may be too late.

FAITH THAT MOVES MOUNTAINS

I assure you: If anyone says to this mountain, "Be lifted up and thrown into the sea," and does not doubt in his heart, but believes that what he says will happen, it will be done for him.

Mark 11:23 HCSB

Because we live in a demanding world, all of us have mountains to climb and mountains to move. Moving those mountains requires faith.

Are you a mountain mover whose faith is evident for all to see? Hopefully so. God needs more women who are willing to move mountains for His glory and for His kingdom.

God walks with you, ready and willing to strengthen you. Accept His strength today. And remember—Jesus taught His disciples that if they had faith, they could move mountains. You can too . . . so with no further ado, let the mountain moving begin.

Let me encourage you to continue to wait with faith. God may not perform a miracle, but He is trustworthy to touch you and make you whole where there used to be a hole.

Lisa Whelchel

Faith sees the invisible, believes the unbelievable, and receives the impossible.

Corrie ten Boom

A TIMELY TIP

You cannot see the future, but God can . . . and you must have faith in His eternal plan for you.

Day 292

PLANS: YOURS AND GOD'S

People may make plans in their minds, but the Lord decides what they will do.
Proverbs 16:9 NCV

If you're like most people, you want things to happen according to your wishes and according to your timetable. But sometimes, God has other plans . . . and He always has the final word.

Are you embittered by a personal tragedy that you did not deserve and cannot understand? If so, it's time to make peace with life. It's time to forgive others, and, if necessary, to forgive yourself. It's time to accept the unchangeable past, to embrace the priceless present, and to have faith in the promise of tomorrow. It's time to trust God completely. And it's time to reclaim the peace—His peace—that can and should be yours. So, if you've encountered unfortunate circumstances that are beyond your power to control, accept those circumstances . . . and trust God. When you do, you can be comforted in the knowledge that your Creator is both loving and wise, and that He understands His plans perfectly, even when you do not.

The will of God for your life is simply that you submit yourself to Him each day and say, "Father, Your will for today is mine. Your pleasure for today is mine. Your work for today is mine. I trust You to be God. You lead me today and I will follow."

Kay Arthur

A TIMELY TIP

Acceptance means learning to trust God more. Today, think of at least one aspect of your life that you've been reluctant to accept, and then prayerfully ask God to help you trust Him more by accepting the past.

THE SEARCH FOR SIGNIFICANCE

For everything, absolutely everything, above and below, visible and invisible, rank after rank after rank of angels—everything got started in him and finds its purpose in him.

Colossians 1:16 MSG

"What on earth does God intend for me to do with my life?" It's an easy question to ask but, for many of us, a difficult question to answer. Why? Because God's purposes aren't always clear to us. Sometimes we wander aimlessly in a wilderness of our own making. And sometimes, we struggle mightily against God in an unsuccessful attempt to find success and happiness through our own means, not His.

If you're a woman who sincerely seeks God's guidance, He will give it. But, He will make His revelations known to you in a way and in a time of His choosing, not yours, so be patient. Even on those difficult days when you are unsure which way to turn, you must never lose sight of these overriding facts: God created you for a reason; He has important work for you to do; and He's waiting patiently for you to do it. The next step is up to you.

Jesus was the Savior Who would deliver them not only from the bondage of sin but also from meaningless wandering through life.

Anne Graham Lotz

A TIMELY TIP

God has a plan for your life, a definite purpose that you can fulfill . . . or not. Your challenge is to pray for God's guidance and to follow wherever He leads.

THE JOYS OF FRIENDSHIP

I give thanks to my God for every remembrance of you.

Philippians 1:3 HCSB

What is a friend? The dictionary defines the word *friend* as "a person who is attached to another by feelings of affection or personal regard." This definition is accurate, as far as it goes, but when we examine the deeper meaning of friendship, so many more descriptors come to mind: trustworthiness, loyalty, helpfulness, kindness, encouragement, humor, and cheerfulness, to mention but a few.

Today, as you consider the many blessings that God has given you, remember to thank Him for the friends He has chosen to place along your path. May you be a blessing to them, and may they richly bless you today, tomorrow, and every day that you live.

Don't bypass the potential for meaningful friendships just because of differences. Explore them. Embrace them. Love them.

Luci Swindoll

As God perfects us, He keeps us protected from the pride that might otherwise develop by veiling, to some extent, our progress in our own eyes. The light of the glory of His presence shines two ways: it sheds light on the knowledge of God so that we can learn to see Him more clearly, but it also sheds light on ourselves so that we can see our own sin more clearly.

Beth Moore

A TIMELY TIP

The best rule for making friends . . . is the Golden one.

TODAY'S BIBLE READING
Old Testament: Isaiah 61-63
New Testament: 1 Timothy 4

READY. SET. GO!

Do not neglect the gift that is in you.

1 Timothy 4:14 HCSB

God has given you talents and opportunities that are uniquely yours. Are you willing to use your gifts in the way that God intends? And are you willing to summon the discipline that is required to develop your talents and to hone your skills? That's precisely what God wants you to do, and that's precisely what you should desire for yourself.

As you seek to expand your talents, you will undoubtedly encounter stumbling blocks along the way, such as the fear of rejection or the fear of failure. When you do, don't stumble! Just continue to refine your skills, and offer your services to God. And when the time is right, He will use you—but it's up to you to be thoroughly prepared when He does.

Great relief and satisfaction can come from seeking God's priorities for us in each season, discerning what is "best" in the midst of many noble opportunities, and pouring our most excellent energies into those things.

Beth Moore

In the great orchestra we call life, you have an instrument and a song, and you owe it to God to play them both sublimely.

Max Lucado

A TIMELY TIP

God has given you a unique array of talents and opportunities. If you use your gifts wisely, they're multiplied. If you misuse your gifts—or ignore them altogether—they are lost. God is anxious for you to use your gifts . . . are you?

GREAT IS THY FAITHFULNESS

God is faithful, by whom you were called into the fellowship of His Son, Jesus Christ our Lord.

1 Corinthians 1:9 NKJV

God is faithful to us even when we are not faithful to Him. God keeps His promises to us even when we stray far from His will. He continues to love us even when we disobey His commandments. But God does not force His blessings upon us. If we are to experience His love and His grace, we must claim them for ourselves.

Are you tired, discouraged, or fearful? Be comforted: God is with you. Are you confused? Listen to the quiet voice of your Heavenly Father. Are you bitter? Talk with God and seek His guidance. Are you celebrating a great victory? Thank God and praise Him. He is the Giver of all things good. In whatever condition you find yourself, trust God and be comforted. The Father is with you now and forever.

God is always sufficient in perfect proportion to our need.

Beth Moore

It is a joy that God never abandons His children. He guides faithfully all who listen to His directions.

Corrie ten Boom

A TIMELY TIP

Of this you can be sure: God's faithfulness is steadfast, unwavering, and eternal.

INFINITE POSSIBILITIES

Is anything too hard for the LORD?

Genesis 18:14 KJV

Ours is a God of infinite possibilities. But sometimes, because of limited faith and limited understanding, we wrongly assume that God cannot or will not intervene in the affairs of mankind. Such assumptions are simply wrong.

Are you afraid to ask God to do big things in your life? Is your faith threadbare and worn? If so, it's time to abandon your doubts and reclaim your faith in God's promises. God's Holy Word makes it clear: absolutely nothing is impossible for the Lord. And since the Bible means what it says, you can be comforted in the knowledge that the Creator of the universe can do miraculous things in your own life and in the lives of your loved ones. Your challenge, as a believer, is to take God at His word, and to expect the miraculous.

We will see more and more that we are chosen not because of our ability, but because of the Lord's power, which will be demonstrated in our not being able.

Corrie ten Boom

No giant will ever be a match for a big God with a little rock.

Beth Moore

A TIMELY TIP

When you place your faith in God, life becomes a grand adventure energized by the power of God.

GOD'S TIMETABLE

Humble yourselves therefore under the mighty hand of God, so that He may exalt you in due time, casting all your care upon Him, because He cares about you.

1 Peter 5:6-7 HCSB

Sometimes, the hardest thing to do is to wait. This is especially true when we're in a hurry and when we want things to happen now, if not sooner! But God's plan does not always happen in the way that we would like or at the time of our own choosing. Our task—as believing Christians who trust in a benevolent, all knowing Father—is to wait patiently for God to reveal Himself.

We human beings are, by nature, impatient. We know what we want, and we know exactly when we want it: RIGHT NOW! But, God knows better. He has created a world that unfolds according to His own timetable, not ours . . . thank goodness!

When we read of the great Biblical leaders, we see that it was not uncommon for God to ask them to wait, not just a day or two, but for years, until God was ready for them to act.

Gloria Gaither

Waiting on God brings us to the journey's end quicker than our feet.

Mrs. Charles E. Cowman

A TIMELY TIP

You don't know precisely what you need—or when you need it—but God does. So trust His timing.

BEYOND GUILT

There is therefore now no condemnation to those who are in Christ Jesus, who do not walk according to the flesh, but according to the Spirit.

Romans 8:1 NKJV

All of us have sinned. Sometimes our sins result from our own stubborn rebellion against God's commandments. And sometimes, we are swept up in events that are beyond our abilities to control. Under either set of circumstances, we may experience intense feelings of guilt. But God has an answer for the guilt that we feel. That answer, of course, is His forgiveness. When we confess our wrongdoings and repent from them, we are forgiven by the One who created us.

Are you troubled by feelings of guilt or regret? If so, you must repent from your misdeeds, and you must ask your Heavenly Father for His forgiveness. When you do so, He will forgive you completely and without reservation. Then, you must forgive yourself just as God has forgiven you: thoroughly and unconditionally.

If God has forgiven you, why can't you forgive yourself?

Marie T. Freeman

Identify the sin. Confess it. Turn from it. Avoid it at all costs. Live with a clean, forgiven conscience. Don't dwell on what God has forgotten!

Max Lucado

A TIMELY TIP

If you've asked for God's forgiveness, He has given it. But have you forgiven yourself? If not, the best moment to do so is this one.

THE FUTILITY OF BLAME

Walking down the street, Jesus saw a man blind from birth. His disciples asked, "Rabbi, who sinned: this man or his parents, causing him to be born blind?" Jesus said, "You're asking the wrong question. You're looking for someone to blame. There is no such cause-effect here. Look instead for what God can do.

John 9:1-3 MSG

To blame others for our own problems is the height of futility. Yet blaming others is a favorite human pastime. Why? Because blaming is much easier than fixing, and criticizing others is so much easier than improving ourselves. So instead of solving our problems legitimately (by doing the work required to solve them) we are inclined to fret, to blame, and to criticize, while doing precious little else. When we do, our problems, quite predictably, remain unsolved.

Have you acquired the bad habit of blaming others for problems that you could or should solve yourself? If so, you are not only disobeying God's Word, you are also wasting your own precious time. So, instead of looking for someone to blame, look for something to fix, and then get busy fixing it. And as you consider your own situation, remember this: God has a way of helping those who help themselves, but He doesn't spend much time helping those who don't.

Forgiveness is the key which unlocks the door of resentment and the handcuffs of hatred. It breaks the chains of bitterness and the shackles of selfishness.

Corrie ten Boom

A TIMELY TIP

If you take responsibility for your actions, you're headed in the right direction. If you try to blame others, you're headed down a dead-end street.

EXCELLENCE, NOT EXCUSES

And now, children, stay with Christ. Live deeply in Christ. Then we'll be ready for him when he appears, ready to receive him with open arms, with no cause for red-faced guilt or lame excuses when he arrives.

1 John 2:28-29 MSG

We live in a world where excuses are everywhere. And it's precisely because excuses are so numerous that they are also so ineffective. When we hear the words, "I'm sorry but...", most of us know exactly what is to follow: the excuse. The dog ate the homework. Traffic was terrible. It's the company's fault. The boss is to blame. The equipment is broken. We're out of that. And so forth, and so on.

Because we humans are such creative excuse-makers, all of the really good excuses have already been taken. In fact, the high-quality excuses have been used, re-used, over-used, and ab-used. That's why excuses don't work—we've heard them all before.

So, if you're wasting your time trying to concoct a new and improved excuse, don't bother. It's impossible. A far better strategy is this: do the work. Now. And let your excellent work speak loudly and convincingly for itself.

Making up a string of excuses is usually harder than doing the work.

Marie T. Freeman

An excuse is only the skin of a reason stuffed with a lie.

Vance Havner

A TIMELY TIP

If you've acquired the unfortunate habit of making excuses . . . you'd better break that habit before that habit breaks you!

COUNTING YOUR BLESSINGS

Finally, brethren, whatever things are true, whatever things are noble, whatever things are just, whatever things are pure, whatever things are lovely, whatever things are of good report, if there is any virtue and if there is anything praiseworthy—meditate on these things.

Philippians 4:8 NKJV

How will you direct your thoughts today? Will you obey the words of Philippians 4:8 by dwelling upon those things that are true and honorable and right? Or will you allow your thoughts to be hijacked by the negativity that seems to dominate our troubled world? Are you fearful, angry, bored, or worried? Are you so preoccupied with the concerns of this day that you fail to thank God for the promise of eternity? Are you confused, bitter, or pessimistic? If so, God wants to have a little talk with you.

God intends that you experience joy and abundance. So, today and every day hereafter, celebrate the life that God has given you by focusing your thoughts upon those things that are worthy of praise. Today, count your blessings instead of your hardships. And thank the Giver of all things good for gifts that are simply too numerous to count.

The things we think are the things that feed our souls. If we think on pure and lovely things, we shall grow pure and lovely like them; and the converse is equally true.

Hannah Whitall Smith

A TIMELY TIP

A positive attitude leads to positive results; a negative attitude leads elsewhere.

A WALK WITH GOD

For I have given you an example that you also should do just as I have done for you.

John 13:15 HCSB

Each day, we are confronted with countless opportunities to serve God and to follow in the footsteps of His Son. When we do, our Heavenly Father guides our steps and blesses our endeavors. As citizens of a fast-changing world, we face challenges that sometimes leave us feeling overworked, overcommitted, and overwhelmed. But God has different plans for us. He intends that we slow down long enough to praise Him and to glorify His Son. When we do, He lifts our spirits and enriches our lives.

Today provides a glorious opportunity to place yourself in the service of the One who is the Giver of all blessings. May you seek His will, may you trust His word, and may you walk in the footsteps of His Son.

Will you, with a glad and eager surrender, hand yourself and all that concerns you over into his hands? If you will do this, your soul will begin to know something of the joy of union with Christ.

Hannah Whitall Smith

A TIMELY TIP

If you want to be a little more like Christ . . . learn about His teachings, follow in His footsteps, and obey His commandments.

FRIENDS AND FAMILY

As iron sharpens iron, a friend sharpens a friend.

Proverbs 27:17 NLT

A loving family is a treasure from God; so is a trustworthy friend. If you are a member of a close knit, supportive family, offer a word of thanks to your Creator. And if you have a close circle of trustworthy friends, consider yourself richly blessed.

Today, let us praise God for our family and for our friends. God has placed these people along our paths. Let us love them and care for them. And, let us give thanks to the Father for all the people who enrich our lives. These people are, in a very real sense, gifts from God; we should treat them as such.

Perhaps the greatest treasure on earth and one of the only things that will survive this life is human relationships: old friends. We are indeed rich if we have friends. Friends who have loved us through the problems and heartaches of life. Deep, true, joyful friendships. Life is too short and eternity too long to live without old friends.

Gloria Gaither

In friendship, God opens your eyes to the glories of Himself.

Joni Eareckson Tada

A TIMELY TIP

Thank your Creator God for the family and friends He has placed along your path. Cherish those relationships, and do your best to make them flourish.

THE SHEPHERD'S CARE

Your righteousness reaches heaven, God, You who have done great things; God, who is like You?

Psalm 71:19 HCSB

It's a promise that is made over and over again in the Bible: Whatever "it" is, God can handle it.

Life isn't always easy. Far from it! Sometimes, life can be very, very difficult. But even then, even during our darkest moments, we're protected by a loving Heavenly Father. When we're worried, God can reassure us; when we're sad, God can comfort us. When our hearts are broken, God is not just near, He is here. So we must lift our thoughts and prayers to Him. When we do, He will answer our prayers. Why? Because He is our Shepherd, and He has promised to protect us now and forever.

When considering the size of your problems, there are two categories that you should never worry about: the problems that are small enough for you to handle, and the ones that aren't too big for God to handle.

Marie T. Freeman

God's all-sufficiency is a major. Your inability is a minor. Major in majors, not in minors.

Corrie ten Boom

A TIMELY TIP

God wants to provide for you and your loved ones. When you trust your life and your future to God, He will provide for your needs.

THE GIFT OF GRACE

For by grace you are saved through faith, and this is not from yourselves; it is God's gift—not from works, so that no one can boast.

Ephesians 2:8-9 HCSB

God has given us so many gifts, but none can compare with the gift of salvation. We have not earned our salvation; it is a gift from God. When we accept Christ into our hearts, we are saved by His grace.

God's grace is the ultimate gift, and we owe to Him the ultimate in thanksgiving. Let us praise the Creator for His priceless gift, and let us share the Good News with all who cross our paths. We return our Father's love by accepting His grace and by sharing His message and His love. When we do, we are eternally blessed . . . and the Father smiles.

God does amazing works through prayers that seek to extend His grace to others.

Shirley Dobson

The most amazing thing about grace to the suffering heart and soul is its utter sufficiency.

Bill Bright

A TIMELY TIP

God's grace isn't earned, but freely given—what an amazing, humbling gift.

GOD HEALS US

I have heard your prayer, I have seen your tears; surely I will heal you.

2 Kings 20:5 NKJV

Women of every generation have experienced adversity, and this generation is no different. But, today's women face challenges that previous generations could have scarcely imagined. Thankfully, although the world continues to change, God's love remains constant. And, He remains ready to comfort us and strengthen us whenever we turn to Him. Psalm 147 promises, "He heals the brokenhearted, and binds their wounds" (v. 3). When we are troubled, we must call upon God, and, in His own time and according to His own plan, He will heal us.

God's peace is like a river, not a pond. In other words, a sense of health and well-being, both of which are expressions of the Hebrew shalom, can permeate our homes even when we're in white-water rapids.

Beth Moore

In order to realize the worth of the anchor, we need to feel the stress of the storm.

Corrie ten Boom

A TIMELY TIP

In dealing with difficult situations, view God as your comfort and your strength. And remember: Tough times can also be times of intense personal growth.

A ONE-OF-A-KIND TREASURE

Every word of God is pure; He is a shield to those who put their trust in Him.

Proverbs 30:5 NKJV

God's Word is a roadmap for life here on earth and for life eternal. As Christians, we are called upon to study God's Holy Word, to trust its promises, to follow its commandments, and to share its Good News with the world.

As believers, we must study the Bible and meditate upon its meaning for our lives. Otherwise, we deprive ourselves of a priceless gift from our Creator. God's Holy Word is, indeed, a transforming, life-changing, one-of-a-kind treasure. And, a passing acquaintance with the Good Book is insufficient for Christians who seek to obey God's Word and to understand His will. After all, neither man nor woman should live by bread alone . . .

Weave the unveiling fabric of God's word through your heart and mind. It will hold strong, even if the rest of life unravels.

Gigi Graham Tchividjian

The Holy Spirit is the Spirit of Truth, which means He always works according to and through the Word of God whether you feel Him or not.

Anne Graham Lotz

A TIMELY TIP

God's wisdom is found in God's Word. When you pick up your Bible and read it, you tune into that wisdom. So do the wise thing: make Bible reading an important part of your day. Every day.

ABUNDANT PEACE

And the peace of God, which surpasses every thought, will guard your hearts and your minds in Christ Jesus.

Philippians 4:7 HCSB

Are you the kind of woman who accepts God's spiritual abundance without reservation? If so, you are availing yourself of the peace and the joy that He has promised. Do you sincerely seek the riches that our Savior offers to those who give themselves to Him? Then follow Him. When you do, you will receive the love and the abundance that Jesus offers to those who follow Him.

Seek first the salvation that is available through a personal, passionate relationship with Christ, and then claim the joy, the peace, and the spiritual abundance that the Shepherd offers His sheep.

God has promised us abundance, peace, and eternal life. These treasures are ours for the asking; all we must do is claim them. One of the great mysteries of life is why on earth do so many of us wait so very long to lay claim to God's gifts?

Marie T. Freeman

God is the giver, and we are the receivers. And His richest gifts are bestowed not upon those who do the greatest things, but upon those who accept His abundance and His grace.

Hannah Whitall Smith

A TIMELY TIP

Abundance and obedience go hand-in-hand. Obey God first and expect to receive His abundance second, not vice versa.

Day 310

ACCEPTING GOD'S GIFTS

For God loved the world in this way: He gave His only Son, so that everyone who believes in Him will not perish but have eternal life.

John 3:16 HCSB

God loves you—His love for you is deeper and more profound than you can imagine. God's love for you is so great that He sent His only Son to this earth to die for your sins and to offer you the priceless gift of eternal life.

You must decide whether or not to accept God's gift. Will you ignore it or embrace it? Will you return it or neglect it? Will you invite Christ to dwell in the center of your heart, or will you relegate Him to a position of lesser importance? The decision is yours, and so are the consequences. So choose wisely . . . and choose today.

It's your heart that Jesus longs for: your will to be made His own with self on the cross forever, and Jesus alone on the throne.

Ruth Bell Graham

Every person who has ever been born has the sovereign right to make this same choice—to receive Jesus Christ by faith as God's revelation of Himself, or to reject Him.

Anne Graham Lotz

A TIMELY TIP

The ultimate choice for you is the choice to invite God's Son into your heart. Choose wisely . . . and immediately.

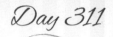
ABOVE AND BEYOND OUR CIRCUMSTANCES

Should we accept only good from God and not adversity?

Job 2:10 HCSB

All of us face difficult days. Sometimes even the most devout Christian women can become discouraged, and you are no exception. After all, you live in a world where expectations can be high and demands can be even higher.

If you find yourself enduring difficult circumstances, remember that God remains in His heaven. If you become discouraged with the direction of your day or your life, turn your thoughts and prayers to Him. He is a God of possibility, not negativity. He will guide you through your difficulties and beyond them . . . far beyond.

Worry is the senseless process of cluttering up tomorrow's opportunities with leftover problems from today.

Barbara Johnson

Crisis brings us face to face with our inadequacy and our inadequacy in turn leads us to the inexhaustible sufficiency of God.

Catherine Marshall

A TIMELY TIP

If it weren't for trouble . . . we might think we could handle our lives by ourselves. Jim Cymbala writes, "Trouble is one of God's great servants because it reminds us how much we continually need the Lord." We should thank the Lord for challenges that bring us closer to Him.

TAKING UP THE CROSS

Then He said to them all, "If anyone wants to come with Me, he must deny himself, take up his cross daily, and follow Me."

Luke 9:23 HCSB

When we have been saved by Christ, we can, if we choose, become passive Christians. We can sit back, secure in our own salvation, and let other believers spread the healing message of Jesus. But to do so is wrong. Instead, we are commanded to become disciples of the One who has saved us, and to do otherwise is a sin of omission with terrible consequences. When Jesus addressed His disciples, He warned them that each one must, "take up his cross daily and follow me" (Luke 9:23 NIV). Christ's message was clear: in order to follow Him, Christ's disciples must deny themselves and, instead, trust Him completely. Nothing has changed since then.

Do you seek to fulfill God's purpose for your life? Then follow Christ. Follow Him by picking up His cross today and every day that you live. Then, you will quickly discover that Christ's love has the power to change everything, including you.

I lived with Indians who made pots out of clay which they used for cooking. Nobody was interested in the pot. Everybody was interested in what was inside. The same clay taken out of the same riverbed, always made in the same design, nothing special about it. Well, I'm a clay pot, and let me not forget it. But, the excellency of the power is of God and not us.

Elisabeth Elliot

A TIMELY TIP

Today, think of at least one single step that you can take to become a better disciple for Christ. Then, take that step.

ENCOURAGEMENT NOW!

Bright eyes cheer the heart; good news strengthens the bones.

Proverbs 15:30 HCSB

Barnabas, a man whose name meant "Son of Encouragement," was a leader in the early Christian church. He was known for his kindness and for his ability to encourage others. Because of Barnabas, many people were introduced to Christ. And today, as believers living in a difficult world, we must seek to imitate the "Son of Encouragement."

We imitate Barnabas when we speak kind words to our families and to our friends. We imitate Barnabas when our actions give credence to our beliefs. We imitate Barnabas when we are generous with our possessions and with our praise. We imitate Barnabas when we give hope to the hopeless and encouragement to the downtrodden.

Today, be like Barnabas: become a source of encouragement to those who cross your path. When you do so, you will quite literally change the world, one person—and one moment—at a time.

If I am asked how we are to get rid of discouragements, I can only say, as I have had to say of so many other wrong spiritual habits, we must give them up. It is never worth while to argue against discouragement. There is only one argument that can meet it, and that is the argument of God.

Hannah Whitall Smith

When we bring sunshine into the lives of others, we're warmed by it ourselves. When we spill a little happiness, it splashes on us.

Barbara Johnson

A TIMELY TIP

When you help other people feel better about themselves, you'll feel better about yourself, too. So what are you waiting for?

A PASSION FOR LIFE

But those who trust in the Lord will renew their strength; they will soar on wings like eagles; they will run and not grow weary; they will walk and not faint.

Isaiah 40:31 HCSB

Are you enthusiastic about your life and your faith? Hopefully so. But if your zest for life has waned, it is now time to redirect your efforts and recharge your spiritual batteries. And that means refocusing your priorities (by putting God first) and counting your blessings (instead of your troubles).

Nothing is more important than your wholehearted commitment to your Creator and to His only begotten Son. Your faith must never be an afterthought; it must be your ultimate priority, your ultimate possession, and your ultimate passion. When you become passionate about your faith, you'll become passionate about your life, too. And God will smile.

If your heart has grown cold, it is because you have moved away from the fire of His presence.

Beth Moore

Don't take hold of a thing unless you want that thing to take hold of you.

E. Stanley Jones

A TIMELY TIP

Don't wait for enthusiasm to find you . . . go looking for it. Look at your life and your relationships as exciting adventures. Don't wait for life to spice itself; spice things up yourself.

THE GREATEST OF THESE

Now these three remain: faith, hope, and love. But the greatest of these is love.

1 Corinthians 13:13 HCSB

The beautiful words of 1st Corinthians 13 remind us that love is God's commandment: Faith is important, of course. So, too, is hope. But, love is more important still. We are commanded (not advised, not encouraged . . . commanded!) to love one another just as Christ loved us (John 13:34). That's a tall order, but as Christians, we are obligated to follow it.

Christ showed His love for us on the cross, and we are called upon to return Christ's love by sharing it. Today, let us spread Christ's love to families, friends, and even strangers, so that through us, others might come to know Him.

Prayer is the ultimate love language. It communicates in ways we can't.

Stormie Omartian

Love is the seed of all hope. It is the enticement to trust, to risk, to try, and to go on.

Gloria Gaither

A TIMELY TIP

God is love, and He expects us to share His love.

TODAY'S BIBLE READING
Old Testament: Jeremiah 51
New Testament: Hebrews 10:23-39

GOD, WORSHIP, AND MARRIAGE

We love Him because He first loved us.

1 John 4:19 NKJV

If you're married, you already know that it takes cooperation and commitment to build a life together. But something else is necessary as well: you and your husband should worship together. When the two of you sincerely embrace God's love, you will feel differently about yourself, your marriage, your family, and your world. When you and your husband embrace God's love together, your marriage will be transformed. And, when the two of you accept the Father's grace and share His love, you will be blessed here on earth and throughout eternity.

So, if you genuinely seek to build a marriage that will stand the test of time, make God the centerpiece. When you do, your love will endure for a lifetime and beyond.

Those who abandon ship the first time it enters a storm miss the calm beyond. And the rougher the storms weathered together, the deeper and stronger real love grows.

Ruth Bell Graham

Marriage is God's idea. He "crafted" it. If your marriage is broken, all the "repairmen" or counselors or seminars you take it to will be unable to fix it; take it to Him. The Creator Who made it in the first place can make it work again.

Anne Graham Lotz

A TIMELY TIP

The best marriages are built upon a shared faith in God. If yours is not, then you're building upon a foundation of sand.

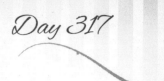

THE BATTLE IS WON

Cast your burden on the Lord, and He will support you; He will never allow the righteous to be shaken.

Psalm 55:22 HCSB

Christians have every reason to live courageously. After all, the ultimate battle has already been won on the cross at Calvary. But even dedicated followers of Christ may find their courage tested by the inevitable disappointments and fears that visit the lives of believers and non-believers alike.

When you find yourself worried about the challenges of today or the uncertainties of tomorrow, you must ask yourself whether or not you are ready to place your concerns and your life in God's all-powerful, all-knowing, all-loving hands. If the answer to that question is yes—as it should be—then you can draw courage today from the source of strength that never fails: your Heavenly Father.

What is courage? It is the ability to be strong in trust, in conviction, in obedience. To be courageous is to step out in faith—to trust and obey, no matter what.

Kay Arthur

A TIMELY TIP

With God as your partner, you have nothing to fear. Why? Because you and God, working together, can handle absolutely anything that comes your way. So the next time you'd like an extra measure of courage, recommit yourself to a true one-on-one relationship with your Creator. When you sincerely turn to Him, He will never fail you.

SOLVING LIFE'S RIDDLES

If you don't know what you're doing, pray to the Father. He loves to help. You'll get his help, and won't be condescended to when you ask for it. Ask boldly, believingly, without a second thought. People who "worry their prayers" are like wind-whipped waves. Don't think you're going to get anything from the Master that way, adrift at sea, keeping all your options open.

James 1:5-8 MSG

L ife presents each of us with countless questions, conundrums, doubts, and problems. Thankfully, the riddles of everyday living are not too difficult to solve if we look for answers in the right places. When we have questions, we should consult God's Word, we should seek the guidance of the Holy Spirit, and we should trust the counsel of God-fearing friends and family members.

Are you facing a difficult decision? Take your concerns to God and avail yourself of the messages and mentors that He has placed along your path. When you do, God will speak to you in His own way and in His own time, and when He does, you can most certainly trust the answers that He gives.

Good and evil both increase at compound interest. That is why the little decisions you and I make every day are of such infinite importance.

C. S. Lewis

Judge everything in the light of Jesus Christ.

Oswald Chambers

A TIMELY TIP

When you're about to make an important decision, take your time and talk to your Creator.

SENSING HIS PRESENCE

Where can I go from your Spirit? Where can I flee from your presence? If I go up to the heavens, you are there; if I make my bed in the depths, you are there. If I rise on the wings of the dawn, if I settle on the far side of the sea, even there your hand will guide me, your right hand will hold me fast.

Psalm 139:7-10 NIV

If God is everywhere, why does He sometimes seem so far away? The answer to that question, of course, has nothing to do with God and everything to do with us.

When we begin each day on our knees, in praise and worship to Him, God often seems very near indeed. But, if we ignore God's presence or—worse yet—rebel against it altogether, the world in which we live becomes a spiritual wasteland.

Today, and every day hereafter, thank God and praise Him. He is the Giver of all things good. Wherever you are, whether you are happy or sad, victorious or vanquished, celebrate God's presence. And be comforted. For He is here.

It is God to whom and with whom we travel, and while He is the End of our journey, He is also at every stopping place.

Elisabeth Elliot

It is God to whom and with whom we travel, while He is the End of our journey, He is also at every stopping place.

Elisabeth Elliot

A TIMELY TIP

God is here, and He wants to establish an intimate relationship with you. When you sincerely reach out to Him, you will sense His presence.

DEFEATING DISCOURAGEMENT

The Lord is the One who will go before you. He will be with you; He will not leave you or forsake you. Do not be afraid or discouraged.

Deuteronomy 31:8 HCSB

When we fail to meet the expectations of others (or, for that matter, the expectations that we have set for ourselves), we may be tempted to abandon hope. Thankfully, on those cloudy days when our strength is sapped and our faith is shaken, there exists a source from which we can draw courage and wisdom. That source is God.

When we seek to form a more intimate and dynamic relationship with our Creator, He renews our spirits and restores our souls. God's promise is made clear in Isaiah 40:31: "But those who wait on the Lord shall renew their strength; they shall mount up with wings like eagles, they shall run and not be weary, they shall walk and not faint" (NKJV). And upon this promise we can—and should—depend.

If I am asked how we are to get rid of discouragements, I can only say, as I have had to say of so many other wrong spiritual habits, we must give them up. It is never worth while to argue against discouragement. There is only one argument that can meet it, and that is the argument of God.

Hannah Whitall Smith

A TIMELY TIP

When things go wrong, it's easy to become discouraged. But those who follow Jesus need never be discouraged because God's promises are true . . . and heaven is eternal.

DECISION-MAKING 101

An indecisive man is unstable in all his ways.

James 1:8 HCSB

From the instant you wake in the morning until the moment you nod off to sleep at night, you have the opportunity to make countless decisions: decisions about the things you do, decisions about the words you speak, and decisions about the thoughts you choose to think.

If you're facing one of life's major decisions, here are some things you can do: 1. Gather as much information as you can. 2. Don't be too impulsive. 3. Rely on the advice of trusted friends and mentors. 4. Pray for guidance. 5. Trust the quiet inner voice of your conscience 6. When the time for action arrives, act. Procrastination is the enemy of progress; don't let it defeat you.

People who can never quite seem to make up their minds usually make themselves miserable. So when in doubt, be decisive. It's the decent way to live.

When we learn to listen to Christ's voice for the details of our daily decisions, we begin to know Him personally.

Catherine Marshall

God always gives His best to those who leave the choice with Him.

Jim Elliot

A TIMELY TIP

Slow down! If you're about to make an important decision, don't be impulsive. Remember: big decisions have big consequences, and if you don't think about those consequences now, you may pay a big price later.

DILIGENCE NOW

Do not lack diligence; be fervent in spirit; serve the Lord.

Romans 12:11 HCSB

God's Word reminds us again and again that our Creator expects us to lead disciplined lives. God doesn't reward laziness, misbehavior, or apathy. To the contrary, He expects believers to behave with dignity and discipline.

We live in a world in which leisure is glorified and indifference is often glamorized. But God has other plans. He did not create us for lives of mediocrity; He created us for far greater things. Life's greatest rewards seldom fall into our laps; to the contrary, our greatest accomplishments usually require lots of work, which is perfectly fine with God. After all, He knows that we're up to the task, and He has big plans for us; may we, as disciplined believers, always be worthy of those plans.

True will power and courage are not only on the battlefield, but also in everyday conquests over our inertia, laziness, and boredom.

D. L. Moody

God cannot build character without our cooperation. If we resist Him, then He chastens us into submission. But, if we submit to Him, then He can accomplish His work. He is not satisfied with a halfway job. God wants a perfect work; He wants a finished product that is mature and complete.

Warren Wiersbe

A TIMELY TIP

If you're a disciplined person, you'll earn big rewards. If you're undisciplined, you won't.

LOOKING BEFORE YOU LEAP

An impulsive vow is a trap; later you'll wish you could get out of it.

Proverbs 20:25 MSG

A re you, at times, just a little bit impulsive? Are you a woman who sometimes looks before she leaps? If so, God wants to have a little chat with you.

God's Word is clear: as believers, we are called to lead lives of discipline, diligence, moderation, and maturity. But the world often tempts us to behave otherwise. Everywhere we turn, or so it seems, we are faced with powerful temptations to behave in undisciplined, ungodly ways. Yet God's Word instructs us to be disciplined in our thoughts and our actions; God's Word warns us against the dangers of impulsive behavior. As believers in a just God, we should act and react accordingly.

When you and I are related to Jesus Christ, our strength and wisdom and peace and joy and love and hope may run out, but His life rushes in to keep us filled to the brim. We are showered with blessings, not because of anything we have or have not done, but simply because of Him.

Anne Graham Lotz

Sometimes, being wise is nothing more than slowing down long enough to think about things before you do them.

Criswell Freeman

A TIMELY TIP

If you can't seem to put the brakes on impulsive behavior . . . you're not praying hard enough.

THE BREAD OF LIFE

I am the bread of life, Jesus told them. "No one who comes to Me will ever be hungry, and no one who believes in Me will ever be thirsty again."

John 6:35 HCSB

He was the Son of God, but He wore a crown of thorns. He was the Savior of mankind, yet He was put to death on a roughhewn cross made of wood. He offered His healing touch to an unsaved world, and yet the same hands that had healed the sick and raised the dead were pierced with nails.

Jesus Christ, the Son of God, was born into humble circumstances. He walked this earth, not as a ruler of men, but as the Savior of mankind. His crucifixion, a torturous punishment that was intended to end His life and His reign, instead became the pivotal event in the history of all humanity.

Jesus is the bread of life. Accept His grace. Share His love. And follow in His footsteps.

In your greatest weakness, turn to your greatest strength, Jesus, and hear Him say, "My grace is sufficient for you, for My strength is made perfect in weakness" (2 Corinthians 12:9, NKJV).

Lisa Whelchel

The crucial question for each of us is this: What do you think of Jesus, and do you yet have a personal acquaintance with Him?

Hannah Whitall Smith

A TIMELY TIP

Today, think about your relationship with Jesus: what it is, what it should be, and what it will be today, tomorrow, and throughout all eternity.

A PROFOUND LOVE

Pursue love and desire spiritual gifts.

1 Corinthians 14:1 HCSB

As a woman, you know the profound love that you hold in your heart for your own family and friends. As a child of God, you can only imagine the infinite love that your Heavenly Father holds for you. God made you in His own image and gave you salvation through the person of His Son Jesus Christ. And now, precisely because you are a wondrous creation treasured by God, a question presents itself: What will you do in response to the Creator's love? Will you ignore it or embrace it?

When you embrace God's love, your life's purpose is forever changed. When you embrace God's love, you feel differently about yourself, your neighbors, your family, and your world. More importantly, you share God's message—and His love—with others. Your Heavenly Father—a God of infinite love and mercy—is waiting to embrace you with open arms. Accept His love today and forever.

Only a love that has no regard for vessels and jars—appearances or image—only a love that will lavish its most treasured essence on the feet of Jesus can produce the kind of fragrance that draws cynics and believers alike into His presence.

Gloria Gaither

A TIMELY TIP

Today, think about someone you know who, for whatever reason, is difficult to love. Then, think of a good way to express your love for that person, even if you'd rather express some other, less favorable, emotion.

MENTORS THAT MATTER

The lips of the righteous feed many.

Proverbs 10:21 HCSB

Here's a simple yet effective way to strengthen your faith: Choose role models whose faith in God is strong.

When you emulate godly people, you become a more godly person yourself. That's why you should seek out mentors who, by their words and their presence, make you a better person and a better Christian.

Today, as a gift to yourself, select, from your friends and family members, a mentor whose judgement you trust. Then listen carefully to your mentor's advice and be willing to accept that advice, even if accepting it requires effort, or pain, or both. Consider your mentor to be God's gift to you. Thank God for that gift, and use it for the glory of His kingdom.

It takes a wise person to give good advice, but an even wiser person to take it.

Marie T. Freeman

God often keeps us on the path by guiding us through the counsel of friends and trusted spiritual advisors.

Bill Hybels

A TIMELY TIP

When it comes to mentors, you need them. When it comes to mentoring, they need you.

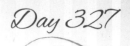

A PASSIONATE LIFE

Never be lazy in your work, but serve the Lord enthusiastically.

Romans 12:11 NLT

Are you passionate about your life, your loved ones, your work, and your faith? As a believer who has been saved by a risen Christ, you should be.

As a thoughtful Christian, you have every reason to be enthusiastic about life, but sometimes the inevitable struggles of life may cause you to feel decidedly unenthusiastic. If you feel that your enthusiasm is slowly fading away, it's time to slow down, to rest, to count your blessings, and to pray. When you feel worried or weary, you must pray fervently for God to renew your sense of wonderment and excitement. Life with God can be—and should be—a glorious adventure. Revel in it. When you do, God will most certainly smile upon your work and your life.

How much of our lives are, well, so daily. How often our hours are filled with the mundane, seemingly unimportant things that have to be done, whether at home or work. These very "daily" tasks could become a celebration of praise. "It is through consecration," someone has said, "that drudgery is made divine."

Gigi Graham Tchividjian

If your heart has grown cold, it is because you have moved away from the fire of His presence.

Beth Moore

A TIMELY TIP

Involve yourself in activities that you can support wholeheartedly and enthusiastically. It's easier to celebrate life when you're passionately involved in life.

YOUR REAL RICHES

Naked I came from my mother's womb, and naked I will leave this life. The Lord gives, and the Lord takes away. Praise the name of the Lord.

Job 1:21 HCSB

Martin Luther observed, "Many things I have tried to grasp and have lost. That which I have placed in God's hands I still have." How true. Earthly riches are transitory; spiritual riches are not.

In our demanding world, financial security can be a good thing, but spiritual prosperity is profoundly more important. Certainly we all need the basic necessities of life, but once we've acquired those necessities, enough is enough. Why? Because our real riches are not of this world. We are never really rich until we are rich in spirit.

I have held many things in my hands, and I have lost them all; but whatever I have placed in God's hands, that I still possess.

Corrie ten Boom

It's sobering to contemplate how much time, effort, sacrifice, compromise, and attention we give to acquiring and increasing our supply of something that is totally insignificant in eternity.

Anne Graham Lotz

A TIMELY TIP

The world says, "Buy more stuff." God says, "Stuff isn't important." Believe God.

REAL REPENTANCE

I preached to those in Damascus first, and to those in Jerusalem and in all the region of Judea, and to the Gentiles, that they should repent and turn to God, and do works worthy of repentance.

Acts 26:20 HCSB

Who among us has sinned? All of us. But the good news is this: When we do ask God's forgiveness and turn our hearts to Him, He forgives us absolutely and completely.

Genuine repentance requires more than simply offering God apologies for our misdeeds. Real repentance may start with feelings of sorrow and remorse, but it ends only when we turn away from the sin that has heretofore distanced us from our Creator. In truth, we offer our most meaningful apologies to God, not with our words, but with our actions. As long as we are still engaged in sin, we may be "repenting," but we have not fully "repented." So, if there is an aspect of your life that is distancing you from your God, ask for His forgiveness, and—just as importantly— stop sinning. Now.

If we do not deal with sin, our spiritual lives become stagnant and we lose our attractiveness and usefulness to God.

Anne Graham Lotz

When true repentance comes, God will not hesitate for a moment to forgive, cast the sins in the sea of forgetfulness, and put the child on the road to restoration.

Beth Moore

A TIMELY TIP

If you're engaged in behavior that is displeasing to God, repent today— tomorrow may be too late.

A WISE MOVE

Now if any of you lacks wisdom, he should ask God, who gives to all generously and without criticizing, and it will be given to him.

James 1:5 HCSB

D o you seek wisdom for yourself and for your family? Of course you do. But, as a thoughtful woman living in a society that is filled with temptations and distractions, you know that it's all too easy for parents and children alike to stray far from the source of the ultimate wisdom: God's Holy Word.

When you commit yourself to daily study of God's Word—and when you live according to His commandments—you will become wise . . . in time. So, as a way of understanding God's plan for your life, study His Word and live by it. When you do, you will accumulate a storehouse of wisdom that will enrich your own life and the lives of your family members, your friends, and the world.

Knowledge can be found in books or in school. Wisdom, on the other hand, starts with God . . . and ends there.

Marie T. Freeman

He teaches us, not just to let us see ourselves correctly, but to help us see Him correctly.

Kathy Troccoli

A TIMELY TIP

Jesus made radical sacrifices for you, and now He's asking you to make radical changes for Him. Are you willing to be a radical Christian? If so, you will be blessed for your willingness to serve God and to walk faithfully and closely in the footsteps of His only begotten Son.

MAKING PEACE WITH YOUR PAST

Forget about what's happened; don't keep going over old history. Be alert, be present. I'm about to do something brand-new. It's bursting out! Don't you see it? There it is! I'm making a road through the desert, rivers in the badlands.

Isaiah 43:18–19 MSG

Have you made peace with your past? If so, congratulations. But, if you are mired in the quicksand of regret, it's time to plan your escape. How can you do so? By accepting what has been and by trusting God for what will be.

Because you are human, you may be slow to forget yesterday's disappointments. But, if you sincerely seek to focus your hopes and energies on the future, then you must find ways to accept the past, no matter how difficult it may be to do so. So, if you have not yet made peace with the past, today is the day to declare an end to all hostilities. When you do, you can then turn your thoughts to wondrous promises of God and to the glorious future that He has in store for you.

We can't just put our pasts behind us. We've got to put our pasts in front of God.

Beth Moore

You cannot change the past, but you can control your own attitude.

Barbara Johnson

A TIMELY TIP

The past is past, so don't invest all your energy there. If you're focused on the past, change your focus. If you're living in the past, it's time to stop living there.

THE CORNERSTONE

Let us fix our eyes on Jesus, the author and perfecter of our faith, who for the joy set before him endured the cross, scorning its shame, and sat down at the right hand of the throne of God.

Hebrews 12:2 NIV

I s Christ the focus of your life? Are you fired with enthusiasm for Him? Are you an energized Christian who allows God's Son to reign over every aspect of your day? Make no mistake: that's exactly what God intends for you to do.

God has given you the gift of eternal life through His Son. In response to God's priceless gift, you are instructed to focus your thoughts, your prayers, and your energies upon God and His only begotten Son. To do so, you must resist the subtle yet powerful temptation to become a "spiritual dabbler." A person who dabbles in the Christian faith is unwilling to place God above all other things. Resist that temptation; make God the cornerstone and the touchstone of your life. When you do, He will give you all the strength and wisdom you need to live victoriously for Him.

When Jesus is in our midst, He brings His limitless power along as well. But, Jesus must be in the middle, all eyes and hearts focused on Him.

Shirley Dobson

Give me the person who says, "This one thing I do, and not these fifty things I dabble in."

D. L. Moody

A TIMELY TIP

Whether you are talking to someone or working at your job, focus your attention on the task at hand. There is an important difference between "investing yourself" and "going through the motions."

IN A HURRY?

The Lord is good to those who wait for Him, to the soul who seeks Him. It is good that one should hope and wait quietly for the salvation of the Lord.

Lamentations 3:25-26 NKJV

A re you a woman in a hurry? If so, you may be in for a few disappointments. Why? Because life has a way of unfolding according to God's timetable, not yours. That's why life requires patience . . . and lots of it!

Lamentations 3:25-26 reminds us that, "The Lord is wonderfully good to those who wait for him and seek him. So it is good to wait quietly for salvation from the Lord" (NIV). But, for most of us, waiting quietly for God is difficult because we're in such a hurry for things to happen!

The next time you find your patience tested to the limit, slow down and trust God. Sometimes, we must wait patiently for Him, and that's as it should be. After all, think how patient God has been with us.

Let me encourage you to continue to wait with faith. God may not perform a miracle, but He is trustworthy to touch you and make you whole where there used to be a hole.

Lisa Whelchel

When life is difficult, God wants us to have a faith that trusts and waits.

Kay Arthur

A TIMELY TIP

With patience and faith, you can endure almost any hardship and overcome almost any setback. So be patient with yourself, with your situation, and with your Creator.

KEEPING POSSESSIONS IN PERSPECTIVE

And He told them, "Watch out and be on guard against all greed, because one's life is not in the abundance of his possessions."

Luke 12:15 HCSB

All too often, we focus our thoughts and energies on the accumulation of earthly treasures, leaving precious little time to accumulate the only treasures that really matter: the spiritual kind. Our material possessions have the potential to do great good or terrible harm, depending upon how we choose to use them. As believers, our instructions are clear: we must use our possessions in accordance with God's commandments, and we must be faithful stewards of the gifts He has seen fit to bestow upon us.

Today, let us honor God by placing no other gods before Him. God comes first; everything else comes next—and "everything else" most certainly includes all of our earthly possessions.

When we put people before possessions in our hearts, we are sowing seeds of enduring satisfaction.

Beverly LaHaye

Our ultimate aim in life is not to be healthy, wealthy, prosperous, or problem free. Our ultimate aim in life is to bring glory to God.

Anne Graham Lotz

A TIMELY TIP

Everything we have is on loan from God. Holocaust survivor Corrie ten Boom writes, "I have held many things in my hands, and I have lost them all; but whatever I have placed in God's hands, that I still possess." Remember: your real riches are in heaven, so conduct yourself accordingly.

Day 335

SPIRITUAL RENEWAL

Therefore if anyone is in Christ, he is a new creature; the old things passed away; behold, new things have come.

2 Corinthians 5:17 HCSB

Even the most inspired Christian women can, from time to time, find themselves running on empty. The demands of daily life can drain us of our strength and rob us of the joy that is rightfully ours in Christ.

Are you tired or troubled? Turn your heart toward God in prayer. Are you weak or worried? Take the time—or, more accurately, make the time—to delve deeply into God's Holy Word. Are you spiritually depleted? Call upon fellow believers to support you, and call upon Christ to renew your spirit and your life. When you do, you'll discover that the Creator of the universe stands always ready and always able to create a new sense of wonderment and joy in you.

He is the God of wholeness and restoration.

Stormie Omartian

It is important that we take time out for ourselves—for relaxation, for refreshment.

Ruth Bell Graham

A TIMELY TIP

God wants to give you peace, and He wants to renew your spirit. It's up to you to slow down and give Him a chance to do so.

HIS TRANSFORMING POWER

Your old sinful self has died, and your new life is kept with Christ in God.

Colossians 3:3 NCV

God's hand has the power to transform your day and your life. Your task is to accept Christ's grace with a humble, thankful heart as you receive the "new life" that can be yours through Him. Righteous believers who fashion their days around Jesus see the world differently; they act differently, and they feel differently about themselves and their neighbors. Hopefully, you, too, will be such a believer.

Do you desire to improve some aspect of your life? If so, don't expect changing circumstances to miraculously transform you into the person you want to become. Transformation starts with God, and it starts in the quiet corners of a willing human heart—like yours.

God's work is not in buildings, but in transformed lives.

Ruth Bell Graham

In the midst of the pressure and the heat, I am confident His hand is on my life, developing my faith until I display His glory, transforming me into a vessel of honor that pleases Him!

Anne Graham Lotz

A TIMELY TIP

Jesus made radical sacrifices for you, and now He's asking you to make radical changes for Him. Are you willing to be a radical Christian? If so, you will be blessed for your willingness to serve God and to walk faithfully and closely in the footsteps of His only begotten Son.

SHARING WORDS OF HOPE

And let us be concerned about one another in order to promote love and good works.

Hebrews 10:24 HCSB

Hope, like other human emotions, is contagious. When we associate with hope-filled Christians, we are encouraged by their faith and optimism. But, if we spend too much time in the company of naysayers and pessimists, our attitudes, like theirs, tend to be cynical and negative.

Are you a hopeful, optimistic, encouraging believer? And do you associate with like-minded people? Hopefully so. As a faithful follower of the One from Galilee, you have every reason to be hopeful, and you have every reason to share your hopes with others. So today, look for reasons to celebrate God's endless blessings. And while you're at it, look for people who will join you in the celebration. You'll be better for their company, and they'll be better for yours.

The glory of friendship is not the outstretched hand, or the kindly smile, or the joy of companionship. It is the spiritual inspiration that comes to one when he discovers that someone else believes in him and is willing to trust him with his friendship.

Corrie ten Boom

A TIMELY TIP

Today, challenge your faith by finding at least three people who need your encouragement, and then give them as much encouragement as you can. Be generous with your words, with pats on the back, and with your prayers. And remember: encouragement is contagious. You can't lift other people up without lifting yourself up, too.

FACING LIFE'S TRIALS

So because of Christ, I am pleased in weaknesses, in insults, in catastrophes, in persecutions, and in pressures. For when I am weak, then I am strong.

2 Corinthians 12:10 HCSB

Life is a tapestry of good days and difficult days, with good days predominating. During the good days, we are tempted to take our blessings for granted (a temptation that we must resist with all our might). But, during life's difficult days, we discover precisely what we're made of. And more importantly, we discover what our faith is made of.

Has your faith been put to the test yet? If so, then you know that with God's help, you can endure life's darker days. But if you have not yet faced the inevitable trials and tragedies of life-here-on-earth, don't worry: you will. And when your faith is put to the test, rest assured that God is perfectly willing—and always ready—to give you strength for the struggle.

God knows exactly how much you can take, and He will never permit you to reach a breaking point.

Barbara Johnson

God is the only one who can make the valley of trouble a door of hope.

Catherine Marshall

A TIMELY TIP

If you're going through difficult times, consider it an opportunity for spiritual growth. Elisabeth Elliot correctly observes, "God's curriculum will always include lessons we wish we could skip. With an intimate understanding of our deepest needs and individual capacities, He chooses our curriculum." So ask yourself this question: "What is God trying to teach me today?"

PRACTICAL CHRISTIANITY

Therefore, get your minds ready for action, being self-disciplined, and set your hope completely on the grace to be brought to you at the revelation of Jesus Christ.

1 Peter 1:13 HCSB

As Christians, we must do our best to ensure that our actions are accurate reflections of our beliefs. Our theology must be demonstrated, not only by our words but, more importantly, by our actions. In short, we should be practical believers, quick to act whenever we see an opportunity to serve God.

Are you the kind of practical Christian woman who is willing to dig in and do what needs to be done when it needs to be done? If so, congratulations: God acknowledges your service and blesses it. But if you find yourself more interested in the fine points of theology than in the needs of your neighbors, it's time to rearrange your priorities. God needs believers who are willing to roll up their sleeves and go to work for Him. Count yourself among that number. Theology is a good thing unless it interferes with God's work. And it's up to you to make certain that your theology doesn't.

Every time you refuse to face up to life and its problems, you weaken your character.

E. Stanley Jones

A TIMELY TIP

Pick out one important obligation that you've been putting off. Then, take at least one specific step toward the completion of the task you've been avoiding. Even if you don't finish the job, you'll discover that it's easier to finish a job that you've already begun than to finish a job that you've never started.

BEYOND BITTERNESS

Don't insist on getting even; that's not for you to do. "I'll do the judging," says God. "I'll take care of it."

Romans 12:19 MSG

Bitterness is a spiritual sickness. It will consume your soul; it is dangerous to your emotional health. It can destroy you if you let it . . . so don't let it! If you are caught up in intense feelings of anger or resentment, you know all too well the destructive power of these emotions. How can you rid yourself of these feelings? First, you must prayerfully ask God to cleanse your heart. Then, you must learn to catch yourself whenever thoughts of bitterness or hatred begin to attack you. Your challenge is this: You must learn to resist negative thoughts before they hijack your emotions.

Matthew 5:22 teaches us that if we judge our brothers and sisters, we, too, will be subject to judgement. Let us refrain, then, from judging our neighbors. Instead, let us forgive them and love them, while leaving their judgement to a far more capable authority: the One who sits on His throne in heaven.

Bitterness is a spiritual cancer, a rapidly growing malignancy that can consume your life. Bitterness cannot be ignored but must be healed at the very core, and only Christ can heal bitterness.

Beth Moore

A TIMELY TIP

Blaming others is easy . . . but it's usually wrong. Fixing mistakes is harder . . . but it's usually right.

MID-COURSE CORRECTIONS

The sensible see danger and take cover; the foolish keep going and are punished.

Proverbs 27:12 HCSB

In our fast-paced world, everyday life has become an exercise in managing change. Our circumstances change; our relationships change; our bodies change. We grow older every day, as does our world. Thankfully, God does not change. He is eternal, as are the truths that are found in His Holy Word.

Are you facing one of life's inevitable "mid-course corrections"? If so, you must place your faith, your trust, and your life in the hands of the One who does not change: your Heavenly Father. He is the unmoving rock upon which you must construct this day and every day. When you do, you are secure.

Mistakes offer the possibility for redemption and a new start in God's kingdom. No matter what you're guilty of, God can restore your innocence.

Barbara Johnson

You will never change your life until you change something you do daily.

John Maxwell

A TIMELY TIP

As you face uncertain times, make sure to build your future on a firm foundation: the unshakable foundation of God's eternal promises.

OUR CHILDREN, OUR HOPE

Let the little children come to Me; don't stop them, for the kingdom of God belongs to such as these.

Mark 10:14 HCSB

Every child is different, but every child is similar in this respect: he or she is a priceless gift from the Father above. And, with the Father's gift comes immense responsibilities.

Our children are our most precious resource. And, as responsible adults, we must create homes in which the future generation can grow and flourish.

Today, let us pray for our children . . . all of them. Let us pray for children here at home and for children around the world. Every child is God's child. May we, as concerned adults, behave—and pray—accordingly.

Children must be valued as our most priceless possession.

James Dobson

Our primary responsibility is to be sure our children grow up in homes where God is honored and the love of Christ reigns.

Billy Graham

A TIMELY TIP

Our children are not really our possessions; our youngsters are, in truth, God's children. They belong to Him, and He entrusts them to our care for a little while. And then, we must let them go.

LIVING IN CHRIST'S LOVE

So now, little children, remain in Him, so that when He appears we may have boldness and not be ashamed before Him at His coming.

1 John 2:28-29 HCSB

E ven though we are imperfect, fallible human beings, even though we have fallen far short of God's commandments, Christ loves us still. His love is perfect and steadfast; it does not waver—it does not change. Our task, as believers, is to accept Christ's love and to encourage others to do likewise.

In today's troubled world, we all need the love and the peace that is found through the Son of God. Thankfully, Christ's love has no limits; it can encircle all of us. And it's up to each of us to ensure that it does.

It has been the faith of the Son of God who loves me and gave Himself for me that has held me in the darkest valley and the hottest fires and the deepest waters.

Elisabeth Elliot

Christ is like a river that is continually flowing. There are always fresh supplies of water coming from the fountain-head, so that a man may live by it and be supplied with water all his life. So Christ is an ever-flowing fountain; he is continually supplying his people, and the fountain is not spent. They who live upon Christ may have fresh supplies from him for all eternity; they may have an increase of blessedness that is new, and new still, and which never will come to an end.

Jonathan Edwards

A TIMELY TIP

Today and every day, give thanks for Christ's sacrifice . . . it is the ultimate expression of His love for you.

TODAY'S BIBLE READING
Old Testament: Daniel 11-12
New Testament: Revelation 2

HIS POWER AND YOURS

When we were baptized, we were buried with Christ and shared his death. So, just as Christ was raised from the dead by the wonderful power of the Father, we also can live a new life.

Romans 6:4 NCV

When you invite Christ to rule over your heart, you avail yourself of His power. And make no mistake about it: You and Christ, working together, can do miraculous things. In fact, miraculous things are exactly what Christ intends for you to do, but He won't force you to do great things on His behalf. The decision to become a full-fledged participant in His power is a decision that you must make for yourself.

In John 14:12, Christ make this promise: "I tell you the truth, whoever believes in me will do the same things that I do" (NCV). So trust the Savior's promise, and expect a miracle in His name.

The amount of power you experience to live a victorious, triumphant Christian life is directly proportional to the freedom you give the Spirit to be Lord of your life!

Anne Graham Lotz

I now know the power of the risen Lord! He lives! The dawn of Easter has broken in my own soul! My night is gone!

Mrs. Charles E. Cowman

A TIMELY TIP

When you form a genuine partnership with God, you can do amazing things. So make God your partner in every aspect of your life.

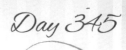

FINDING CONTENTMENT

I am able to do all things through Him who strengthens me.

Philippians 4:13 HCSB

Where can we find contentment? Is it a result of wealth, or power, or beauty, or fame? Hardly. Genuine contentment is a gift from God to those who trust Him and follow His commandments.

Our modern world seems preoccupied with the search for happiness. We are bombarded with messages telling us that happiness depends upon the acquisition of material possessions. These messages are false. Enduring peace is not the result of our acquisitions; it is a spiritual gift from God to those who obey Him and accept His will.

If we don't find contentment in God, we will never find it anywhere else. But, if we seek Him and obey Him, we will be blessed with an inner peace that is beyond human understanding. When God dwells at the center of our lives, peace and contentment will belong to us just as surely as we belong to God.

We will never be happy until we make God the source of our fulfillment and the answer to our longings.

Stormie Omartian

If we know we have pleased God, contentment will be our consolation, for what pleases God will please us.

Kay Arthur

A TIMELY TIP

God offers you His peace, His protection, and His promises. If you accept these gifts, you will be content.

BEYOND ANXIETY

In the multitude of my anxieties within me, Your comforts delight my soul.

Psalm 94:19 NKJV

God calls us to live above and beyond anxiety. God calls us to live by faith, not by fear. He instructs us to trust Him completely, this day and forever. But sometimes, trusting God is difficult, especially when we become caught up in the incessant demands of an anxious world.

When you feel anxious—and you will—return your thoughts to God's love. Then, take your concerns to Him in prayer, and to the best of your ability, leave them there. Whatever "it" is, God is big enough to handle it. Let Him. Now.

The moment anxious thoughts invade your mind, go to the Lord in prayer. Look first to God. Then, you will see the cause of your anxiety in a whole new light.

Kay Arthur

Worry is a cycle of inefficient thoughts whirling around a center of fear.

Corrie ten Boom

A TIMELY TIP

Remembering God's faithfulness in the past can give you peace for today and hope for tomorrow.

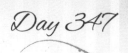

KEEPING UP APPEARANCES

We justify our actions by appearances; God examines our motives.

Proverbs 21:2 MSG

The world sees you as you appear to be; God sees you as you really are . . . He sees your heart, and He understands your intentions. The opinions of others should be relatively unimportant to you; however, God's view of you—His understanding of your actions, your thoughts, and your motivations—should be vitally important.

Few things in life are more futile than "keeping up appearances" for the sake of neighbors. What is important, of course, is pleasing your Father in heaven. You please Him when your intentions are pure and your actions are just.

Outside appearances, things like the clothes you wear or the car you drive, are important to other people but totally unimportant to God. Trust God.

Marie T. Freeman

If the narrative of the Scriptures teaches us anything, from the serpent in the Garden to the carpenter in Nazareth, it teaches us that things are rarely what they seem, that we shouldn't be fooled by appearances.

John Eldredge

A TIMELY TIP

Don't be too worried about what you look like on the outside. Be more concerned about the kind of person you are on the inside. God loves you just like you are . . . and now, it's your turn to do the same thing.

THE DIRECTION OF YOUR THOUGHTS

My cup runs over. Surely goodness and mercy shall follow me all the days of my life; and I will dwell in the house of the Lord Forever.

Psalm 23:5-6 NKJV

God has given you free will, including the ability to influence the direction and the tone of your thoughts. And, here's how God wants you to direct those thoughts: "Finally brothers, whatever is true, whatever is honorable, whatever is just, whatever is pure, whatever is lovely, whatever is commendable—if there is any moral excellence and if there is any praise—dwell on these things" (Philippians 4:8 HCSB).

The quality of your attitude will help determine the quality of your life, so you must guard your thoughts accordingly. If you make up your mind to approach life with a healthy mixture of realism and optimism, you'll be rewarded. But, if you allow yourself to fall into the unfortunate habit of negative thinking, you will doom yourself to unhappiness, or mediocrity, or worse. So, the next time you find yourself dwelling upon the negative aspects of your life, refocus your attention on things positive. That's the wise way to direct your thoughts.

Attitude is all-important. Let the soul take a quiet attitude of faith and love toward God, and from there on, the responsibility is God's. He will make good on His commitments.

A. W. Tozer

A TIMELY TIP

If you're a Christian, you have every reason on earth—and in heaven—to have a positive attitude.

COURAGE DURING TIMES OF CHANGE

Therefore don't worry about tomorrow, because tomorrow will worry about itself. Each day has enough trouble of its own.

Matthew 6:34 HCSB

Are you anxious about situations that you cannot control? Take your anxieties to God. Are you troubled about changes that threaten to disrupt your life? Take your troubles to Him. Does your corner of the world seem to be trembling beneath your feet? Seek protection from the One who cannot be moved.

The same God who created the universe will protect you if you ask Him . . . so ask Him . . . and then serve Him with willing hands and a trusting heart. And rest assured that the world may change moment by moment, but God's love endures—unfathomable and unchanging—forever.

Live for today, but hold your hands open to tomorrow. Anticipate the future and its changes with joy. There is a seed of God's love in every event, every circumstance, every unpleasant situation in which you may find yourself.

Barbara Johnson

A TIMELY TIP

When it comes to making big changes or big purchases, proceed slowly. Otherwise, you may find yourself uncomfortably perched atop a merry-go-round that is much easier to start than it is to stop.

CHOOSING WISELY

But the wisdom that is from above is first pure, then peaceable, gentle, willing to yield, full of mercy and good fruits, without partiality and without hypocrisy.

James 3:17 NKJV

Because we are creatures of free will, we make choices—lots of them. When we make choices that are pleasing to our Heavenly Father, we are blessed. When we make choices that cause us to walk in the footsteps of God's Son, we enjoy the abundance that Christ has promised to those who follow Him. But when make choices that are displeasing to God, we sow seeds that have the potential to bring forth a bitter harvest.

Today, as you encounter the challenges of everyday living, you will make hundreds of choices. Choose wisely. Make your thoughts and your actions pleasing to God. And remember: every choice that is displeasing to Him is the wrong choice—no exceptions.

Faith is not a feeling; it is action. It is a willed choice.

Elisabeth Elliot

Every time you make a choice, you are turning the central part of you, the part that chooses, into something a little different from what it was before.

C. S. Lewis

A TIMELY TIP

Little decisions, when taken together over a long period of time, can have big consequences. So remember that when it comes to matters of health, fitness, stress, and spirituality, there are no small decisions.

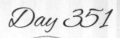
Day 351

HIS INFINITE LOVE

For I am persuaded that neither death nor life, nor angels nor rulers, nor things present, nor things to come, nor powers, nor height, nor depth, nor any other created thing will have the power to separate us from the love of God that is in Christ Jesus our Lord!

Romans 8:38-39 HCSB

Christ's love for you is personal. He loves you so much that He gave His life in order that you might spend all eternity with Him. Christ loves you individually and intimately; His is a love unbounded by time or circumstance. Are you willing to experience an intimate relationship with Him? Your Savior is waiting patiently; don't make Him wait a single minute longer. Embrace His love today.

I am Thine, O Lord; / I have heard Thy voice, / And it told Thy love to me. / But I long to rise in the arms of faith / And be closer drawn to Thee.

Fanny Crosby

Christ is with us . . . and the warmth is contagious.

Joni Eareckson Tada

A TIMELY TIP

Jesus is the light of the world. Make sure that you capturing and reflecting His light.

A TIME TO REST

Come to Me, all you who labor and are heavy laden, and I will give you rest. Take My yoke upon you and learn from Me, for I am gentle and lowly in heart, and you will find rest for your souls. For My yoke is easy and My burden is light.

Matthew 11:28-30 NKJV

Sometimes, the struggles of life can drain us of our strength. When we find ourselves tired, discouraged, or worse, there is a source from which we can draw the power needed to recharge our spiritual batteries. That source, of course, is God.

God expects us to work hard, but He also intends for us to rest. When we fail to take the rest that we need, we do a disservice to ourselves and to our families.

Is your spiritual battery running low? Is your energy on the wane? Are your emotions frayed? If so, it's time to turn your thoughts and your prayers to God. And when you're finished, it's time to rest.

Life is strenuous. See that your clock does not run down.

Mrs. Charles E. Cowman

Oh, the tranquil joy of that dear retreat, / Where the Savior bids thee rest, / With steadfast hope, and a trusting faith, / In His love secure and blest.

Fanny Crosby

A TIMELY TIP

God wants you to get enough rest. The world wants you to burn the candle at both ends. Trust God.

JOY AND THE CHRISTIAN LIFE

Light shines on those who do right; joy belongs to those who are honest. Rejoice in the Lord, you who do right. Praise his holy name.

Psalm 97:11-12 NCV

God's Word makes it clear: He intends that His joy should become our joy. The Lord intends that believers should share His love with His joy in their hearts. Yet sometimes, amid the inevitable hustle and bustle of life-here-on-earth, we can forfeit—albeit temporarily—God's joy as we wrestle with the challenges of daily living.

Joni Eareckson Tada spoke for Christian women of every generation when she observed, "I wanted the deepest part of me to vibrate with that ancient yet familiar longing, that desire for something that would fill and overflow my soul."

If, today, your heart is heavy, open the door of your soul to Christ. He will give you peace and joy. And if you already have the joy of Christ in your heart, share it freely, just as Christ freely shared His joy with you.

As I contemplate all the sacrifices required in order to live a life that is totally focused on Jesus Christ and His eternal kingdom, the joy seeps out of my heart onto my face in a smile of deep satisfaction.

Anne Graham Lotz

God gives to us a heavenly gift called joy, radically different in quality from any natural joy.

Elisabeth Elliot

A TIMELY TIP

Joy does not depend upon your circumstances; it depends upon your thoughts and upon your relationship with God.

THE WORLD . . . AND YOU

Don't copy the behavior and customs of this world, but let God transform you into a new person by changing the way you think.

Romans 12:2 NLT

We live in the world, but we must not worship it. Our duty is to place God first and everything else second. But because we are fallible beings with imperfect faith, placing God in His rightful place is often difficult. In fact, at every turn, or so it seems, we are tempted to do otherwise.

The 21st-century world is a noisy, distracting place filled with countless opportunities to stray from God's will. The world seems to cry, "Worship me with your time, your money, your energy, and your thoughts!" But God commands otherwise: He commands us to worship Him and Him alone; everything else must be secondary.

As we have by faith said no to sin, so we should by faith say yes to God and set our minds on things above, where Christ is seated in the heavenlies.

Vonette Bright

The more we stuff ourselves with material pleasures, the less we seem to appreciate life.

Barbara Johnson

A TIMELY TIP

The world's power to distract, detour, and destroy is formidable. Thankfully, God's power is even greater.

THE TREASURE HUNT

For where your treasure is, there your heart will be also.

Luke 12:34 NKJV

All of humanity is engaged in a colossal, worldwide treasure hunt. Some people seek treasure from earthly sources, treasures such as material wealth or public acclaim; others seek God's treasures by making Him the cornerstone of their lives.

What kind of treasure hunter are you? Are you so caught up in the demands of everyday living that you sometimes allow the search for worldly treasures to become your primary focus? If so, it's time to think long and hard about what you value, and why. All the items on your daily to-do list are not created equal. That's why you must put first things first by placing God in His rightful place: first place. The world's treasures are difficult to find and difficult to keep; God's treasures are ever-present and everlasting. Which treasures, then, will you claim as your own?

It's sobering to contemplate how much time, effort, sacrifice, compromise, and attention we give to acquiring and increasing our supply of something that is totally insignificant in eternity.

Anne Graham Lotz

A TIMELY TIP

Do you find yourself wrapped up in the material world? If so, it's time to reorder your priorities and reassess your values. Today, think long and hard about the priorities and values that guide your decision-making. And then, when you finally put all that material stuff in perspective, begin storing up riches that will endure throughout eternity—the spiritual kind.

AT PEACE WITH YOUR PURPOSE

But now in Christ Jesus you who once were far off have been brought near by the blood of Christ. For He Himself is our peace.

Ephesians 2:13–14 NKJV

Are you at peace with the direction of your life? If you're a Christian, you should be. Perhaps you seek a new direction or a sense of renewed purpose, but those feelings should never rob you of the genuine peace that can and should be yours through a personal relationship with Jesus.

Have you found the lasting peace that can be yours through Jesus, or are you still rushing after the illusion of "peace and happiness" that our world promises but cannot deliver? Today, as a gift to yourself, to your family, and to your friends, claim the inner peace that is your spiritual birthright: the peace of Jesus Christ.

Prayer guards hearts and minds and causes God to bring peace out of chaos.

Beth Moore

In the center of a hurricane there is absolute quiet and peace. There is no safer place than in the center of the will of God.

Corrie ten Boom

A TIMELY TIP

God offers peace that passes human understanding . . . and He wants you to make His peace your peace.

CONSTANT PRAISE

Through Him then, let us continually offer up a sacrifice of praise to God, that is, the fruit of lips that give thanks to His name.

Hebrews 13:15 NASB

The Bible makes it clear: it pays to praise God. But sometimes, we allow ourselves to become so preoccupied with the demands of daily life that we forget to say "Thank You" to the Giver of all good gifts.

Worship and praise should be a part of everything we do. Otherwise, we quickly lose perspective as we fall prey to the demands of the moment.

Do you sincerely desire to be a worthy servant of the One who has given you eternal love and eternal life? Then praise Him for who He is and for what He has done for you. Praise Him all day long, every day, for as long as you live . . . and then for all eternity.

God is worthy of our praise and is pleased when we come before Him with thanksgiving.

Shirley Dobson

The time for universal praise is sure to come some day. Let us begin to do our part now.

Hannah Whitall Smith

A TIMELY TIP

Remember that it always pays to praise your Creator. That's why thoughtful believers (like you) make it a habit to carve out quiet moments throughout the day to praise God.

Day 358

TODAY'S BIBLE READING
Old Testament: Habakkuk 1-3
New Testament: Revelation 16

GOD IS HERE

Draw near to God, and He will draw near to you.

James 4:8 HCSB

God is constantly making Himself available to you; therefore, when you approach Him obediently and sincerely, you will most certainly find Him: God is always near. Whenever it seems to you that God is distant, disinterested, or altogether absent, you may rest assured that your feelings are a reflection of your own emotional state, not an indication of God's absence.

If, during life's darker days, you seek to establish a closer relationship with Him, you can do so because God is not just near, He is here.

Has he taken over your heart? Perhaps he resides there, but does he preside there?

Vance Havner

I now know the power of the risen Lord! He lives! The dawn of Easter has broken in my own soul! My night is gone!

Mrs. Charles E. Cowman

A TIMELY TIP

Where is your focus today? Remember that it's important to focus your thoughts on Jesus first.

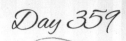
HONORING GOD

Honor GOD with everything you own; give him the first and the best. Your barns will burst, your wine vats will brim over.

Proverbs 3:9-10 MSG

Whom will you choose to honor today? If you honor God and place Him at the center of your life, every day is a cause for celebration. But if you fail to honor your Heavenly Father, you're asking for trouble, and lots of it.

At times, your life is probably hectic, demanding, and complicated. When the demands of life leave you rushing from place to place with scarcely a moment to spare, you may fail to pause and thank your Creator for the blessings He has bestowed upon you. But that's a big mistake. So honor God for who He is and for what He has done for you. And don't just honor Him on Sunday morning. Praise Him all day long, every day, for as long as you live . . . and then for all eternity.

The Holy Spirit testifies of Jesus. So when you are filled with the Holy Spirit you speak about our Lord and really live to His honor.

Corrie ten Boom

Praise opens the window of our hearts, preparing us to walk more closely with God. Prayer raises the window of our spirit, enabling us to listen more clearly to the Father.

Max Lucado

A TIMELY TIP

God has given you everything. You must honor Him with your words, your actions, and your prayers.

ENTHUSIASTIC DISCIPLESHIP

Don't work only while being watched, in order to please men, but as slaves of Christ, do God's will from your heart. Render service with a good attitude, as to the Lord and not to men.

Ephesians 6:6-7 HCSB

With whom will you choose to walk today? Will you walk with shortsighted people who honor the ways of the world, or will you walk with the Son of God? Jesus walks with you. Are you walking with Him? Hopefully, you will choose to walk with Him today and every day of your life. Jesus has called upon believers of every generation (and that includes you) to follow in His footsteps. And God's Word promises that when you follow in Christ's footsteps, you will learn how to live freely and lightly (Matthew 11:28-30).

Jesus doesn't want you to be a run-of-the-mill, follow-the-crowd kind of person. Jesus wants you to be a "new creation" through Him. And that's exactly what you should want for yourself, too. Jesus deserves your extreme enthusiasm; the world deserves it; and you deserve the experience of sharing it.

When Jesus put the little child in the midst of His disciples, He did not tell the little child to become like His disciples; He told the disciples to become like the little child.

Ruth Bell Graham

A life lived in God is not lived on the plane of feelings, but of the will.

Elisabeth Elliot

A TIMELY TIP

Talk is cheap. Real ministry has legs. When it comes to being a disciple, make sure that you back up your words with deeds.

LIVING IN AN ANXIOUS WORLD

Cast all your anxiety on him because he cares for you.

1 Peter 5:7 NIV

We live in a world that often breeds anxiety and fear. When we come face-to-face with tough times, we may fall prey to discouragement, doubt, or depression. But our Father in heaven has other plans. God has promised that we may lead lives of abundance, not anxiety. In fact, His Word instructs us to "be anxious for nothing" (Philippians 4:6). But how can we put our fears to rest? By taking those fears to God and leaving them there.

As you face the challenges of daily life, you may find yourself becoming anxious, troubled, discouraged, or fearful. If so, turn every one of your concerns over to your Heavenly Father. The same God who created the universe will comfort you if you ask Him . . . so ask Him and trust Him. And then watch in amazement as your anxieties melt into the warmth of His loving hands.

When you are anxious, it means that you aren't trusting God completely; it means that you aren't trusting God to take care your needs.

Stormie Omartian

So often we pray and then fret anxiously, waiting for God to hurry up and do something. All the while God is waiting for us to calm down, so He can do something through us.

Corrie ten Boom

A TIMELY TIP

Divide your areas of concern into two categories: those you can control and those you cannot. Resolve never to waste time or energy worrying about the latter.

ULTIMATE ACCOUNTABILITY

We encouraged, comforted, and implored each one of you to walk worthy of God, who calls you into His own kingdom and glory.

1 Thessalonians 2:12 HCSB

For most of us, it is a daunting thought: one day, perhaps soon, we'll come face-to-face with our Heavenly Father, and we'll be called to account for our actions here on earth. Our personal histories will certainly not be surprising to God; He already knows everything about us. But the full scope of our activities may be surprising to us: some of us will be pleasantly surprised; others will not be.

Today, do whatever you can to ensure that your thoughts and your deeds are pleasing to your Creator. Because you will, at some point in future, be called to account for your actions. And the future may be sooner than you think.

There may be no trumpet sound or loud applause when we make a right decision, just a calm sense of resolution and peace.

Gloria Gaither

Don't worry about what you do not understand. Worry about what you do understand in the Bible but do not live by.

Corrie ten Boom

A TIMELY TIP

Ask yourself if your behavior has been radically changed by your unfolding relationship with God. If the answer to this question is unclear to you—or if the honest answer is a resounding no—think of a single step you can take, a positive change in your life, that will bring you closer to your Creator.

ABUNDANT LIVING

I came so they can have real and eternal life, more and better life than they ever dreamed of.

John 10:10 MSG

The familiar words of John 10:10 should serve as a daily reminder: Christ came to this earth so that we might experience His abundance, His love, and His gift of eternal life. But as every woman knows, some days are so busy and so hurried that abundance seems a distant promise. It is not. Every day, we can claim the spiritual abundance that God promises for our lives . . . and we should.

Christ is the ultimate Savior of mankind and the personal Savior of those who believe in Him. As His servants, we should place Him at the very center of our lives. And, every day that God gives us breath, we should share Christ's love and His abundance with a world that needs both.

If you want purpose and meaning and satisfaction and fulfillment and peace and hope and joy and abundant life that lasts forever, look to Jesus.

Anne Graham Lotz

Get ready for God to show you not only His pleasure, but His approval.

Joni Eareckson Tada

A TIMELY TIP

Abundant living may or may not include material wealth, but abundant living always includes the spiritual riches that you receive when you obey God's Word.

LIFE ETERNAL

In a little while the world will see Me no longer, but you will see Me. Because I live, you will live too.

John 14:19 HCSB

How marvelous it is that God became a man and walked among us. Had He not chosen to do so, we might feel removed from a distant Creator. But ours is not a distant God. Ours is a God who understands—far better than we ever could—the essence of what it means to be human.

God understands our hopes, our fears, and our temptations. He understands what it means to be angry and what it costs to forgive. He knows the heart, the conscience, and the soul of every person who has ever lived, including you. And God has a plan of salvation that is intended for you. Accept it. Accept God's gift through the person of His Son Christ Jesus, and then rest assured: God walked among us so that you might have eternal life; amazing though it may seem, He did it for you.

If you are a believer, your judgment will not determine your eternal destiny. Christ's finished work on Calvary was applied to you the moment you accepted Christ as Savior.

Beth Moore

A TIMELY TIP

People love talking about religion, and everybody has their own opinions, but ultimately only one opinion counts . . . God's. Talk to your friends about God's promise of eternal life—what that promise means to you and what it should mean to them.

Day 365

COMMISSIONED TO WITNESS

Go, therefore, and make disciples of all nations, baptizing them in the name of the Father and of the Son and of the Holy Spirit, teaching them to observe everything I have commanded you. And remember, I am with you always, to the end of the age.

Matthew 28:19-20 HCSB

After His resurrection, Jesus addressed His disciples. As recorded in the 28th chapter of Matthew, Christ instructed His followers to share His message with the world. This "Great Commission" applies to Christians of every generation, including our own.

As believers, we are called to share the Good News of Jesus with our families, with our neighbors, and with the world. Christ commanded His disciples to become fishers of men. We must do likewise, and we must do so today. Tomorrow may indeed be too late.

Our commission is quite specific. We are told to be His witness to all nations. For us, as His disciples, to refuse any part of this commission frustrates the love of Jesus Christ, the Son of God.

Catherine Marshall

Witnessing is not something that we do for the Lord; it is something that He does through us if we are filled with the Holy Spirit.

Warren Wiersbe

A TIMELY TIP

The best day to respond to Christ's Great Commission is this day.

Notes and Favorite Scripture

Notes and Favorite Scripture

Notes and Favorite Scripture

Notes and Favorite Scripture

Notes and Favorite Scripture

Notes and Favorite Scripture

Notes and Favorite Scripture

Notes and Favorite Scripture

Notes and Favorite Scripture

Notes and Favorite Scripture

Notes and Favorite Scripture